Making Care Count

Making Care Count

A Century of Gender, Race, and Paid Care Work

MIGNON DUFFY

RUTGERS UNIVERSITY PRESS
New Brunswick, New Jersey, and London

Library of Congress Cataloging-in-Publication Data

Duffy, Mignon.
    Making care count : a century of gender, race, and paid care work / Mignon Duffy.
      p. cm.
    Includes bibliographical references and index.
    ISBN 978–0–8135–4960–6 (hbk. : alk. paper) — ISBN 978–0–8135–4961–3
(pbk. : alk. paper)
     1. Service industries workers—United States.   2. Caregivers—United States.
3. Household employees—United States.   4. Social service—United States.
5. Sexual division of labor—United States.   I. Title.
    HD8039.S452U638   2011
    331.7′6136210973—dc22

                                 2010024092

A British Cataloging-in-Publication record for this book is available from the
British Library.

Visit our Web site: http://rutgerspress.rutgers.edu

Manufactured in the United States of America

For my parents, Michael and D'Neil Duffy

Contents

List of Figures   *ix*
Acknowledgments   *xi*

	Introduction	*1*
Chapter 1	Conceptualizing Care	*9*
Chapter 2	Domestic Workers: Many Hands, Heavy Work	*20*
Chapter 3	Transforming Nurturance, Creating Expert Care	*42*
Chapter 4	Managing Nurturant Care in the New Economy	*75*
Chapter 5	Doing the Dirty Work	*113*
Chapter 6	Making Care Count	*129*

Appendix: Data and Methods   *147*
Notes   *153*
Index   *177*

Figures

2.1. Female private household workers by race-ethnicity and birthplace, 1900 (in percentages)   23

2.2. Number of private household workers, 1900–1990   25

2.3. Female private household workers by race-ethnicity and birthplace, 1950 (in percentages)   27

2.4. Female private household workers by race-ethnicity and birthplace, 1990 (in percentages)   30

2.5. Number of nannies and housekeepers, 1980–2007   32

3.1. Number of nurturant care workers, 1900–1950   43

3.2. Nurturant care workers by race-ethnicity and birthplace, 1900 and 1950 (in percentages)   44

3.3. Number of workers in selected health-care occupations, 1900–1950   50

3.4. Women in selected health-care occupations, 1900–1950 (in percentages) 52

3.5. Selected health-care workers by race-ethnicity and birthplace, 1900 (in percentages)   53

3.6. Selected health-care workers by race-ethnicity and birthplace, 1950 (in percentages)   53

3.7. Number of teachers, 1900–1950   60

3.8. Race-ethnicity and birthplace of teachers, 1900 and 1950 (in percentages) 62

3.9. Number of workers in selected social service occupations, 1900–1950   66

3.10. Women in selected social service occupations, 1900–1950 (in percentages) 67

3.11. Selected social service workers by race-ethnicity and birthplace, 1900 (in percentages)   68

3.12. Selected social service workers by race-ethnicity and birthplace, 1950 (in percentages)   68

4.1. Number of nurturant care workers by occupational group, 1950–2007   78

4.2.   Nurturant care workers by race-ethnicity and birthplace, 1950–2007 (in percentages)   *79*

4.3.   Number of workers in selected health-care occupations, 1950–2007   *80*

4.4.   Women in selected health-care occupations, 1950–2007 (in percentages)   *84*

4.5.   Selected health-care workers by race-ethnicity and birthplace, 1950 (in percentages)   *85*

4.6.   Selected health-care workers by race-ethnicity and birthplace, 2007 (in percentages)   *85*

4.7.   Number of teachers and child-care workers, 1950–2007   *93*

4.8.   Selected education and child-care workers by race-ethnicity and birthplace, 1970 (in percentages)   *95*

4.9.   Selected education and child-care workers by race-ethnicity and birthplace, 2007 (in percentages)   *98*

4.10. Number of workers in mental health and social service occupations, 1950–2007   *106*

4.11. Women in selected mental health and social service occupations, 1960–2007 (in percentages)   *107*

4.12. Selected mental health and social service workers by race-ethnicity and birthplace, 1970 (in percentages)   *109*

4.13. Selected mental health and social service workers by race-ethnicity and birthplace, 2007 (in percentages)   *109*

5.1.   Cleaning, food, and laundry workers by race-ethnicity and birthplace, 1900–2007 (in percentages)   *115*

5.2.   Number of cleaning, food, and laundry workers, 1900–2007   *116*

5.3.   Selected hospital workers by race-ethnicity and birthplace, 2007 (in percentages)   *125*

Acknowledgments

I find it a bit difficult to know where to start to thank the many people who have been part of this book in one way or another. Since this is a book about care, it seems appropriate to begin with my own circle of care. My parents, Michael and D'Neil Duffy, are my rock and foundation in every way. Their role in making this book a possibility began long before I ever dreamed of writing a book at all. My husband, Gary Jorgensen, is as steadfast, loving, and generous a partner in life as one could ever hope for. And my children, Ben and Rebecca, constantly remind me of just how true it is that care is never a one-way proposition. Rebecca's request for her own copy of the book once it has a real cover and Ben's imitation of his reading it to his grandchildren years from now will be my most treasured reviews.

My friends—Kim and Anna McMaken-Marsh, Anna Allocco, and Heather Calvin especially—went above and beyond the call of duty to make me feel like I had a village behind me during what can feel like a very solitary process. And my children not only get amazing care but also learn how to be contributing members of a caring community at Lexington Montessori School. I also thank the board and school leadership at LMS for giving me an opportunity to have something else to be passionate about in my volunteer work there during the time I have been immersed in this book project.

My writing group partners—Karen Hansen and Debi Osnowitz—have read every word of this manuscript, some parts multiple times. Karen was one of the first people to believe in this project and has been my mentor, my colleague, and my friend throughout. Karen's experience with big unruly research, her remarkable ability to navigate through theoretical quagmires, and her generosity in sharing her experience and friendship have been for me wonderful gifts. Debi has shared her keen editor's eye, her wisdom about publishing, and her huge knowledge of scholarly literature. Karen and Debi have been my critics, my cheerleaders, my editors, and my advisors as this project has become a book. I cannot imagine having done it without them, and everyone should be so lucky as I to have such gifted scholars and good friends to write with.

Michael Duffy, in a true labor of love, also read the whole manuscript with his editor's eye. And I am grateful to Nancy Folbre, Clare Hammonds, and Katherine Rosa for their reads of various chapters and their willingness to provide feedback. Clare was also the force behind getting the endnotes into shape, and her diligence and extensive knowledge of the care work literature made her research assistance in the final stages of the project extremely valuable.

My colleagues at the University of Massachusetts Lowell—especially the faculty associates at the Center for Women and Work—have given me both emotional support and practical advice. And Daniel Egan, the chair of the Sociology Department, has provided critical mentoring and guidance during my time at UML. The university also gave me the opportunity to take a pre-tenure sabbatical during a crucial writing period, and I am grateful for this institutional support. During my time at UML I have also had the opportunity to collaborate with Nancy Folbre and Randy Albelda through a University of Massachusetts grant. Working with two people who have thought so deeply about gender, care, and work has been an honor and a privilege, and my conversations with Randy and Nancy have certainly helped challenge and shape my thinking about these issues.

I cannot say enough good things about the people who work at the Minnesota Population Center with the Integrated Public Use Microdata Series (IPUMS). They have created a remarkable tool for scholars, and during the time I have been working on this project, the amount of data available and the accessibility to that data for all kinds of users has only gotten better. The staff members are exemplars of professionalism and responsiveness. In particular, I want to thank Trent Alexander. For ten years, I have e-mailed and called him with obscure questions about census data, and for ten years he has responded to me quickly, with clear answers, thoughtful insight, and good humor. Also, thanks to Paula England for leading me to IPUMS in the first place.

Virginia Woolf, one of my heroines, has said that in order to write, a woman needs a room of her own. Thank you for giving me that space to Lisa Hatch at Brandeis University, the Gulf Shores public library, the Waltham public library, Karen Hansen (for her office), Heather Calvin and Emily Bottis (for their child-free house), and Michael and D'Neil Duffy (for rooms in their house as well as in various timeshares over the years). The Boston Library Consortium and the Minuteman Library Network have also been invaluable resources.

Before this project was a book, it was a dissertation. In addition to Karen Hansen, who served as the chair, I want to thank the other members of my dissertation committee—Janet Giele, Carmen Sirianni, Grant Ritter, and Juliet Schor. I received funding from Brandeis University for a Dissertation Year Fellowship, and the Missy Carter Dissertation Fellowship from the Women's Studies Research Center. I was also part of a feminist dissertation support group that was critical to my success as a graduate student, and I thank all the members of that group—especially Julia Gittleman and Diane Purvin—for being my community during the dissertation process.

Last, but definitely not least, I am extraordinarily grateful to the editors I have worked with at Rutgers University Press—to Adi Hovav for believing in the project early on; to Marlie Wasserman for always making time in her busy schedule to shepherd the book along; and to Peter Mickulas for his interest in and understanding of the project, despite having been thrown into it in midstream.

Making Care Count

Introduction

IN EVERY SOCIETY, children have to be raised—taught whatever they need to know to survive in their particular time and place. They also have to be fed, bathed, diapered, and taken care of when they are sick or hurt. Homes need to be maintained, kitchens need to be stocked and cleaned, meals need to be prepared, and clothing needs to be laundered. People who are elderly, ill, or disabled need care. These are some of the most fundamental tasks of a society, and the daily labor of these activities can involve both monotonous drudgery and untold rewards for those performing them. These jobs cannot be outsourced overseas, because they involve the most intimate spaces of our everyday lives—our homes, our bodies, our families.

The nature of these tasks may vary widely across place and across historical time. In one era, raising children means teaching them the work of the family farm, while in another, it means sending them to formal schooling. In one place, cleaning the house may involve vacuuming and silver polishing, while in another it might mean using a broom to sweep a dirt floor. Applying leeches, changing wound dressings, comforting with a song, or performing complex surgery have all been part of caring for the sick at one time or another. For those recognized as mentally ill, care may mean institutionalization, treatment with counseling, or prescribed medication. And just as the nature of this work is culturally and historically bound, so is the system for distributing its labor.

In the United States, as in many other societies, a gendered division of labor has ensured that women perform many of these tasks as unpaid family work. But the country also has more than twenty million nannies, housekeepers, day-care workers, nurses, doctors, teachers, home-care aides, social workers, and other care workers. This book is about these workers—those paid to perform some of the most intimate labors in U.S. society.

Why Care About Care Workers?

The most obvious reason to pay attention to care workers is that meeting the most basic needs of our society relies on their labor. And this labor force is riddled with problems: child-care workers earn among the lowest wages in the country; registered nurses are under increasing pressure in an environment of understaffing and expanding demands; housekeepers and nannies who are undocumented immigrants have little guarantee of fair treatment; and an exponentially growing number of health-care support workers like hospital orderlies and home-care aides work for low wages under difficult conditions. These kinds of problems are certainly not unique to the care sector, but in these cases there are immediate human consequences not only for the workers and their families but also for those in their care. The wages and working conditions of care workers are directly linked to the quality and availability of care. Occupations that offer little opportunity for advancement, low wages, and difficult working conditions cannot consistently attract enough talented individuals to fill them. And we cannot expect the best care possible from workers worn down by the pressures of understaffing, by having to hold down multiple jobs, or by both. Understanding the paid care sector is critical to moving toward solutions to the current crisis in care in the United States.

The second reason to study the paid care sector is that its division of labor is crucial territory for analyzing the intersections of gender, racial-ethnic, and class inequalities.[1] Feminists have understood the gendered division of labor that assigns care of home and family to women to be one of the linchpins of systematic gender inequality across U.S. society.[2] The basic argument is that women's responsibility for unpaid work in the home disadvantages them in the labor market, both through periodic or long-term absences and through the burden of the second shift that wage-earning women still bear in the home.[3] These labor-market disadvantages contribute to women's earning less than men as well as to the glass ceiling that makes it more challenging for women to advance to the highest levels of power in the workplace. In turn, this inequality at the macro level maintains material constraints and ideological norms that uphold the gendered division of labor in the home. That is, women with less access to economic resources and less societal power have less leverage in individual relationships with men. This dynamic is aggravated by the fact that many of the jobs in which women have been concentrated have been seen as paid versions of the jobs they do at home—taking care of children, watching over the sick, and cleaning people's houses and hospital rooms. The often low wage levels in these occupations make women even more economically vulnerable.

But as Evelyn Nakano Glenn has pointed out, feminist analysis has largely ignored racial-ethnic, class, and citizenship differences among women, and most theoretical treatments of racial-ethnic inequality focus on the paid labor market and pay scant attention to gender. Nakano Glenn argues that analysis of the racial division of care work is "key to the distinct exploitation of women of color . . . and essential to the development of an integrated model of race and gender."[4] The distribution of care work, paid and unpaid, has both shaped and been shaped by the history of gender, racial-ethnic, and class divisions in the United States. To analyze the intersection of these inequalities requires an understanding of their relationship to care work.

The Stories We Tell

That there is a care crisis in the United States is not news to anyone who has missed work to take care of a sick child, worried about how to care for an aging relative, tried to find child care for a new baby, or stayed in a hospital unit where staffing shortages spread nurses thin. But how did we get to this point? And where do we go from here? Our collective understanding of the answers to the first question informs our answers to the second. While there is certainly no consensus in the popular imagination (or in the scholarly literature) about the causes of the contemporary care crisis, two narratives seem to resonate with particular strength.

The first story line contrasts a present in which children and the elderly are cared for in cold institutional settings with an idealized past in which families took care of their own. According to this account, as more and more women entered the paid labor force, the care work that they used to do in the home for free was outsourced. So, while in the past a daughter might have cared for her elderly mother in the daughter's home, now her mother is in a nursing home. And the child that used to come home to a plate of warm cookies baked by his mother now goes to an after-school program or is picked up by a nanny. These are the kinds of images associated with the outsourcing narrative, images that point to a society that has lost its way, a country that has become fundamentally less caring. Politicians and pundits who lament the decline of the family—some of whom advocate the large-scale return of women to full-time homemaking as the solution to the care crisis—enthusiastically embrace this interpretation of history.

But it is not just conservatives who describe the transformation of care in the twentieth century as a movement from family to market. Although feminist scholars point to very different solutions from those conservatives favor, many of their analyses that focus on the commercialization, commodification, or marketization of care share the same basic assumption. For example, Arlie Hochschild has contrasted the "traditional" model of care, represented by the homemaker mother, with two models she says exist in contemporary life: the "postmodern" and the "cold-modern." In the postmodern model, women enter the paid labor force but are still expected to provide the majority of the care for the family, resulting in a decline in the time and energy devoted to care. The cold-modern model is represented by "impersonal institutional care in year-round ten-hour daycare and old-age homes."[5] Based on these descriptions, women's entrance into the labor force has resulted in a care deficit, which impersonal market solutions fill unsatisfactorily. Hochschild does not propose a return to the traditional model, but rather a "warm-modern" model that combines some institutional care with equal participation in family care from women and men. She considers the family the default for care and sees marketization as having had a negative impact.

Deborah Stone has also criticized the "wrenching" of care out of families and into the labor market: "Caring comes from the private world of love, intimacy, families, and friendship, but much of it is now done in the public world of work, organizations, markets, and governments. Just as farm and craft labor were once wrenched out of the family and brought into a system of work controlled from outside, caring work is increasingly separated from the personal relationships in which it naturally arises and is performed instead in a system of managed and waged labor."[6] Stone goes on to describe a number of dimensions along which the values of care and the values of paid work clash, creating difficult conflicts for caregivers as well as undermining the quality of care that the paid labor market can provide. Again, a story of movement from family to market is linked to a decline in care.

Although the twentieth century has seen many dramatic changes related to care, the historical analysis in the following chapters demonstrates that the changes lie in not just the *who* and the *where* of care, but more fundamentally in the *what* of care. Demographic shifts, technological advances, and changing cultural norms over the past one hundred years have created a radically different system of physical and mental health care, new demands for elder care, and distinct expectations about the care of children and young people. The popular outsourcing story line at once overstates and underestimates the transformation of care over the last century.

A second narrative that has found some audience both in the popular press and in the scholarly literature is what I call the "serfdom saved the women's movement" story line. I borrow that phrase from the title of an article in a popular newsmagazine, which berated professional women for exploiting immigrant women as nannies and housekeepers to do the care work when they traded home for career. Scholars have used somewhat less inflammatory language to make similar arguments. For example, in her 1999 book *Care and Equality*, Mona Harrington warned: "We are heading towards hardening inequality in the creation of a new, low-wage servant class to do our caretaking for us." In her view, by "depending on these workers, we create not just a servant class but one made up of racial and ethnic minorities." This story line builds on the first narrative: as middle- and upper-class White women entered the paid labor force, their care work was outsourced to racial-ethnic and immigrant women in the form of low-wage and often exploitative paid care jobs.[7]

I want to emphasize that any scholarly and popular attention to racial-ethnic inequalities related to paid care work shines a light on an area of inquiry that has to date been far too often ignored. Feminists must include race-ethnicity, class, and other inequalities in their analyses of gender, and recent interest in exploring connections between racial-ethnic stratification and paid care work is critically important—and in fact was the inspiration for this project. In particular, linking the privileges of some groups of women to the exploitation of other groups of women is the kind of analysis that feminists must not shy away from. Having said that, my research shows that the "serfdom saved the women's movement" story line is simplistic and not grounded in historical and contemporary evidence. My goal in this book is to provide an overarching historical analysis of the intersections of gender, racial-ethnic, and class inequalities with paid care to illuminate the complex realities behind these straightforward narratives.

About This Book

At its core, *Making Care Count* is a historical analysis of the paid care labor force. As a feminist sociologist, I believe that patterns of social inequality are not fixed or predetermined by biology, but are shaped by cultural and economic factors. If that is true, then an understanding of historical forces is critical to analyzing contemporary social problems.[8] This book documents and interrogates the twentieth-century history of paid care work as a whole, drawing on an in-depth analysis of U.S. Census data as well as a range of individual occupational histories. Throughout the book I focus on change and continuity in the social organization and cultural construction of the labor of care and its relationship to gender, racial-ethnic, and class inequalities.

The backbone of the book is an analysis of U.S. Census data from 1900 to 2007. Using samples from the Integrated Public Use Microdata Series (IPUMS), I have analyzed the growth as well as the demographic changes in the paid care labor force throughout the twentieth century.[9] Large nationally representative samples from the U.S. Census for each decade from 1900 through 2000 and from the American Community Survey for each year from 2000 through 2007 have allowed me to construct population estimates and demographic breakdowns for paid care occupations. The IPUMS datasets are intended to facilitate historical comparison and overall are the best available samples for studying the labor force historically; where particular issues of comparability occur, I have noted them. To flesh out the story around the data, I have relied heavily on individual occupational histories. Although many of the occupations included in this book have been well studied individually, analyzing them as a group yields important new insights that contribute to the growing body of scholarship examining care work.

To decide which occupations to include, I have used a broad conceptualization of care for reasons I explain thoroughly in the next chapter, "Conceptualizing Care." I include any occupation in which the primary task involves "maintaining people both on a daily basis and intergenerationally" (physical and mental health, meal preparation, cleaning, personal care, and care of children and youth).[10] This definition is meant to capture the whole range of intimate labors that keep our society going—the child-care worker changing a diaper, the elementary school teacher reading with a student, the nursing home aide giving a resident a bath, the nurse monitoring the condition of a critically ill patient, the housekeeper emptying the dishwasher, and the hospital cafeteria worker preparing food to meet varying dietary needs.

Within this broad conceptualization of care work, I distinguish between *nurturant* and *nonnurturant* care work. Nurturant care includes labor that is inherently relational, that is, the core labor of nurturant care workers—nurses, child-care workers, physicians, teachers, social workers—involves intimate and face-to-face relationship with the people they are caring for. Nonnurturant care is the labor that undergirds nurturant care but may not be relational at all— the work of housekeepers, hospital laundry operatives, nursing home cafeteria workers, and health-care orderlies. These workers perform labor that is often out of sight or at least does not involve explicit relationship with those being cared for.

Chapter 2, "Domestic Workers: Many Hands, Heavy Work," unravels the historical story of domestic servants, by far the most numerous paid care workers in the late nineteenth and early twentieth centuries. In many homes, these workers were involved in every aspect of care work. How do we understand the decline of this occupation in the twentieth century—and has that decline been reversed in recent decades? This chapter addresses that question as well as the complex set of issues about who has done this work over time.

Understanding the evolution of domestic service provides important context for analyzing the development of other care occupations during the course of the twentieth century. In addition, perhaps nowhere have the intersections of gender, race-ethnicity, class, and care work been better studied than in the field of domestic service. The analyses of inequalities in this job of last resort provide a framework for examining the development of other care occupations and of care work as a broad category.

Chapter 3, "Transforming Nurturance, Creating Expert Care," focuses on the dramatic change in the nurturant care sector at the dawn of the twentieth century. During this time, economic and cultural shifts led to the redefinition and reorganization of nurturance across health care, education and child care, and social services. Paid care workers in the twentieth century are performing fundamentally different work from their nineteenth-century predecessors, and this chapter explores the origins of that transformation. The strong gendered and racialized dimensions of nurturant care were established during this critical period, when care became the domain of experts.

Chapter 4, "Managing Care in the New Economy," explores the impact of cost cutting and political retrenchment on the work of paid care in the last decades of the twentieth century. The overall trends toward routinization and bureaucratic control led to the squeezing out of the relational aspects of care work as well as some loss of autonomy for many care workers. Importantly, during this time, nurturant care became even more heavily feminized and racial-ethnic hierarchies more entrenched.

Within the nurturant care sector, there are important and meaningful divisions of labor by race-ethnicity, citizenship, and class. However, those inequalities come into starker focus when one also considers the nonnurturant aspects of care work. Chapter 5, "Doing the Dirty Work," describes the evolution of the jobs of cleaning, food preparation and service, and laundry and finds that both the gender and racial-ethnic dynamics of these nonrelational components of domestic labor have developed quite differently from their nurturant counterparts. Do some of the frameworks developed to analyze domestic service help us understand contemporary inequalities related to nonnurturant care work? How do race-ethnicity, citizenship, class, and gender intersect to make these some of the lowest-paid and least-rewarded jobs in the economy? This chapter makes clear the limitations of focusing exclusively on nurturant care for capturing a full picture of racial-ethnic and class divides.

The final chapter, "Making Care Count," looks to the future and suggests some implications for the project of social change from the perspective of a historical understanding. Solving the care crisis requires an approach that combines recognizing the uniqueness of nurturant care with placing all care work in a larger economic context. Addressing the ways in which the occupational structure of paid care reinforces gender and racial-ethnic inequalities demands attention both to the cultural construction of care work and to broad structural divides. Alice Kessler-Harris has noted that "without a history, public policy follows the path of social myth."[11] My hope is that the macro-historical analysis in *Making Care Count* will be useful in pointing the way toward more effective and humane public policy that ensures both economic justice and quality care.

A Note on Measuring Race

The measurement of race in the U.S. Census has been the subject of much controversy and debate, and the enumeration of racial categories has changed many times over the decades. The IPUMS datasets include a standardized variable measuring race, an additional variable identifying Hispanic origin, and a detailed variable identifying birthplace. In my analysis, I combined these measures to create a new set of mutually exclusive categories: White U.S. born, Black U.S. born, Hispanic U.S. born, other U.S. born, and foreign born. The categorical choice is a strategic one based on the social construction of racial-ethnic categories in the United States rather than on the inherent conceptual validity of the categories. These broad characterizations allow me to examine general historical trends at a national level. Following the example of Nakano Glenn, throughout the book I use the term "racial-ethnic" to "refer collectively to groups that have been socially constructed and constituted as racially as well as culturally distinct from European Americans."[12]

Chapter 1   Conceptualizing Care

SUPREME COURT JUSTICE POTTER STEWART famously said that although he could not provide a clear definition of pornography, "I know it when I see it."[1] In many ways, the same could be said of "care work." The term has become something of a buzzword among scholars and advocates, and it is often used in ways that assume a shared implicit understanding of what care is. However, as with pornography, when it comes to specifying which particular jobs or particular workers should be included as care, there are as many definitions as there are scholars. In an undergraduate textbook on care, Francesca Cancian and Stacey Oliker define the concept this way: "feelings of affection and responsibility combined with actions that provide responsively for an individual's personal needs or well-being, in a face-to-face relationship."[2] This definition exemplifies what I call the "nurturant care perspective," and variations on this characterization of care can be found increasingly throughout the literature.[3]

When applied to paid care, a nurturance definition includes nurses, doctors, teachers, child-care workers, social workers, psychotherapists, and personal care attendants. These occupations demand intensive relational work that is geared toward improving the personal well-being of others. Examining these workers as a group whose jobs share key characteristics has led to important theoretical insights and empirical findings. The chapters that follow build on this emergent body of scholarship to examine the intertwining histories of nurturant care occupations, the shifting and contradictory construction of relationality in these jobs, and the ways nurturance has intersected with gender, racial-ethnic, and class inequalities.

I also include some workers not usually considered care workers by those who define care based on the relational content of the job: housecleaners, school cafeteria workers, kitchen workers in nursing homes, hospital laundry workers, and building cleaners. I devote a chapter to domestic service, which in its early twentieth-century incarnation may have included some nurturant care roles along with many hours of scrubbing floors, doing laundry, and other tasks that require more physical labor and less direct relationship with others. In this chapter I explore the theoretical foundations of nurturant care as a concept and explain why I do not limit my analysis to these relational roles.[4]

While nurturant care theory illuminates many important pieces of the care-inequalities puzzle, it obscures others. In particular, an approach to care work that focuses exclusively on relationality does not provide a clear picture of critical racial-ethnic and class hierarchies. I use the concept of nurturant care and look beyond it to more fully understand the historical development of the occupational structure of paid care. I draw on an earlier feminist conceptualization of women's intimate labors—the notion of reproductive labor—to describe some of the antecedents of theoretical ideas about care, as well as to reveal some of the limitations of a nurturance perspective.

Reproductive Labor: Making Women's Work Visible

The development of the concept of reproductive labor was part of a movement to challenge the invisibility of women's unpaid labor in the home. The bifurcation of activities into separate spheres of home and work dates back to the Industrial Revolution, when large numbers of men left family farms for factories, and women in many families took primary charge of the substantial labor of maintaining a home. While a gendered division of labor has a long history in the United States, in an agricultural economy almost all work took place in and around the home—from planting and harvesting crops to tending fires for heat and cooking to sewing and laundering clothes. The boundaries between work and family were not clearly defined in this environment, and so neither gender could lay exclusive claim to one or the other. With industrialization, the newly organized gendered division of labor became the basis of a gendered definition of work: what men did in the market for pay was work, and what women did in the home for free was housework or domestic work.[5] The ideology of separate spheres, a private one inhabited by women and a public one inhabited by men, became a central organizing idea of social life and of work in the United States.

The clear ideological demarcation between private female domesticity and public male work did not always reflect people's lived realities. Throughout the nineteenth century (and well into the twentieth in rural areas), women who did not work outside the home often engaged in income-generating activities such as taking in boarders or hiring out their services to do sewing, laundry, or other piece-work tasks. Particular groups of women were also a presence in the paid labor force throughout the nineteenth century—Black women working in agricultural fields in the South, immigrant women working in northern factories, and many White U.S.-born women without the means to live in the world of separate spheres. And of course, there were always women who chose to engage in paid labor despite the cultural prohibition against it. During the twentieth century, as women's labor-force participation expanded, the notion of separate spheres less and less reflected the reality of even many middle- and upper-class married women. And, despite the ideological construction of the domestic sphere as one supported purely by the unpaid labor of love, paid workers have a long history of contributing to domestic labor.

Nevertheless, the exclusive equation of work with the male public sphere was one of the linchpins of the ideology of separate spheres and has shown remarkable persistence over the centuries. Even today, ask a woman whose primary activity is taking care of her home, her children, or both what she does, and she is likely to respond, "I don't work." Feminist scholars and activists building on Marxist traditions developed the concept of reproductive labor to name women's domestic labor as *work*, and as such, an important part of the economic and social structure. Defining domestic labor as work also challenged the notion that its activities were part of women's natural role.

The concept of reproductive labor was first introduced by Karl Marx and Friedrich Engels. Marx viewed production as one of the central tasks of a society; Engels used the term "reproductive labor" to refer to the activities involved in maintaining and reproducing the labor force.[6] Workers would not be able to work, or at least not as productively, without being fed, having clean clothes, and having a clean bed to sleep in. Viewed through this lens, women's unpaid activities in the home are indispensable to the functioning of a market economy. In addition, raising children contributes directly to the future labor force. Thus, what may at first glance appear to be private and removed from the world of market work is actually intimately and inextricably connected to it. Feminist scholars who developed this idea of reproductive labor emphasized a woman's unpaid domestic labor not just as a benefit to her family, but as central to the continued existence of society.[7]

One of the major obstacles to reframing reproductive labor as work has been the notion that what women do in the home for their own families is part of their natural role.[8] Activities strongly associated with the feminine sphere of domesticity are "not seen as learned, skilled, required, but only the expression of the character or style of women in general."[9] Unpaid domestic labor not only goes unremunerated, but also is detached from the associations of skill, moral worth, and dignity that accompany the designation of an activity as work. Part of the project of feminist analysis of reproductive labor has been to name the intimate labor of the home as work, thereby making it more visible and socially recognized.

The concept of reproductive labor has also been used to analyze paid work. While there is disagreement about the specific boundaries of paid reproductive labor, it is generally defined to include labor involved in "maintaining people both on a daily basis and intergenerationally" (physical and mental health, meal preparation, cleaning, personal care, and care of children and youth).[10] Like unpaid domestic labor, paid reproductive labor is framed as essential to the functioning and continuation of the labor force. Through the lens of reproductive labor, women's predominance in occupations like teaching, child care, home health care, housecleaning, and kitchen work is an extension of their association with these tasks in the domestic realm. Scholars have also argued that paid reproductive labor, like unpaid domestic work, has been vulnerable to invisibility as "real work" because of its characterization as the expression of women's natural role.

In some discussions, the terms "care work," "domestic labor," and "reproductive labor" are used almost interchangeably. However, despite some overlaps, the increasingly prominent nurturance perspective on care work is distinct from an understanding of reproductive labor in important theoretical and practical ways. The definition of nurturant care I presented at the opening of this chapter defines care work in terms of its emotional content and relational context, in contrast to the identification of the role of reproductive labor in the larger economic structure as its defining characteristic. Practically, the definitions include many of the same jobs—nurses, teachers, child-care workers, psychologists, and home health-care aides. A definition of care work based on nurturance, however, excludes some workers usually considered as engaged in reproductive labor, among them housecleaners, kitchen workers, and hospital laundry workers, whose work does not usually happen in a face-to-face relationship. A closer look at the theoretical roots of nurturant care illuminates both the similarities and the differences between the conceptualization of care work as reproductive labor and its framing as nurturance.

Nurturant Care: Focusing on Relationship

Nurturant care theory draws on a broad range of scholarship, including feminist analysis of the welfare state, legal studies, economics, ethics, and philosophy. At its most theoretical level, care has been presented as a practice or ethic that encompasses interdependence, nurturance, and relationship, in contrast to the dominant U.S. values of competition, individualism, and rationality.

Feminist psychologists have argued that those engaged in the practice of care learn a fundamentally different way of thinking about the world that incorporates emotional responsiveness and relationality.[11] Feminist philosophers advocate moving away from individualistic notions of justice to a broad ethic of care that builds a sense of shared collective responsibility for each other and our world.[12] And feminist economists use the language of care to insert the lived experiences of love, obligation, and reciprocity into an economic theory that supposes those things not to exist.[13] In a society in which emotion and nurturance have been characterized as "feminine" in contrast to the "masculine" qualities of rationality and individualism, care theorists have argued either explicitly or implicitly for the acknowledgement of the missing feminine pieces to these masculinized discourses.

In the context of this broad theoretical construction of nurturant care, a number of tensions emerge in thinking about care as paid work. On the one hand, scholars want to raise societal recognition of the value of care in all its forms, including paid care work. One way to do that is to adopt an approach that focuses on making visible the labor and skills involved in care (a conceptualization that has parallels with reproductive labor). On the other hand, many want to preserve the distinctiveness of care as a practice and resist subsuming it into the masculinized language of market labor. While reproductive labor is situated as enabling the labor market, care theorists often pose nurturant care as antithetical to market values. Using market-based language like "skill" and "labor" to describe care fits it into a market-based model, and many care theorists would like to challenge that model at a fundamental level.

Another tension for nurturant care theorists conceptualizing paid care work is how to deal with the contested notion of dependency. Feminist scholars have mounted a strong critique of the way U.S. culture and policy stigmatize certain types of dependency. In this society, structured around an ideology of individualism and self-sufficiency, dependency has been much maligned. Few examples illustrate this stigma more clearly than the discourse of welfare reform in the 1990s that demonized single mothers receiving welfare for being "dependent" and insisted on their becoming "independent" by getting a job.[14] Feminist critics have pointed out that the dependent status of poor mothers is at least in part a result of their unrecognized but critically important unpaid role, caring for children who are by definition dependent. Theorists also point to other more invisible instances of dependency in U.S. society—for example, the subsidizing of middle-class homeowners through tax deductions and the dependence of male workers on the unpaid labor of their wives. Care theorists argue that dependency is a reality of social life that should be recognized and celebrated rather than denied and stigmatized. Joan Tronto has suggested that acknowledging dependency threatens the foundations of the U.S. value system: "If humans need care, then that fact belies the presupposition of the rational, autonomous individual."[15] Nurturant care theorists propose replacing a marginalizing language of dependency with an integrated discourse of care based on the interdependence and reciprocal ethical obligation among all members of a society.[16]

Moving from this broad philosophical argument to a microlevel view of the relationship between one caregiver and one care receiver, researchers have also found notions of dependency inadequate to describe real care relationships. The description of one human being (say, a child or an elderly nursing-home patient) as dependent on another (say, a parent or a nursing assistant) does not capture the complexity of those relationships. Scholars have argued that even in these apparently lopsided caregiving relationships, the interaction is still just that—a two-way street. Tronto and Berenice Fisher, who have identified four phases of care—caring about, taking care of, caregiving, and care receiving—argue that care should be seen as embedded in relationship rather than as a one-way dispersal of services to a dependent recipient.[17] Of course, many examples of care are less apparently lopsided: the elderly spouses who help each other, the grown child who takes care of a parent, and the individual in a wheelchair who may need assistance bathing but teaches a classroom full of children. Again, care theorists argue that unilaterally labeling any individual or group "dependent" belies the complex web of interdependence in any society, as well as in any individual human relationship.

The goals of moving beyond the masculinized discourse of the market and the stigmatized discourse of dependency have led to broad definitions of care. Tronto and Fisher, for example, define care as "a species activity that includes everything that we do to maintain, continue, and repair our world so that we can live in it as well as possible. That world includes our bodies, our selves, and our environment, all of which we seek to interweave in a complex, life-sustaining web."[18] Yet, despite the existence of these broad ethical frameworks, many scholars distinguish different types of care. Norwegian sociologist Kari Waerness makes a distinction between caring for dependents, caring for superiors, and caring in symmetrical relations, arguing that "caring for dependents, those members of society who by normal social standards are unable to take care of themselves, is the field of caring that most clearly is a concern both for social policy and for feminists."[19] In a similar vein, feminist legal scholar Martha Albertson Fineman has noted that the "inevitable" dependencies of childhood, old age, disability, and illness are rooted in biology and apply in some way to all or most members of a society at some point in their lives. According to Fineman, it is the inevitability and universality of these dependencies that "support the assertion of collective responsibility" and create an ethical responsibility to care at a societal level.[20]

How do paid workers fit into this discourse? Nurturant care theorists have pointed out that individuals who care for those who are young, old, ill, or disabled often find themselves dependent in some way as well. If their care work is unpaid, then they are dependent on other sources of economic support, whether family members or the government. Many paid care workers at the low end of the wage spectrum also experience continued economic dependence. This dependence is "derivative" in the sense that it is based on certain members of a society taking on the responsibility of caring for those in a stage of inevitable dependency, and theorists have argued that our ethical responsibility to care must extend to these caretakers as well. In effect, those providing care to inevitable dependents cannot do it without broader support, a circumstance that extends the sphere of societal responsibility and ethical obligation.[21]

Cancian and Oliker's definition of nurturant care that I introduced at the beginning of this chapter—"feelings of affection and responsibility combined with actions that provide responsively for an individual's personal needs or well-being, in a face-to-face relationship"—captures three elements common to the discussions I have characterized as the nurturant care perspective.[22] First, it focuses on the meeting of personal needs; second, it emphasizes the relational context of care; and finally, it includes not just actions but feelings and emotional responsiveness. In discussions of paid work, scholars have used a combination of these elements to define a particular group of workers as care workers.

The first element of a nurturance definition of care work often concerns meeting personal needs or contributing to human well-being, development, or capabilities. Nurturant care scholars examining paid care draw on the strong ethical argument that sees workers who care for inevitable dependents as deserving social support. However, given the problematic nature of the concept of dependency, many avoid using the term "dependent" in favor of more neutral language that addresses meeting needs. Of course, a mechanic and a day-care worker both meet the needs of their customer—but there is something more intimate, more personal, and more developmental about the needs being met by the day-care worker. An emphasis on the labor involved in nurturant care work as meeting personal needs or contributing to personal development is a way to distinguish it from other types of service work without relying on notions of dependency.

The second and related element of a definition of nurturant care work is that these personal or developmental needs are met in a relational context. The intimate nature of the tasks involved in nurturant care requires a face-to-face relationship, and care work defined in this way is inherently interpersonal.

When a child gets hurt, the mother who reads the child's feelings and soothes the child at the same time she cleans the cut and puts on a Band-aid is engaged in care work. Paid care workers such as nurses, home health-care aides, and child-care workers employ a complex set of interpersonal skills in performing their jobs.[23] But the father who brings home the money to buy the Band-aids or the janitor who cleans the hospital room is not considered a nurturant care worker. Nurturant care work names a particular kind of activity that is personal and relational in nature.

The third element of a nurturance definition of care, its emotional dimension, is closely related to the interpersonal nature of care work. As Cancian and Oliker's definition implies, some argue that to be considered care—or at least to be considered *good* care—the tasks of meeting an individual's needs in a relational context must be accompanied by an emotional connection. Arlie Hochschild coined the term "emotional labor" to refer to "the management of feeling to create a publicly observable facial and bodily display."[24] The concept of emotional labor has been widely used to analyze the experiences of workers across the service sector whose work demands that they project particular emotions as part of their job—the flight attendant who must smile and make passengers feel safe, the retail sales associate who must follow a script that demonstrates enthusiastic helpfulness. Some scholars have conceptualized care work as a specific type of emotional labor, the expectation for many care workers being not only a display of emotion but also a genuine emotional connection.[25] The interpersonal and intimate work of care is linked to this emotional labor and to relationship in a way that identifies care work as a unique practice.

Intersections and Inequalities: The Role of Race-Ethnicity and Class

Although conceptualizations of reproductive labor and nurturant care theory are both founded in a gendered analysis, attention to racial-ethnic and other divisions within these fields is more recent. Dorothy Roberts has argued that an analysis of domestic service shows clear racial-ethnic and class divisions of reproductive labor among women:

> Some work in the home is considered spiritual: it is valued highly because it is thought to be essential to the proper functioning of the household and the moral upbringing of children. Other domestic work is considered menial: it is devalued because it is strenuous and unpleasant and thought to require little moral or intellectual skill. While the ideological opposition of home and work distinguishes men from women, the ideological distinction between spiritual and menial

> housework fosters inequality among women. Spiritual housework is associated with privileged white women; menial housework is associated with minority, immigrant, and working class women.[26]

In the nineteenth century in homes where domestic servants were employed, they performed the domestic tasks considered the most menial—scrubbing floors and washing out laundry, taking care of the bodily needs of children and adults in the household, and preparing and cleaning up after meals. By contrast, the mistress of the home retained supervisory power over the whole household and acted as hostess for guests and moral guide for children. Women's lived experience of domestic work was more varied than this dichotomous characterization would suggest, as we will see later. Nonetheless, these ideological divisions within reproductive labor are crucial to understanding the intersecting constructions of gender, racial-ethnic, and class inequalities.

Evelyn Nakano Glenn has demonstrated that the racial-ethnic division of paid reproductive labor in the contemporary service sector shows remarkable continuities with this hierarchical division of domestic work. White women are disproportionately engaged in the occupations with supervisory capacity, a public relational element, and some degree of moral authority: registered nurse, teacher, social worker. Racial-ethnic women are concentrated in the "heavy, dirty, 'back-room' chores of cooking and serving food in restaurants and cafeterias, cleaning rooms in hotels and office buildings, and caring for the elderly and ill in hospitals and nursing homes, including cleaning rooms, making beds, changing bed pans, and preparing food."[27] Within the paid care workforce, these racial-ethnic and class divisions persist and are interconnected with the gendered associations of the work.

Nurturant care theorists have also explored the role of race-ethnicity and other inequalities in perceptions of dependence and ideals of care. Feminist historians of welfare policy in the United States have documented the shift from a program of mothers' pensions, created to provide economic support to single mothers so that they could stay home to care for their young children, to its newest incarnation as a program that above all else requires paid work for this group of women.[28] Although there are many reasons for this shift, a strong argument has been made that the expectation of full-time unpaid care work has been the province primarily of middle- and upper-class White women, while racial-ethnic, working-class, and immigrant mothers have always been expected to work in the paid labor force. The evolution of the welfare program offers a telling illustration of the impact of these differing norms around unpaid care as the demographic makeup of the population receiving welfare changed over time. These differing expectations of care for different groups of women are critical to understanding the connections between care and inequalities.

But, importantly, if the divide between spiritual and menial labor is one of the major axes of racial-ethnic and class stratification within reproductive labor, then a focus on nurturant care actually obscures this axis in the context of paid care work. Nurturant care is by definition relational, and those back-room jobs like the hospital janitor or the housekeeper or the cafeteria worker would not be considered nurturant care work. Nurturant care includes only jobs that have some association with the spiritual dimension of domestic labor. Although important racial-ethnic hierarchies exist within nurturant care, some of the most significant concentrations of racial-ethnic workers are in the jobs that I call nonnurturant (these are Roberts's menial jobs).

A Framework for Understanding Care, Value, and Inequalities

To identify nurturant care workers in this volume, I borrow the following criteria directly from the work of Paula England, Michelle Budig, and Nancy Folbre: (1) the job should entail providing face-to-face service to clients, not to managers or other employees; (2) providing face-to-face service should comprise a major part of the worker's time; and (3) the face-to-face service must develop the human capabilities of the recipient, which might include physical and mental health, physical skills, cognitive skills, or emotional skills.[29] This definition is very clear in its use of two of the three characteristics of nurturant care as developed in the theoretical literature on the topic: the meeting of personal or developmental needs and the relational and interpersonal context of nurturant care. It does not include a measure of the emotional content of the job, in large part because whether a worker establishes an emotional connection with a care recipient is much more an individual characteristic than an occupational one. In my analysis, I explore how expectations of emotional connection affect workers in these occupations.

My construction of nurturant care differs in one important way from the one England and her colleagues present: I have limited my discussion to nurturant care work that also meets the criteria of the definition of reproductive labor.[30] When I looked at the overlap between the workers included under a definition of nurturant care and under a definition of reproductive labor, I had a group of workers—including nurses, teachers, child-care workers, and personal care attendants—almost identical to the workers considered by nurturant care scholars to be caring for inevitable dependents. I agree with Waerness that it is with this group that feminist analysis and social policy should be most concerned, and so it is on this group that I focus in this book.[31]

I also incorporate some analysis of workers who are included by a broader definition of reproductive labor but excluded by a definition of nurturant care, focusing on those engaged in cleaning, laundry, and food preparation and service occupations. My primary motive for including these workers in the analysis was to explore the full scope of the racialized hierarchy between spiritual and menial labor discussed by Roberts and Nakano Glenn. I sometimes refer to these occupations as a group as "nonnurturant care" or "nonnurturant reproductive labor," and I also draw on Nakano Glenn's terminology of "dirty work." To refer to the entire universe of occupations—from child-care workers and teachers to nurses and social workers to janitors and cafeteria workers—I use the more general terms "reproductive labor" or "care work."

Discrete categorization of any complex human activity is inherently problematic. Many care occupations have both nurturant and nonnurturant components—the nanny who also cleans the kitchen, the nursing-home worker who empties bedpans but also comforts residents in their most profound sorrows. And there will inevitably be some disagreement with my choice of which workers to include—and exclude—from the overall category of care workers. I persist in the effort to define a care sector despite the ambiguities of doing so because of the fundamental assumption of the concept of care: there is a group of tasks that share some basic characteristics that are inextricably intertwined with the public and private value of the work. I have used a broad examination of care work to begin to untangle some of those questions of value, the core of which remains largely unchanged by disagreement around the edges of the boundaries of care. And, although I have used clear definitional boundaries to quantify numbers and demographic breakdowns of care workers over time, I have also tried to provide enough context to communicate the nuance and complexity that can sometimes get lost in the project of measurement.

In addition, while the boundaries between spiritual and menial work or between nurturant care work and other types of labor are not rigid, these have historically been socially constructed as dichotomous categories. Moreover, when one divides jobs and workers into discrete categories, those groups rarely end up reaping equal societal recognition and reward. Just as workers who are "skilled" occupy a higher place in the labor market hierarchy than those considered "unskilled," these other dichotomous constructions can also be used to divide workers by gender, race-ethnicity, or class. Here I explore the lived realities of care work and all the boundaries that work straddles. I also analyze the ways in which care occupations have been constructed ideologically, often as on one side or the other of these various divides—because how work and workers get labeled has material consequences, and only by making these hierarchies visible can we hope to understand them well enough to challenge them.

Chapter 2 Domestic Workers

Many Hands, Heavy Work

IN HER WELL-KNOWN fictional portrayal of nineteenth-century family life, *Home*, Catharine Maria Sedgwick explains that the family "did not regard their servant as a hireling, but as a member of the family, who, from her humble position in it, was entitled to their protection and care."[1] Maria W. Stewart, an African American women's rights activist who had worked as a domestic servant from a young age, described service very differently: "Tell me no more of southern slavery; for with few exceptions . . . I consider our condition but little better than that."[2] Taken together, these two voices capture many of the profound contradictions of domestic service in the nineteenth century, when servants could be described, depending on one's perspective, as family members or as slaves. These workers performed a whole range of nurturant and nonnurturant tasks in perhaps the most intimate venue—private homes.

It is difficult to overestimate the importance of domestic service in the United States during the second half of the 1800s, both to women workers and to reproductive labor. During this time period, nearly every middle- and upper-class family employed at least one domestic servant, and some wealthier families employed an entire staff to carry out the daily functions of their households. Ninety percent of these workers were women, and until 1870, at least 50 percent of employed women in the United States were domestic servants. In 1870, there was one servant for every eight U.S. families, and in some cities the ratio was as high as one to four.[3] Paid reproductive labor in the twentieth century has its roots in the nineteenth century with these workers who represent some of the earliest and most ubiquitous paid care workers in U.S. history.[4]

From Ubiquity to the Underground: The Shifting Economic and Cultural Context of Domestic Service

The context for private household work at the dawn of the twenty-first century is certainly different from the world of servants 150 years ago, and yet some patterns of gender and racial-ethnic inequality have shown remarkable persistence. From the emergence of domestic service as a rigidly hierarchical occupation to its precipitous numerical decline to its more recent incarnations, its story provides a critical foundation for understanding the development of paid care work in the United States.

THE DOMESTIC SERVICE MODEL TAKES HOLD: 1800–1900

The work of maintaining a household in the agricultural economy of the nineteenth century has been described as "exhausting, backbreaking, [and] unceasing."[5] Food preparation often began with tending a garden and caring for animals, and involved laborious and time-consuming tasks such as canning and preserving, churning butter, and baking bread. Cooking was done on coal stoves or woodstoves that required constant tending. Laundry was so labor intensive that in many households an entire day of the week was devoted to boiling clothes in huge tubs, scrubbing them on the washboard, wringing them out, and hanging them to dry. Floors had to be scrubbed, water collected, and heating fires maintained.[6] In a large number of families—even those not considered particularly well-off—hired domestic servants worked alongside the women and children of the house to accomplish these daunting tasks.[7]

In addition to the physical maintenance of the home, domestic servants were involved in many other aspects of reproductive labor. It was common for families to hire servants to care for children, sit with ill family members, or help with a new baby.[8] While the twentieth century would see a shift of some of this type of care to institutions like hospitals and preschools, in the 1800s most care happened in private homes. And for families who could afford to hire servants, paid workers were a big part of providing that care.

For much of the nineteenth century, the term "servant" was used far less frequently to describe these workers than the term "hired girl." These workers were overwhelmingly young women, old enough to be helpful but not yet married. Families often hired the daughters of neighbors or friends and saw their role as part employer and part mentor. Young women who had helped their own families with household tasks perfected their domestic skills as hired girls to prepare themselves for marriage. These young women may have lived in the homes of their employers at least temporarily but often came from homes nearby and traveled back and forth. Hiring help was an unorganized activity that varied seasonally or with changing family needs, not an occupational category that distinguished particular individuals. While they were engaged in very difficult labor, these hired girls often ate with the family and shared in family activities, not subjected to the rigid distinctions that would come to characterize domestic service.[9]

If the hired-girl model was prevalent in New England and in westward expansion, in the pre–Civil War South, domestic labor was performed overwhelmingly by slaves. Like paid servants, slaves participated in every aspect of reproductive labor, from food production and preservation to cleaning to child care. The line between slave and master/mistress was clearly drawn, and slaves were subjected to brutal treatment; the harsh working conditions and immediate punishment that characterized slave labor in the plantation fields extended to domestic labor. Slave children often supplied household labor, especially during the most labor-intensive times on the plantation when many female slaves worked in the fields alongside men. The racial exploitation inherent in the master/mistress–slave relationship would in many ways be incorporated in later models of domestic service.[10]

The language of domestic service began to emerge in the early to mid-nineteenth century in northern urban centers, where the twin forces of industrialization and urbanization were creating an environment in which families hired strangers on the labor market rather than making informal arrangements with family and neighbors to help with reproductive labor. The shift from an agricultural economy to an increasingly industrial one brought with it changes in family ideology.[11] For the new urban middle class, the family became the refuge for men coming home from a long day away at work, with an increasing emphasis on times of private family togetherness. A model of domestic service that emphasized more rigid divisions between family and servants fit this emerging ideology. Unlike hired girls, domestic servants ate apart from the family, lived in separate and often woefully inadequate quarters, and were bound by constant and clear reminders of their status in every way, from uniforms to forms of address.[12]

The mid-1800s also brought about supply-side shifts that contributed to this redefinition of the domestic servant role. In the 1840s and 1850s, large waves of young single Irish women arrived in the growing cities of the United States. They were spurred on by the famine and desperation in their homeland and by targeted efforts by middle- and upper-class Americans to attract them to service positions. During the turbulence of industrialization, increasing economic pressure on all poor families produced a more ready supply of both immigrant and U.S.-born women willing to take on the role of servant. In the South, domestic service was one of the only occupations open to newly free

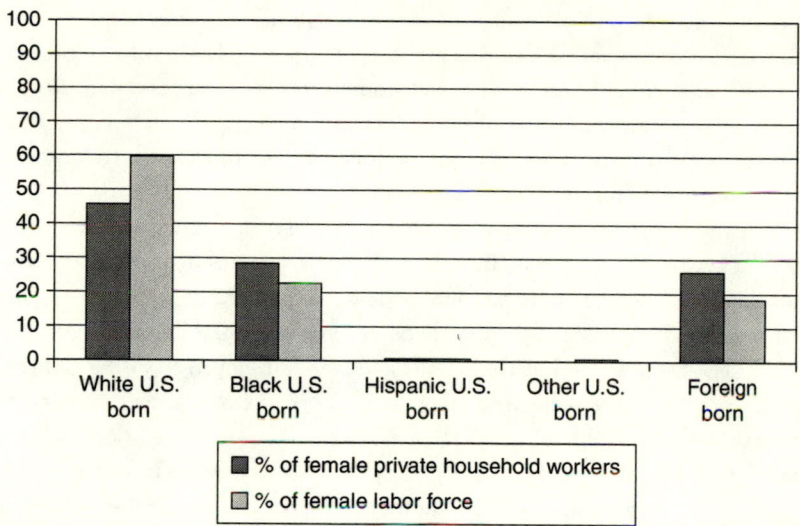

Figure 2.1. Female private household workers by race-ethnicity and birthplace, 1900 (in percentages) *Source: Calculated by author using U.S. Census data (1900) available through the Integrated Public Use Microdata Series (IPUMS).*

Black women, and the rigid separation between servant and employer also accorded with racist ideologies and the legacy of slavery. By 1900, a model of domestic service was entrenched in urban centers, while in rural areas the hired-girl model persisted well into the twentieth century.[13]

Although alternative occupational choices in factories and offices were open to some women by 1900, domestic service still then employed almost 1.4 million workers, more than one-quarter of the female labor force.[14] The largest group of domestic workers—over 40 percent—were White U.S.-born women (see figure 2.1), an underrepresentation compared to the 60 percent of White U.S.-born women in the female labor force as a whole. These numbers indicate the high representation of Black and foreign-born women among private household workers and mask even more pronounced concentrations of these groups in particular regions of the country.

In northern cities, Irish immigrants remained the core of the domestic service workforce.[15] Nationally, 26 percent of private household workers were foreign born, and an additional 18 percent came from families where one or both parents were foreign born, meaning that almost half the domestic servants in the United States in 1900 came from immigrant families. The majority of these were from Ireland, but by 1900 domestic service had begun to attract substantial numbers of young women from Germany and the

Scandinavian countries. Among these immigrants and daughters of immigrants, 94 percent were unmarried and 80 percent were in their teens or twenties. While there were a few widowed women in this group, the majority had never been married. Service, although perhaps more rigidly defined by ideology, remained a transitional occupation for many young immigrant women, a stepping-stone to marriage or a better job.[16]

In the South, the occupation of domestic service remained dominated by Black women, who had inherited slavery's racialized division of labor. Nationally, Black U.S.-born women made up 28 percent of domestic servants, compared to 22 percent of the female labor force overall. Almost 75 percent of Black U.S.-born women in the labor force were employed in either domestic service or agriculture, reflecting severe occupational constraints that persisted fifty years after emancipation. Because of these curtailed occupational choices and the expectation (and often necessity) for Black women to remain in the labor force after marriage, service was much less frequently a transitional stage for Black women. Over 30 percent of Black U.S.-born private household workers were married, and of those who were not married, a large number were widowed or divorced. About half were more than thirty years old, and more than a quarter were over forty. Despite the similarities in the content of domestic labor, the context differed dramatically by racial-ethnic group.

In 1900, servants continued to be engaged in every aspect of reproductive labor. A fully staffed household might include numerous maids to clean and maintain the rooms of the house, laundresses to do the washing and ironing, a cooking staff to prepare and serve meals, a nursemaid to attend to the children, personal care staff for the adults, and a head housekeeper and butler to manage and oversee the rest of the domestic staff. In the majority of middle-class households in the United States, all these functions were combined in the job of a single domestic servant, often called a "maid of all work."[17] While well over half of private household workers still lived in the homes of their employers at the turn of the century, increasing numbers returned to their own homes in the evenings. This pattern developed particularly among Black U.S.-born domestic workers, of whom almost 70 percent reported that they were living in their own household or that of a family member.[18] A desire to balance work with one's family needs was partly behind this trend, as Black women were more likely to be balancing paid care with unpaid care work in their own families.

DOMESTIC SERVICE IN TRANSITION: 1900–1950
Although the increase in private household employment that had characterized the nineteenth century continued through the first several decades of the

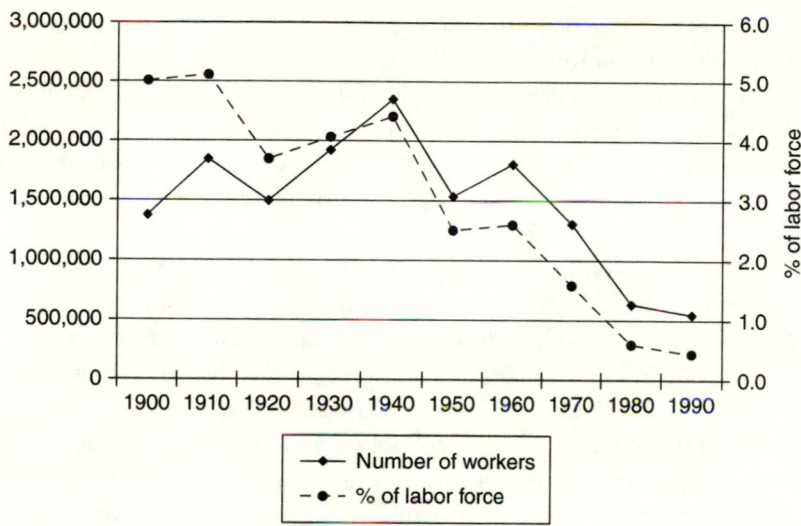

Figure 2.2. Number of private household workers, 1900–1990 *Source: Calculated by author using U.S. Census data (1900–1990) available through the Integrated Public Use Microdata Series (IPUMS).*

twentieth, the overall story of the twentieth century is the dramatically declining presence of domestic servants as paid care workers (see figure 2.2). Nonetheless, absolute numbers of domestic servants continued to rise until the 1930s.[19] Between 1900 and 1940, the number of domestic workers rose from 1.4 to 2.4 million. In contrast to the accelerating growth of the previous century, this reflects a slowdown relative to the continued expansion of the overall labor force. By 1960 a numerical decline had begun that would characterize the remainder of the century.

This slowdown in the growth of domestic service was largely the result of societal shifts that limited the supply of domestic servants. First, the occupational choices available to women—particularly to U.S.-born White women—continued to expand. Technological innovation and expanding consumer demand in the post–World War I era intensified the growth of the manufacturing sector, and factory employment became a viable alternative for increasing numbers of women with little or no formal education. As education became more accessible to certain groups of women, and corporate bureaucratization created specialized positions, many women found jobs as secretaries, saleswomen, clerks, cashiers, stenographers, or typists.[20] The expansion of nurturant care jobs like teaching and nursing also created opportunities for some women. While jobs requiring education remained primarily the domain of middle-class U.S.-born White women, factories provided alternatives to service for immigrant women as well.

A second factor limiting the supply of domestic servants was the drastically reduced number of immigrant women in the labor force as a result of draconian immigration restrictions in the 1920s.[21] In 1900, over 20 percent of the U.S. labor force was foreign born; by 1940, the number had dropped to less than 12 percent. Finally, during this same time period, child-labor laws and the movement toward compulsory education removed the youngest girls (a cohort that had worked in domestic service in substantial numbers) from the labor market. World War II further accelerated women's labor-force participation, and by midcentury these converging trends had greatly reduced the number of women available and willing to take on domestic service positions.

At the same time, a series of technological innovations transformed the nature of household work itself. In the beginning decades of the twentieth century, the introduction of washing machines and electric and gas stoves, as well as the new and widespread availability of running water and electricity in homes, dramatically reduced the amount of physical labor necessary to run a household.[22] By the 1950s, popular women's magazines were promising that housewives could be "liberated" from housework by a range of new appliances from vacuum cleaners to blenders.[23] Although these technological advances developed more quickly in urban areas, by midcentury the day-to-day experience of household labor had changed dramatically even in rural homes. Industrialization also shifted some tasks, such as processing food and making clothing, out of the home and into factories, so household labor for most families no longer included such time-intensive work.[24] The very real decrease in the amount of physical work that needed to be done in private homes also contributed to the decline in domestic service.

The net impact of industrialization on household labor must also take into account ideological shifts that somewhat mitigated the effects of these technological innovations. The gendered separation of public/work and private/family spheres that had begun during the industrial revolution intensified through the first half of the twentieth century, as did the expectation that middle- and upper-class women should be perfect housekeepers and mothers. Although new technologies may have eased the physical burden of domestic work in some areas, standards of cleanliness and beauty in the home increased simultaneously. So while most women in the post–World War II era did not have to spend an entire day doing laundry, the cultural image of the middle-class housewife in particular was exemplified by happy women in TV commercials scrubbing away at their shiny white bathtubs.[25] In the public imagination, the domestic sphere had become the exclusive domain of women, and a woman's worth was intimately connected to how clean her bathroom was, how little dust was on her furniture, and how often she baked cookies.

Linked to the development of this ideology of separate spheres, changing economic structures and fertility patterns fueled a transformation in how Americans viewed childhood. Once essential productive members of the family farm economy, children were increasingly held up as "precious," to be nurtured and protected from "real life" rather than contributors to it.[26] The resulting focus on child care, combined with higher expectations for household cleanliness, created new forms of household labor at the same time that technological changes made others obsolete.[27]

These labor-market, technological, and ideological transformations all contributed not only to declining rates of private household work but also to a reconfiguration of the remaining domestic service workforce. By 1950, reflecting the curtailment of immigration, foreign-born workers represented only about 10 percent of domestic servants; White U.S.-born women, now almost 80 percent of the women in the labor force, made up only 30 percent of domestic servants; U.S.-born Black women made up the remaining almost 60 percent, despite being only 10 percent of the female labor force overall (see figure 2.3). In contrast to the range (relatively speaking) of occupational opportunities available to White women in this period, Black women were

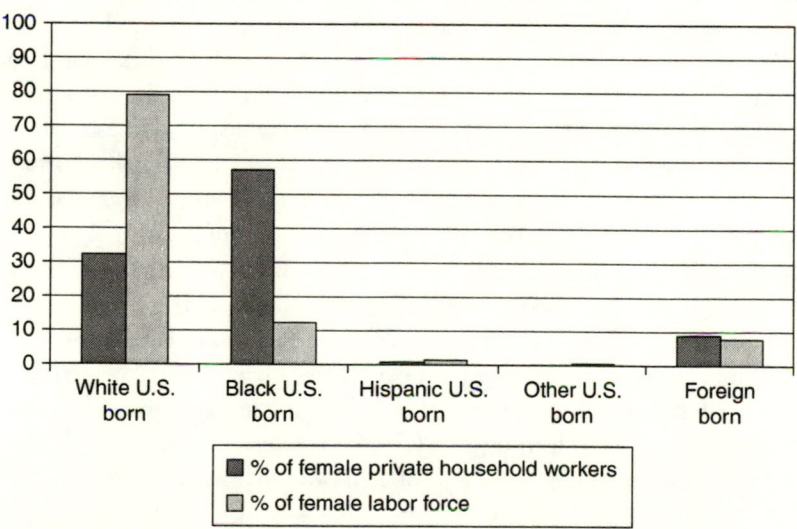

Figure 2.3. Female private household workers by race-ethnicity and birthplace, 1950 (in percentages) *Source: Calculated by author using U.S. Census data (1950) available through the Integrated Public Use Microdata Series (IPUMS).*

still severely constrained. Over 40 percent of Black U.S.-born women in the labor force in 1950 were employed as domestic servants. As had always been the case in the South, the Black women who now dominated domestic service in cities across the Northeast and Midwest as well were older and more likely to be married than their immigrant predecessors.[28] In 1950, the mean age for domestic servants across the country was 40.6 years old, and almost 40 percent were married. While there were still important regional variations, in large part domestic service had ceased to be a transitional occupation for young women and had become a lifelong and sometimes intergenerational "occupational ghetto" for Black women with few other options.[29]

In part because of this dominance of Black women in the occupation, by 1950 the shift from live-in to live-out work was almost complete (only 13 percent of domestic servants in that year lived in the homes of their employers). Black women who had families of their own to care for and were dealing with the rigid segregation of the pre–civil rights era drove the move away from a live-in model.[30] A live-out model was also more compatible with a new family ideology among White middle- and upper-class employers, which emphasized the centrality and inviolability of the nuclear family unit. As family privacy became more prized, houses became smaller and budgets tighter, adding to the pressures to hire domestic workers on a live-out basis.[31]

The increased racialization of domestic service magnified the rigid enforcement of boundaries as well as the heavy workload that had come to define the occupation, despite the potential for improved conditions from living out. In the 1950s, domestic servants continued to work long hours, limiting the time they were able to spend at home; further, they now had to pay for room and board on wages that had not increased from live-in levels.[32] Servants were often confined to particular rooms in their employer's house and had little control over such fundamental things as when they ate or when they took breaks. These workers often performed some of the dirtiest and most physically demanding tasks in the new domestic order—scrubbing bathrooms, vacuuming, mopping, and dusting.[33] An increase in restaurants and hospitals meant that fewer domestic workers cooked family meals or cared for the sick, but child care remained an important part of the job for many.[34] Nevertheless, even as rates of domestic service declined and the context for household labor was transformed, at midcentury the 1.5 million women employed as domestic workers remained an important part of care work in private homes.

THE "DEATH" OF DOMESTIC SERVICE: 1950–1990

In the second half of the twentieth century, a number of trends converged to turn the slowdown in the growth of domestic service into a steep decline.

By 1990, the number of domestic servants had dropped to just over 500,000 (see figure 2.2), less than one-quarter of the number in 1940.[35] This substantial drop occurred at the same time the total labor force more than doubled. From an occupation that once employed more than half the female labor force, domestic service now represented less than 1 percent of it, reflecting in large part expanding labor-force alternatives for some women.

During the 1960s and 1970s, the civil rights movement and the women's movement opened up new occupational choices for Black women. Like White women before them, when Black women had other choices, they left domestic service in large numbers.[36] Some observers argued at the time that these social movements toward a more egalitarian ideal had made the master-servant relationship upon which domestic service was based obsolete, and the occupation was declared "dead" two decades before the end of the twentieth century.[37] At the same time, the health-care industry and the food preparation and service industry continued to expand at a phenomenal rate. By the end of the century, the remaining domestic servants were rarely asked to prepare family meals, and the practice of hiring women to sit with the sick or help with a new baby had long since given way to hospital care.[38]

These trends led not only to a significant decrease in the overall number of domestic servants, but also to important reconfigurations of the occupation. Similar to the pattern at the beginning of the century, over 40 percent of domestic workers were now White U.S.-born women, reflecting the exodus of Black women from domestic labor and the entrance of a new smaller group of immigrant women (see figure 2.4). Although still overrepresented among domestic workers (at twice the rate of their participation in the labor force), Black U.S.-born women made up only 20 percent of the domestic workforce in 1990 (compared to 60 percent in 1950). By contrast, Hispanic women (both U.S. and foreign born), who were barely visible through most of the century, made up almost one-fourth of domestic servants in 1990. These shifts reflect transformations in the U.S. labor force. After many decades of decline, immigrant representation in the labor force reached a low of just over 5 percent of workers in 1970. Since that time, new waves of migration have brought immigrants from Mexico, Central America, and Asia in increasing numbers.[39] By 1990, immigrant workers made up 10 percent of the labor force overall, still lower than their almost 25 percent early in the century but a 100 percent increase over twenty years earlier. Domestic service is one of the occupations populated by this growing immigrant workforce.

Although immigrant women are again today a growing presence among domestic servants, the context of their employment is quite different from that of their Irish predecessors a century ago. Interestingly, the mean age (41.6

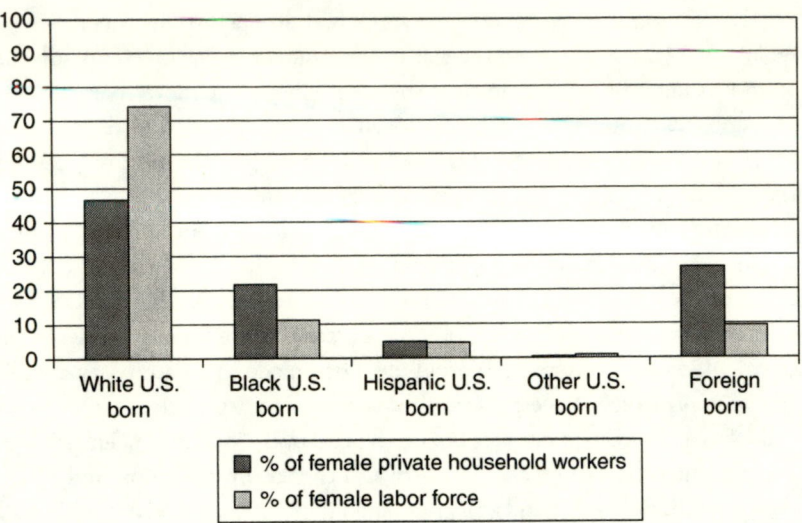

Figure 2.4. Female private household workers by race-ethnicity and birthplace, 1990 (in percentages) *Source: Calculated by author using U.S. Census data (1990) available through the Integrated Public Use Microdata Series (IPUMS).*

years old) and the percentage of domestic servants who are married (40 percent) are very close to the numbers for 1950. Perhaps most significantly, almost 70 percent of domestic servants in 1990 reported having at least one child.[40] As a number of scholars have documented, in some of these cases, the children have remained in the country of origin, creating "global care chains": an immigrant woman is caring for children of a U.S. family while money she sends home helps someone else (a grandmother or aunt perhaps) provide daily care for her own children elsewhere on the globe.[41] Eighty percent of Hispanic domestic workers in 1990 were foreign born, and the job does not tend to be passed from mother to daughter in the way that was often true for midcentury Black domestics.[42] And although the occupation overall remained primarily live out (only 7 percent of domestic servants reported living in the home of their employer), live-in positions are often the first step for new immigrants. The language of servitude has largely been replaced, and these workers are usually called "nannies" or "housekeepers" rather than "servants." Whatever their titles, domestic workers in single private households are often called upon to assist with a range of child-care and housekeeping duties.[43]

After 1990, the U.S. Census Bureau changed its occupational coding system and for the first time in at least one hundred years did not categorize "private household workers" as a separate occupation. U.S. Census occupation categories have changed many times during the century, of course, but private household occupations had remained an identifiable category throughout. In an attempt to better standardize the coding of occupations (based on the content of a job) and industry (based on the location of a job), the 2000 U.S. Census uses an industry code for workers in private households that includes a range of people from accountants to mechanics to chauffeurs. Perhaps this coding decision also reflected the wider cultural assumption that the occupation of domestic service was a relic of the past. Whatever the reason, this reorganization makes it impossible to directly compare rates of domestic labor at the dawn of the twenty-first century with earlier eras—problematic when some observers are arguing that this occupation, once declared dead, is again on the rise.

A NEW SERVANT CLASS? 1990–2007

The assumption that the number of domestic servants is growing again at the dawn of the twenty-first century runs through many contemporary analyses— despite the fact that this assumption has not been documented on a national level.[44] Observers attribute the purported renewal of domestic service to the convergence of two trends. First, scholars suggest that rising immigration rates, particularly from Mexico and Central America, provide a new pool of workers available for domestic service. Second, such observers point to a care deficit created by increasing care needs (particularly among the elderly and disabled) combined with a decreasing supply of unpaid care as a result of women's large-scale entry into the paid labor force. One empirical study that documented expanding rates of domestic service in two Southern California cities between 1980 and 1990 also emphasized that rising economic inequality allows some families to hire domestic help and forces financially constrained workers to take these largely undesirable jobs.[45] Given the changes in data collection, it is difficult to tell whether these identified growth pockets were isolated instances with unique circumstances or whether they foretold a national trend.

To address this question, I have constructed an alternate measure of the number of domestic workers by combining the industry codes and occupation codes for the latter decades of the twentieth century and up to the most current data available. The results of this analysis appear in figure 2.5, where I identify those coded as housekeepers/maids or child-care workers within the industry code of private households.[46] While this measure does not capture exactly the same universe of workers as the more precise occupational category, it is clear from comparing the 1980 and 1990 estimates to those generated by the use of the occupational code (figure 2.2) that the estimates are close.

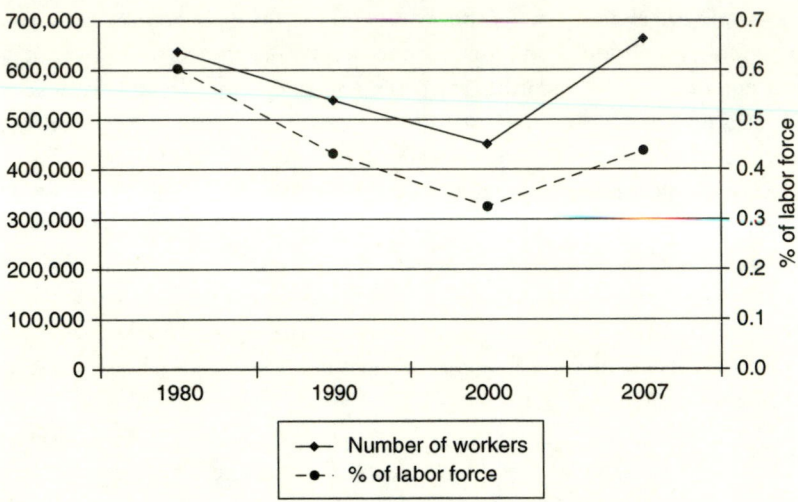

Figure 2.5. Number of nannies and housekeepers, 1980–2007 *Source: Calculated by author using data from the U.S. Census (1980–2000) and from the American Community Survey (2007) available through the Integrated Public Use Microdata Series (IPUMS).*

Despite particular metropolitan areas that showed an increase in rates of domestic service as early as the 1980s, the overall national trend continued downward through 2000. But the years since 2000 have shown an increase at the national level in the number of nannies and housekeepers, as well as a small increase in the proportion of the labor force represented by these workers. This growth is significant in that it reverses a long trend of decline, calling into question the notion that domestic service as an occupation has been rendered obsolete by increasingly egalitarian ideals and technological and social change. The future direction of this occupation, considered a job of last resort by many generations of women, is now unclear.

What is certain is that the cultural and economic context is quite different for these nannies and housekeepers than for domestic servants a century ago. Even given the possibility of recent and future growth, traditionally defined domestic service positions today represent only a tiny fraction of paid reproductive labor. Other forms of private household labor—housecleaning services and home-care services—have become increasingly prominent. And institutional forms of care work—hospitals, nursing homes, and child-care centers—also continue to expand. A century of changing attitudes toward immigration has led to increasing scrutiny of undocumented immigrants, as well as of informal economic arrangements like the ones that were common in hiring domestic help in the nineteenth century. While domestic service was once ubiquitous, today's nannies and housekeepers are in many ways underground.

Invisible Work, Women's Work, and Dirty Work: Understanding the Social Construction and Material Realities of Domestic Labor

Perhaps nowhere have the intersections of gender, racial-ethnic, and class inequalities with paid care work been more extensively studied than in both historical and contemporary analyses of private household work. Examining the historical development of the occupation in light of these analytical explanations provides important insights not only into domestic service, but also into the story of paid care work more broadly.

A JOB OF LAST RESORT

The historical story of domestic service describes jobs that women leave when they can. One scholar of nineteenth-century domestic service observed: "In most cases only people in desperate financial straits, those who considered service a brief interlude to better things, or those who could not find employment elsewhere became servants."[47] The twentieth-century evolution of the work demonstrates that as groups of women gained access to alternative occupational choices, they left domestic service in large numbers.

The unique context of private household service in many ways leaves workers vulnerable to exploitation. The boundaries of a domestic worker's job are often blurred by both the diffuse nature of the work itself and the individualistic nature of the employment relationship.[48] Care work is not easy to break down into a series of identifiable tasks. An hour in the life of a nanny may look like this: make lunch for child, wipe child's nose, rock child to sleep, return to bedroom three times for water, clean kitchen, get child from bedroom and comfort after bad dream, help child get shoes on while teaching child how to do it, and on and on. And while housekeeping tasks in theory may be more easily broken down, in practice nannies and housekeepers perform an unpredictable and seemingly never-ending series of child-care and housekeeping tasks. In the nineteenth century, the average domestic servant worked eleven to twelve hours a day, seven days a week.[49] Two hundred years later, one nanny/housekeeper describes her job this way: "Even though it's paid well, you are sinking in the amount of your work. Even while you are ironing the clothes, they can still call you to the kitchen to wash the plates."[50] The content of the work of domestic servants in the nineteenth century (boiling laundry and scrubbing floors) was quite different from the work of contemporary nannies and housekeepers (making peanut butter-and-jelly sandwiches and cleaning toilets). But the constants have been long hours and heavy workloads.

Live-in domestic workers are the most vulnerable to expanding job demands by employers and to employer control over their time. This was a chief complaint of many of the servants Lucy Maynard Salmon surveyed in 1890, one of whom said: "You are mistress of no time of your own."[51] Live-in domestic workers in the late twentieth century still reported working an average of sixty-four hours a week, and for these workers the lines between work and nonwork are blurred by the constancy of their presence in the home of their employer.[52] Although live-out workers report more control over their hours, that control sometimes comes at a price, as employers demand the same amount of work in fewer hours.[53]

One of the dynamics that contributes to a high degree of employer control over the time of domestic workers is the individualistic nature of the employer-employee relationship. In contrast to jobs in which employees are embedded in an organizational structure, domestic workers are employed by a single family, and in most cases their work is directed by a single person.[54] Structurally, domestic workers are isolated from their peers and have no recourse to managers or supervisors if they feel they are being treated unfairly.[55] This context gives employers a tremendous amount of power, which is magnified when the employer-employee relationship also reflects power differences related to race-ethnicity, class, and citizenship. Employer power is also reinforced by the fact that the worksite is a private home, an intimate venue that provides many opportunities for intense employer scrutiny. While there have been some innovative efforts among domestic workers throughout the century to organize and push for change, these attempts have been relatively localized.[56] In 2008, the primary tool used by private household workers who feel they are being treated unfairly remains the same as it was in 1900: to quit and seek employment with another family.[57]

Expanding work demands and intense employer control are buttressed by the relational nature of care work in private homes. Even as the symbolic boundaries between servant and family became more rigidly enforced, in practice domestic servants throughout the nineteenth and twentieth centuries interacted with the women and children of the house regularly. Within the confines of a private home, interaction and the development of a relationship between employing woman and domestic are almost inevitable. That relationship can take on many different forms, and domestic workers have been harshly treated and patronized, as well as treated as confidants or competitors.[58] Theoretically, the intimate relational nature of this employment situation could lead to more dignified and respectful treatment for private household workers. While this may occur in some homes, often the obligations of relationship actually intensify the heavy work demands of domestic service.

The relational context creates a situation in which employers may justify and in some cases expect more work without more pay. And employees' feelings of obligation to the individuals they work for and with daily may make it harder for them to enforce boundaries around work hours and demands. These relational obligations are most extreme in contemporary nanny situations, where the relationship between the nanny and the child is central.

In individual cases, women may have chosen domestic service for a variety of reasons. In the nineteenth century, factory work in the North and agricultural work in the South both involved working under harsh physical conditions. Some women chose domestic service as a more "healthy" alternative.[59] Some Black women in the twentieth century reported that they chose live-out domestic work because it gave them more independence than factory work.[60] A study of Hispanic domestic workers in the late twentieth century points out that, "on the one hand, cleaning houses is degrading and embarrassing; on the other, domestic service can be higher paying, more autonomous, and less dehumanizing than other low-status, low-skilled occupations."[61] What is striking is that the choice of domestic service is always posed against a bleak slate of alternatives. As we have seen, the historical record is clear that as groups of women gained access to a wider range of occupational alternatives, they left domestic service in large numbers.

DOLLARS AND DIGNITY

While wages for domestic service have never been high, it is notable that low wages have not been the chief complaint of private household workers. In fact, a substantial number of the respondents to Salmon's 1890 survey cited pay as one of the reasons they entered domestic service.[62] It is difficult to quantify the earnings of domestic servants at the turn of the century because in so many cases room and board were included as part of a servant's compensation. But relative to other jobs available to women at the time—and this is key—the pay was comparable and in some cases perhaps higher when room and board were considered.[63] W.E.B. Du Bois observed in 1899 that the primary problem with domestic service is not wages, but the stigma.[64] Similarly, the number one disadvantage of domestic service cited by Salmon's respondents was "pride, social conditions, and unwillingness to be called servants."[65]

Through the course of the twentieth century, there has been considerable variation in wage levels as well as in the attitudes of domestic workers toward their wages.[66] Qualitative studies find that domestic workers' descriptions of their wages vary from "fine" to "slave wages,"[67] and that reported wages vary significantly even within the same geographic locale.[68] In 1950, the median earnings for full-time year-round private household workers was $850 a year ($7,700 in 2010 dollars), compared to an overall median wage of $2,350 ($21,300 in 2010 dollars) for the full-time labor force.[69] It should be noted that this ranks among the lowest median earnings for any occupation in that year. In 1990, median earnings for full-time private household workers again fell near the bottom of the occupational earnings hierarchy at $9,980 a year ($16,700 in 2010 dollars), compared to an overall median of $23,000 ($38,400 in 2010 dollars).

These national averages do mask important variations. Mary Romero has observed that "both micro- and macro-levels of analysis demonstrate how immigrants and non-migrants who are racialized and gendered are positioned on the continuum of household labor as domestics, nannies, or au pairs, and differentiated by wages, benefits, and overall working conditions."[70] U.S. Census wage data bears this out: in 1990 some domestic workers earned as much as $50,000. But only about 5 percent of full-time private household workers earned more than the labor-force median of $23,000. As a whole, contemporary private household work is low-wage work that rarely provides benefits such as paid vacations, medical insurance, and sick days.[71]

The wage level of domestic work reflects a labor-market hierarchy based on particular notions of skill and economic value. Despite the challenges to quantifying wages in this occupation, it is clear that if we measure value economically, private household work is in a very low position. What emerges from the many excellent qualitative studies of domestic service in the late twentieth century is that, at least in the perception of the workers themselves, the social valuation of their jobs has not changed much since the days when domestic servants complained of the stigma of their job to Lucy Maynard Salmon. Over and over again, nannies and housekeepers speak of the lack of respect and dignity afforded those in their position.[72] They experience this lack of social value as both a generalized judgment about the job and in daily acts of dehumanization. This issue of social valuation is so intense that in the 1990s when a group of domestic workers in Los Angeles created a list of goals for changing the occupation, "respect for our rights and dignity as a person" was in the number one position, ahead of fair pay.[73]

THE INVISIBLE LABOR OF WOMEN'S WORK

Being invisible is antithetical to being valued, and domestic workers are vulnerable to a number of intersecting dynamics that render their work (and sometimes their persons) invisible. Domestic labor, both in its content and in its location, is firmly anchored in the private, feminine, nonwork sphere. The ideological division of labor into gendered separate spheres has not been a neutral process, as the identification of the public labor of men as work has provided it with legitimacy, economic rewards, and social standing that have not been afforded private household labor.[74] The construction of cleaning, cooking, and caring tasks as not work is powerful enough that even when these tasks are paid, they retain strong associations with the private sphere of women's unrecognized labor. In the case of private household employment, this invisibility is exacerbated by the work's location in private homes. The informality of the economic arrangements that have characterized domestic service—from "hired girls" to "under the table" nannies and housekeepers— both reflect and reinforce the construction of this labor as somehow distinct from a legitimate job.

The invisibility of domestic labor as work extends quite literally to the legal sphere. Many New Deal social welfare laws, including Social Security benefits, did not include domestic servants. Domestic workers have also been systematically excluded from protective labor legislation like the National Labor Relations Act, Occupational Health and Safety regulations, and workers' compensation programs. In the first half of the twentieth century, as many of these policies were being formulated, domestic work was vulnerable not only to association with the domestic sphere but also to racial bias. A number of scholars have documented that the exclusion of domestic labor and agriculture from Social Security effectively denied coverage to the majority of Black workers.[75] Even when reformed Social Security laws required employers to pay Social Security taxes for their domestic workers, their frequent noncompliance effectively excluded many employees. Judith Rollins has observed among her respondents that "the prevalence of disregard for the law [requiring payment of Social Security taxes] and the comfort expressed with that disregard by both domestics and employers suggests that women may see domestic work as exceptional, not quite as legitimate a job as others, not to be taken entirely seriously as an employer-employee relationship."[76]

Part of the ideological scaffolding of separate spheres is the argument that women are "naturally" suited to the private sphere of family (and men to the world of commerce and production). Making a home clean and welcoming, preparing meals, and caring for children are all tasks that have been strongly associated with essential elements of femininity. Throughout the twentieth century, to be a woman—or at least to be a good woman—meant being the mistress of this domestic realm. The construction of these tasks as part of woman's fundamental nature and role in society obscures the skill and effort that goes into them, adding another layer of invisibility to the labor of domestic work.[77]

DOING THE DIRTY WORK

Ironically, the preservation of this notion of femininity for White middle- and upper-class women has depended on the simultaneous division of repro- ductive labor into what Dorothy Roberts labels "spiritual" and "menial" work.[78] For middle- and upper-class White women in the nineteenth cen- tury, mastery of the private/feminine sphere required them to be ladies, deli- cate and refined. Yet the work of maintaining a home was dirty, messy, and physically demanding. The ideology of separate spheres was built on the strong association of the domestic realm with the purported feminine virtues of moral and spiritual superiority. The nineteenth century also saw married women increasingly expected to be emotionally available and sexually attrac- tive for their husbands.[79] One scholar of nineteenth-century domestic service observed that "servants were needed to spare American women the dirt, monotony, and drudgery of their own homes."[80] By delegating many of the most physically demanding and dirty tasks to their servants, women could both keep a nice home and maintain their status as ladies of the house, their feminine moral authority and loving guidance uninterrupted by the menial tasks of housekeeping. And they could provide their husbands with good meals and fresh laundry with soft, clean hands. So, for some middle- and upper-class married women, living up to the ideals of feminine domesticity actually required hiring other women to perform the dirty work of keeping house.

Of course, many women who could not afford to hire domestic servants remained trapped in these paradoxical expectations of femininity. For many middle- and working-class families, the sheer amount of labor required to run a home in the nineteenth and early twentieth centuries meant that the women and often the children of the home worked alongside hired girls. But the distinction between spiritual and menial housework was an important ideological construct that in many ways enabled the gendered division of labor. As the domestic service model became more entrenched, and especially as the occupation became more racialized, this hierarchy became increasingly attached to racial-ethnic divisions as well.[81]

In the middle decades of the twentieth century, Black women's domi- nance in private household service coincided with the intensification of the cult of domesticity and the idealization of impossibly conflicting images of femininity. Phyllis Palmer has argued that middle-class housewives in the 1950s needed domestic servants for both practical and ideological reasons. Practically, to maintain one's home and one's body in the pristine condition required by the code of angelic womanhood was a tricky business, and having other hands to do the dirty work certainly helped. But Palmer argues that the juxtaposition of the Black domestic servant with the White housewife also served to reinforce the White woman's image as good, pure, and moral in contrast to the construction of the Black woman as bad, sexually impure, and dirty.[82] So, the division between spiritual and menial housework during this era was intimately linked to broader social constructions of gender and racial-ethnic identity and inequality.[83]

The period around the 1950s was also the pinnacle of the idealization of the nuclear family norm in the history of the United States. The premium put on family privacy required more than ever that servants be practically invisible. The rigid boundaries in this period between domestic servants and their employing families were also linked to race-ethnicity in important ways. The pioneering feminist Simone de Beauvoir analyzed the process by which people in dominant groups in a society turn those in subordinate groups into "the Other."[84] Naming a group or individual as other is part of the process of dehumanization and therefore a way to rationalize unequal treatment. To the extent that employers could identify the women working for them as other—a process facilitated by those women being of a different racial-ethnic origin—employers were more easily able to render these women invisible, nonfamily members in the sacred space of the family home.[85]

The high concentration of Black women in domestic service for many decades makes these links to racial-ethnic inequalities particularly salient. But even in the 1950s, over 30 percent of domestic servants were White U.S.-born women, and the racial-ethnic configuration of private household workers has varied from region to region and city to city.[86] Both the macrosociological forces and the microsociological relationships have differed in their manifestations across a range of situations. In some settings, class more than race was linked to these various constructions of invisibility and the menial. In the late twentieth century, the increasing presence of foreign-born Hispanic women among domestic workers conflates racial-ethnic identity with immigration status in a way not true for earlier generations. Hondagneu-Sotelo points out that these women are differentiated by both race-ethnicity and citizenship, whereas domestics in previous eras tended to be either White immigrants or Black U.S.-born women.[87] The precarious material as well as legal circumstances of many of these women, the constraints created by a lack of English skills for some, and the distance between women and their own children all make foreign-born Hispanic domestic workers especially vulnerable to exploitation.[88] The common thread in all these stories is the construction of women's work in the home as of very low value as labor—and of the paid work of domestic servants as the very lowest.

Did Serfdom Save the Women's Movement?

Consider this passage from an article entitled "How Serfdom Saved the Women's Movement" that appeared in a popular newsmagazine in 2004:

> And so, because of these petty, almost laughably low concerns—the unmade beds, the children with their endless questions, the crumbs and jelly on the counter, the tendency of a good fight over housework to stop the talking and the kissing and the, well, you know—one of the most profound cultural revolutions in American history came perilously close to running aground. And then, like magic, as though the fairy godmother of women's liberation had waved a starry wand, the whole problem got solved. . . . With the arrival of a cheap, easily exploited army of poor and luckless women—fleeing famine, war, the worst kind of poverty, leaving behind their children to do it, facing the possibility of rape or death on the expensive and secret journey—one of the noblest tenets of second-wave feminism collapsed like a house of cards. The new immigrants were met at the docks not by a highly organized and politically powerful group of American women intent on bettering the lot of their sex but, rather, by an equally large army of educated professional-class women with booming careers who needed their children looked after and their houses cleaned.[89]

This direct link—between a recent rise in domestic service and the women's movement and increasing labor-force participation by middle- and upper-class women—is a common theme in analyses of contemporary paid household labor. These analyses point to profound racial-ethnic and class inequalities that are critical to examine, but there are several problems with this formulation of the issue.

First, as this chapter has shown, the United States has a long history of paid domestic work. In fact, even if this occupation is on the rise, the number of private household nannies and housekeepers at the dawn of the twenty-first century is far smaller than the number of domestic servants one hundred years ago. The outsourcing of domestic labor to paid workers in itself is not a response to women's large-scale entrance into the labor market. During the long historical period when women's opportunities in the labor market really opened up and many women entered the labor force, the number of domestic servants overall *decreased* substantially.

Second, patterns of racial-ethnic inequalities among women around domestic labor also have a long history. The proportion of foreign-born domestic workers in the early twenty-first century is very similar to the proportion in the domestic service workforce one hundred years ago, and the proportion of Black women in the occupation is far lower than it was fifty years ago.

I am not suggesting that inequality is any less problematic because it has a long history, and as I have pointed out, there are certainly ways in which the situations of contemporary domestic workers differ substantially from those of their predecessors. But contemporary inequalities need to be examined as part of a historical process rather than as new phenomena.

Finally, although focusing on inequalities among women is vital, it is also important to maintain a critical lens on the gendered assumptions implicit in arguing that middle-class women are hiring women to look after "their" children and clean "their" houses. Framing the hiring of nannies and housekeepers as a transfer of labor between women leaves intact the notion that domestic labor belongs to women in the first place. It is important to combine this critical lens on racial-ethnic inequalities among women with an analysis of men's participation (or lack thereof) in domestic labor.

Despite my objections to the "serfdom" frame, an important kernel lies at the center of this argument: not only gender but also race-ethnicity, immigration status, and class radically impact the division of care work. My goal in this book is to broaden the analysis beyond the "serfdom saved the women's movement" frame—both by historicizing domestic service and the inequalities within it (as I have done in this chapter) and by examining care work more broadly through this intersectional lens (as I do in the chapters that follow).

Transforming Nurturance, Creating Expert Care

As DOMESTIC SERVICE SAW a precipitous decline in the twentieth century, other forms of paid care work were expanding just as sharply. Hospitals and medical centers became the primary delivery sites of health care, which meant a growing number of positions for doctors, nurses, and other specialized health-care workers. As more and more children attended school, the number of teachers at all levels of education increased. The work of serving the poor and others in need, once defined as charity, became more associated with expert intervention, resulting in the creation of many jobs for social workers and other human services professionals. All these care workers—doctors, nurses, nursing aides, teachers, social workers, psychologists—have become part of a highly gendered sector of the labor force in which nurturance has been closely linked to ideals of White middle-class femininity.

The growth of nurturant care work, which I have defined as face-to-face service work that develops the human capabilities of the recipient, is one of the prominent stories of the twentieth century. In this chapter, I examine the roots of these specialized care occupations in the late nineteenth and early twentieth centuries, when some of the same economic and cultural developments that led to the reconfiguration of household labor and of domestic service also led to the emergence of large institutional care structures and expert care workers. In this process, expectations of what it means to care for a child, for an ill person, or for an individual's mental health were fundamentally transformed. As occupational categories were defined (or redefined) to meet these needs, they were constructed in gendered and racialized ways. Patterns of sex segregation and racial-ethnic stratification among nurturant care workers reflect both a remarkably changed context for care work and important continuities with patterns in domestic service.

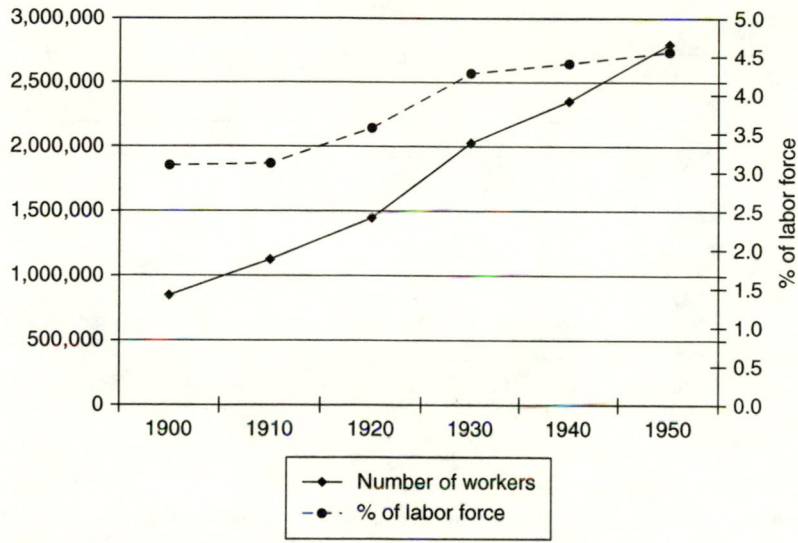

Figure 3.1. Number of nurturant care workers, 1900–1950 *Source: Calculated by author using U.S. Census data (1900–1950) available through the Integrated Public Use Microdata Series (IPUMS).*

The specialized nurturant care occupations that began to emerge in the nineteenth century grew exponentially in the twentieth. Considered as a group, the 850,000 nurturant care workers in 1900 made up only 3 percent of the labor force (see figure 3.1). This number includes doctors, nurses, and other nurturant care workers in health; teachers and child-care workers; and social workers and other human services workers.[1] In the first half of the century, there was steady growth in these sectors of the labor force, and by 1950 between 4 and 5 percent of workers (almost three million people) worked in nurturant care. During these years, the concept of expert care was established and specialized care occupations emerged. In the second half of the century these occupations would expand remarkably.

As a sector, nurturant care since its inception has been associated with women, an association that strengthened over the course of the century. In 1900, women made up just under 55 percent of the nurturant care workforce; by 1950, 66 percent; and almost 80 percent by the end of the century. Nurturant care in the twentieth century not only has been the domain of women, but also has been dominated by White women (see figure 3.2). In 1900, only 66 percent of the labor force was White, yet White U.S.-born workers held 80 percent of nurturant care jobs. In contrast to their overrepresentation in domestic service positions at the turn of the century, immigrant

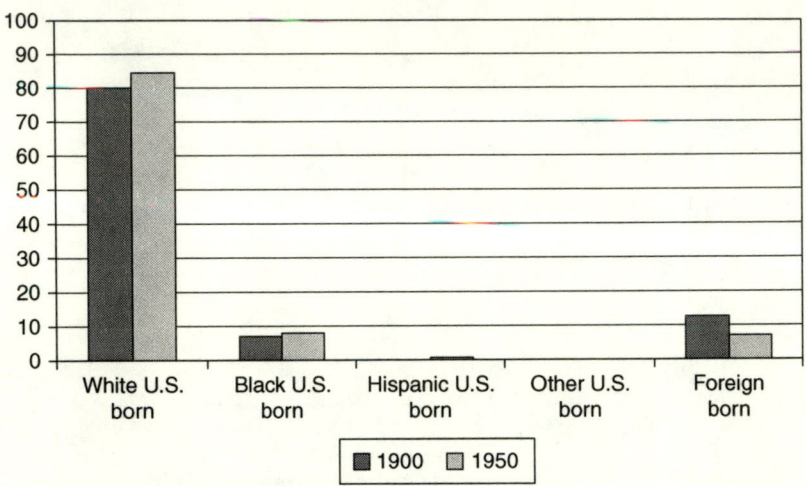

Figure 3.2. Nurturant care workers by race-ethnicity and birthplace, 1900 and 1950 (in percentages) *Source: Calculated by author using U.S. Census data (1900 and 1950) available through the Integrated Public Use Microdata Series (IPUMS).*

and Black women were underrepresented in nurturant care occupations like nursing and teaching. Black U.S.-born workers made up only 7 percent of nurturant care workers, despite being over 12 percent of the labor force (and 22 percent of the female labor force). Foreign-born workers, who made up 22 percent of the labor force, held only 12 percent of nurturant care jobs (compared to 26 percent of domestic service posts).

Between 1900 and 1950, nurturant care occupations like nursing, teaching, and social work were among the limited number of options open to the many White U.S.-born women who entered the labor force. By 1950, 85 percent of nurturant care workers were U.S.-born Whites. The declining number of foreign-born workers in these jobs, as in the labor force overall, was a result of immigration restrictions in the 1920s, as mentioned earlier; representation of Black workers in the nurturant care occupations remained largely unchanged. During a time when Black U.S.-born women made up almost 60 percent of domestic servants, less than 8 percent of nurturant care workers were Black. Nurturant care remained practically—and, as we will see, ideologically—linked to White women.

From Domestic Labor to Expert Care: The Transformation of Nurturance

The expansion of nurturant care occupations is often interpreted as the substitution of paid care for unpaid care in the wake of women's large-scale entrance into the paid labor force. According to this theory, as middle-class women entered the labor force, they began to contract out to paid workers the care work that they had previously performed in the home without pay. This variation on the "serfdom saved the women's movement" construction discussed in the context of domestic service shares many of its problems. Most obviously, large numbers of paid workers were involved in reproductive labor as domestic servants throughout most of the nineteenth century and into the twentieth. Against this backdrop, the expansion of paid nurturant care in the second half of the twentieth century could be seen at least in part as a substitution of one group of workers for another. However, both explanations oversimplify and underestimate the transformation of care work in the twentieth century. Social, economic, and political forces converged in the latter half of the nineteenth century to change the very *nature* of care work. The range of nurturant care occupations that currently exist and their continued growth can be understood only in the context of these fundamental shifts in the material realities and cultural constructions of care.

Technological advances in the late nineteenth and early twentieth centuries had a significant impact on the nature of household labor, as we have seen. The rapid technological change that characterized the twentieth century also had consequences for caregiving, and for the practice of caring for the sick in particular. More broadly, the rise of scientific thinking and the proliferation of specialized expert knowledge have helped shift societal expectations about what it takes to be a competent parent, health-care provider, teacher, or other caregiver. Today's home-care aides, child-care workers, nurses, teachers, and social workers are performing work fundamentally different from that of domestic servants one hundred years ago. The shifting nature of care work has also affected the expectations of family members who perform unpaid care. So we need to understand at least some of the rise in nurturant care occupations not as a substitute for family care (or for paid care by domestic servants) but as a redefinition of the nature of care work itself.

While broad economic forces were important in catalyzing this redefinition, political and ideological forces were equally critical. The link between the labor of nurturant care and the feminine-identified traits of moral guidance, empathy, and compassion became part of the construction of occupations like nursing, teaching, and social work at the dawn of the twentieth century. In some cases, women activists intent on opening up respectable jobs to middle-class women deliberately cultivated this connection, a strategic ideological choice which became not only a persuasive argument to open up jobs to women, but also a mechanism by which middle-class White women could enter the paid labor force with their femininity intact. Despite the often tedious, physically demanding, dirty, and technical nature of the duties of many nineteenth-century nurses and teachers, their jobs were rhetorically constructed as reflective of spiritual notions of femininity.

Simultaneously, the exclusionary policies of educational and workplace institutions curtailed women's access to other professional opportunities. Also, as institutions like schools and hospitals expanded and faced cost pressures, the lower wages offered to women became an attractive incentive to feminize certain portions of the workforce. The confluence of women's activism, institutional sexism, and economic incentives thus led both to the sex segregation of nurturant care jobs and to a gendered definition of this labor. A closer examination of the early twentieth-century development of health care, the care and education of children, and mental health and social service occupations illustrates how nurturant care work was fundamentally transformed.

Healing, House Calls, and Hospitals: The Emergence of Modern Medicine

The enormous health-care industry that dominates medical care in the United States today was in its infancy in 1900; for most of the nineteenth century, people who became ill or disabled were cared for at home.[2] While families may have sought advice from a local healer, the bulk of the care work fell to female relatives and friends, neighbors, and hired girls (and later domestic servants). Where hospitals existed, they functioned not as centers of medical care but as institutional warehouses for the indigent, where ambulatory patients often provided the care for others. Occasionally, women in need of income because of widowhood or separation would profess their occupation as a nurse, and hire themselves out to families specifically to care for the sick. These nurses, along with the mothers, daughters, and wives they assisted, were responsible for tasks as varied as changing bandages, applying leeches or plasters, preparing special foods or tonics, and sitting with patients to monitor their condition and to provide emotional support.

As formal systems of domestic service emerged and expanded, the nurse became one category of domestic worker; nurses were usually older and more likely to be White and U.S. born than the general population of servants. Cultural norms at the time dictated that women care for ill or elderly relatives, and as nursing emerged as a paid occupation, its fundamental link to notions of womanly duty remained strong. Many of the jobs that women were expected to perform in families—taking care of children, nursing babies, and caring for the sick and elderly—were interchangeably referred to as "nursing" when they became paid work. These tasks were considered so much a part of women's natural role that they were not thought of as skills that required training, but as tasks that women could perform because they had practiced them in their own homes or as domestic servants.

In some instances—when a case was particularly serious, when families had access to transportation, or when patients could pay for medical services—families were assisted in judging a patient's needs by a myriad of lay healers, midwives, chiropractors, osteopaths, and physicians. The title "doctor" was applied somewhat loosely in the 1800s, since standards for licensing and training for the most part did not exist. While there were elite physicians whose status derived largely from their family backgrounds and the social standing of their patients, most doctors struggled to earn a living. Before the telephone, doctors' practices depended on families' ability to find them when they were needed, and doctors spent large parts of their days traveling by horse and buggy to patients' homes. Physicians who claimed superior knowledge often met with mistrust among families who believed themselves the best judges of their loved ones' needs. Yet by the dawn of the twentieth century, the transformation of care of the ill from household labor to management and treatment by experts was well under way.

THE PROFESSIONALIZATION OF MEDICINE

Toward the end of the nineteenth century, a number of trends converged to forever alter the landscape of health care in the United States.[3] First, the introduction of the telephone in the 1870s and of the automobile in the 1890s transformed communication and transportation. As telephone communication became more common, patients could contact doctors more easily, and doctors could book patient visits on a more regular schedule. Physicians were among the first large-scale consumers of the automobile; traveling by car allowed them to see more patients in a day, as well as to cover a larger geographic radius. Although these communication and transportation developments often had not reached rural areas, for the growing middle class in the sprawling urban centers at the turn of the century treatment by physicians became much more accessible.

Second, a society becoming more specialized and scientifically oriented increasingly valued the judgment of physicians. As more people had easier access to doctors, they began to rely on a doctor's presence and opinion in ways that would have been impractical and often impossible in earlier eras. Reliance on the professional opinion of doctors was in line with larger social trends of specialization in the industrial economy, including the cultural proliferation of narrow knowledge specialties rather than the assumption of generalized knowledge. Advances in medical science and technology widened the gap between lay knowledge and expert knowledge of medicine. By the 1880s, important discoveries had been made about the bacterial origin of many common diseases, and applications of basic science to curative medicine became much more central. The late 1800s also saw the proliferation of new diagnostic instruments such as the stethoscope that further distanced professional medical practice from lay healing.

Physicians capitalized on these trends to make theirs one of the archetypical professions.[4] Scholars have recognized as professions those occupations that share a number of essential characteristics and generally command high economic and social rewards. First, the professional is in an occupation that requires a high degree of specialized knowledge and is perceived as an expert in their field. Second, professional expertise translates into a high degree of authority, autonomy, and control in the work environment. In the ideal model, professionals are not subject to extensive monitoring by superiors but rather are guided by an ethical code, often formalized, and a strong sense of altruism and service. Professional authority comes not only from skilled service but also from expert judgment.[5]

Paul Starr has pointed out that physicians were able to achieve professional status in the early twentieth century in large part by creating barriers that limited access to the occupation. In the 1870s and 1880s, doctors began a movement to standardize and expand medical licensing laws. By 1901, licensing standards were widespread and gradually began to require higher levels of formal education. While training for doctors had once been largely practical and taken the form of apprenticeships, in the early twentieth century medical education was incorporated into universities, with an emphasis on classroom learning and basic science as well as practical training. Some doctors contested this shift on the grounds that only specialists needed this level of academic training, and that less intensive, more practical training would be enough for doctors to practice everyday medicine.

However, in the first two decades of the twentieth century, medical education became firmly incorporated into the academic model, and physicians became the sole prescribers of pharmaceutical drugs, for the most part replacing door-to-door peddlers and homemade treatments. Organizing what would become one of the most powerful professional associations in the country, the American Medical Association (AMA), physicians had by the 1930s gained control of medicine and established themselves as professionals. By pushing for the formalizing of education requirements and licensing laws, the AMA drew ever-tightening boundaries around the profession. The increasing exclusivity of the occupation raised its value both socially and economically, leading to the rewards as well as the professional authority enjoyed by physicians.

HOSPITALS AND THEIR KEEPERS

The professionalization of medicine was accompanied by a related shift in the primary locus of care from private homes to hospitals and medical offices. As physicians saw more patients and could schedule appointments in advance, and as increasing numbers of patients had access to automobile transportation, it became more practical for physicians to set up offices rather than visit each patient at home. In addition, changing demographic patterns made it more difficult for the ill to be cared for primarily at home, as more and more people left home to go to work each day, and many more were geographically mobile during their working lives. Young workers who moved to cities for jobs often had no nearby family, and fewer families had large extended kin networks to help care for acutely or chronically ill family members.[6] All these trends created the conditions for shifting health care to hospitals. Parallel to the efforts of physicians to solidify their professional status, a group of women activists had been working to transform hospitals, marginalized and stigmatized throughout most of the nineteenth century.

In the post–Civil War era, inspired in part by the work of caring for wounded soldiers on the battlefields, an elite group of female reformers began to advocate for major changes to hospitals. In language similar to that used by social welfare reformers at the time, advocates argued that hospitals needed to offer patients moral guidance and a clean and orderly environment—a description that could not have been further from the reality of hospitals of the mid-nineteenth century. Reformers had a dual agenda: to improve conditions in hospitals, and to provide respectable employment opportunities for the daughters of the new middle class. To that end, the guardians of this new hospital morality were to be trained nurses, women of strong character honed by training and practice. The first hospital-based training program for nurses was opened in 1873. For the first several decades of nursing training, an exploited army of student nurses staffed most hospitals; once women finished their training, they looked for more respectable assignments in private homes. The shift to hospitals as the major employers of most nurses would not be complete until the 1930s, but the reform movement of the late nineteenth century triggered the transformation of hospitals and of nursing into their twentieth-century forms.[7]

Simultaneous changes in medical practice and physician education were an additional factor in the growth of hospitals as generalized health-care centers. Hospital care was more conducive to the use of the diagnostic technology that was gaining importance in turn-of-the-century medicine. In particular, the use of anesthesia and the advent of surgical techniques that required sterile conditions made treatment of acute conditions incompatible with home care.

As educational requirements for doctors tightened, hospitals became the central institutions for physician training as well. Between 1870 and 1930, as some of the labor of caring for the acutely and chronically ill shifted from private homes to hospitals, these institutions underwent the significant growth and reordering that established their central role in the U.S. health-care system.[8]

NEW ORDER, OLD PATTERNS

The introduction of nursing schools increased the number of professional nurses while at the same time providing a constant supply of cheap labor to the emergent hospitals in the form of student nurses. By 1930, with their dominance firmly established, hospitals began to look to trained nurses to perform increasingly complex medical tasks. The hierarchy of the hospital became firmly entrenched: physicians maintained their autonomy and decision-making power, and registered nurses were subservient to the physicians and superior to the attendants, whose ranks were increasingly formalized into specialized positions such as aides, orderlies, and licensed practical nurses. Beginning in the 1920s, the growth in numbers in professional nursing and these attendant occupations swiftly outpaced the growth in the number of physicians (see figure 3.3). Once the norm, practical nurses—nurses who had

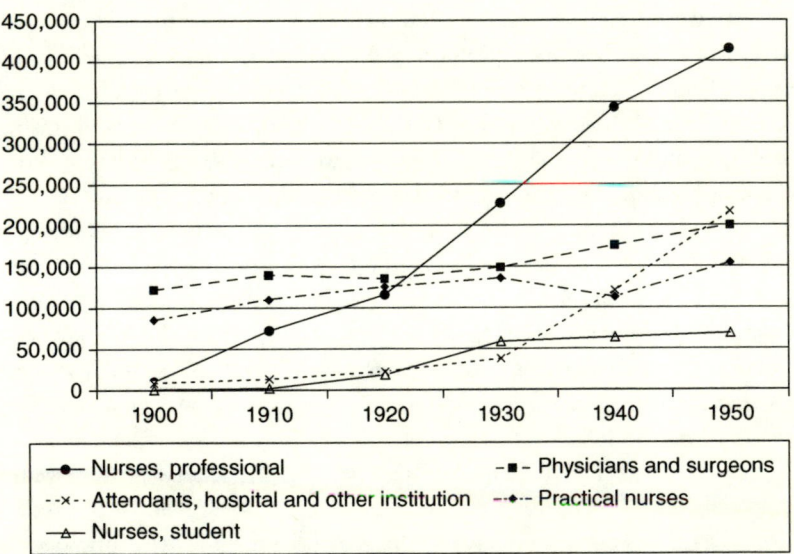

Figure 3.3. Number of workers in selected health-care occupations, 1900–1950
Source: Calculated by author using U.S. Census data (1900–1950) available through the Integrated Public Use Microdata Series (IPUMS).

not gone through formal training—by midcentury were outnumbered by the more formally educated ranks of professional nurses. Interestingly, in the late nineteenth and early twentieth century, as newly trained nurses left hospitals for private duty, hospitals were staffed by students and practical nurses, but by midcentury, hospitals were the domain of the most highly trained nurses, leaving care of the sick at home in the hands of practical nurses, sometimes called "short course" nurses.[9]

The hierarchical organization of the hospital was firmly linked to gender and racial-ethnic inequalities. For physicians, the late nineteenth century was a time of professional consolidation, rising cultural authority, and growing access to economic and political power. Trained and licensed doctors became the proprietors of expert scientific knowledge and diagnostic technology, increasingly turned to as the only reliable arbiters of sound medical practice. The first medical schools, established in the second half of the nineteenth century, were coeducational, and a number of women's medical colleges were founded. In the 1890s, women made up about 10 percent of medical school students, and in several large cities close to 20 percent of trained doctors were women.[10] But around the turn of the century, as medical education was consolidated and assimilated by universities, schools began to erect formal barriers to women's entrance into medical programs. Administrators argued that women should not be trained as doctors since they would not continue to practice after marriage, and well into the 1950s, quotas limited women in medical schools to 5 percent of students.[11] Blacks faced equally significant barriers to entrance into the medical profession, as only two Black medical colleges existed, and many hospitals denied internship opportunities and treatment privileges to Blacks as well. Coupled with the increasing costs of medical education, these discriminatory practices assured that as medicine became professionalized, it also became increasingly homogenous in terms of class, race, and gender. In 1900, women made up less than 5 percent of all physicians (see figure 3.4). In that same year, 89 percent of physicians were White and U.S. born, 10 percent were foreign born, and less than 1 percent were Black (see figure 3.5).

While the sex composition of the medical profession remained relatively constant through the first half of the century, the number of foreign-born physicians increased—despite the sharp decline in the proportion of foreign-born workers in the labor force as a whole. By 1950, when less than 10 percent of the labor force was foreign born (compared to 21 percent in 1900), the proportion of foreign-born physicians had increased to 15 percent of all physicians (from 10 percent in 1900) (see figure 3.6). Almost half the foreign-born doctors in 1950 were from Europe, with the highest concentrations from

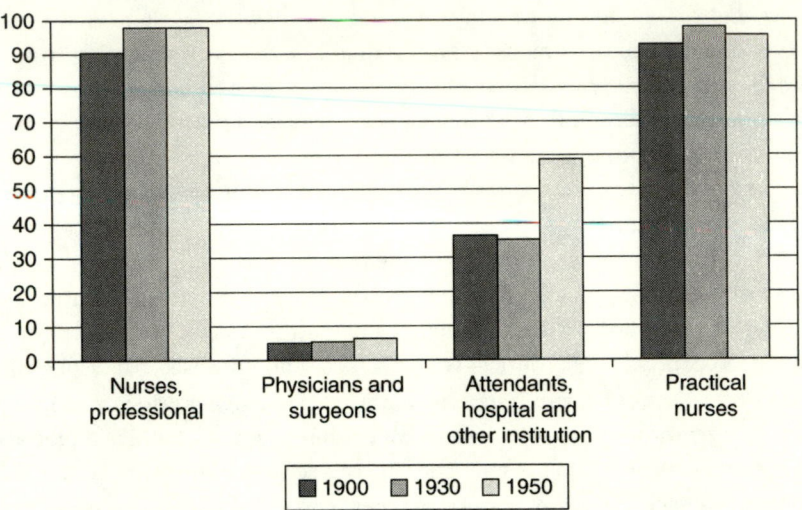

Figure 3.4. Women in selected health-care occupations, 1900–1950 (in percentages)
Source: Calculated by author using U.S. Census data (1900–1950) available through the Integrated Public Use Microdata Series (IPUMS).

Germany, Poland, Austria, and Italy. There were also substantial numbers of doctors from Canada and a smaller group from the Soviet Union. The immigration restrictions created during the 1920s had exclusions for highly skilled workers, so foreign-born doctors were able to continue to enter the country. In particular, World War II led many doctors to flee Eastern Europe and the Soviet Union, and those immigrants were welcomed into the United States.

Although training for doctors was increasingly based on science, early training programs for nurses emphasized character above all. The idea of womanly duty that had characterized both unpaid family nursing and domestic forms of paid nursing remained central to hospital training programs. To transform nursing into a respectable profession for White middle-class women, reformers drew on very specific notions of femininity. They explicitly emphasized feminine-identified character traits—self-sacrifice, altruism, moral purity, and submissiveness—as central to the role of the trained nurse.[12]

As the structure of hospitals consolidated to place nurses below physicians in the hierarchy, decisions about patient diagnosis and management were in the hands of the doctors, and nurses were not only to comply with physician-ordered treatment but also to ensure patient compliance. Despite the rhetoric of moral guardianship, early hospital nursing involved a lot of hard and unpleasant physical labor, such as scrubbing bathrooms, cleaning up vomit,

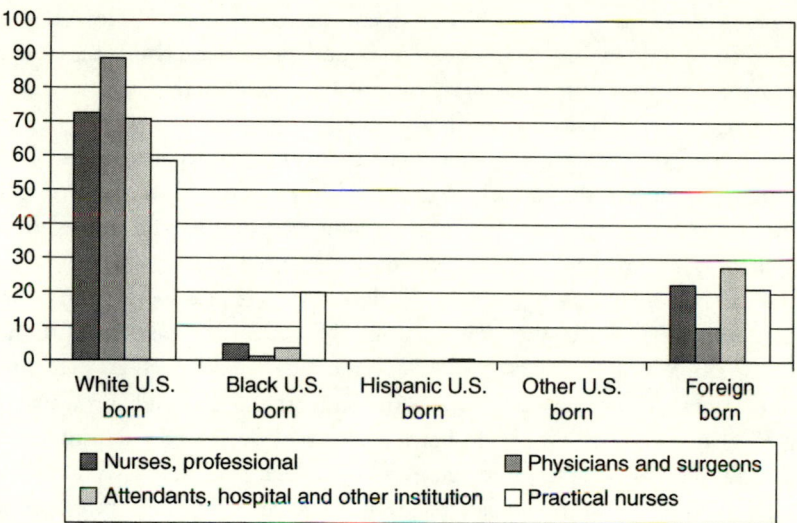

Figure 3.5. Selected health-care workers by race-ethnicity and birthplace, 1900 (in percentages) *Source: Calculated by author using U.S. Census data (1900) available through the Integrated Public Use Microdata Series (IPUMS).*

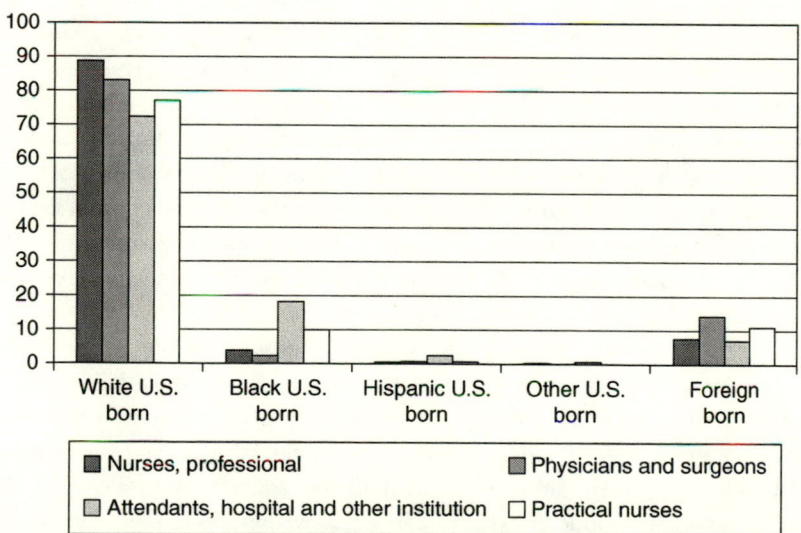

Figure 3.6. Selected health-care workers by race-ethnicity and birthplace, 1950 (in percentages) *Source: Calculated by author using U.S. Census data (1950) available through the Integrated Public Use Microdata Series (IPUMS).*

mopping floors, and washing bloody operating-room sheets.[13] Nevertheless, advocates of trained nursing drew careful boundaries around the occupation to distinguish it from untrained practical nursing, domestic service, and other emerging occupations in the new hospitals.[14]

Trained nurses were the moral guardians and spiritual keepers of the hospital—an image that closely linked to White middle-class ideals of femininity. Throughout the first half of the twentieth century, the trained nurse population was over 90 percent female; by 1950, 98 percent of professional nurses were women (see figure 3.4). Black women were excluded from professional nursing well into the 1960s, and in 1950 almost 90 percent of trained nurses were White and U.S. born (see figure 3.6).[15] Although 20 percent of trained nurses in 1900 were foreign born (largely from England and Canada), by 1950 the number of foreign-born nurses had decreased substantially as immigration was curtailed (see figures 3.5 and 3.6). Exclusionary practices as well as cultural norms had created a group of nurses that was as homogenous as the physician population.

While trained nursing was associated with the feminine, as well as increasingly perceived as skilled labor, practical nurses were judged able to perform only the more menial tasks of nursing care. This ideological construction was connected to the racial-ethnic makeup of the occupation's workers. Like trained nurses, practical nurses were overwhelmingly female, but Black U.S.-born women as well as foreign-born women were overrepresented in their ranks. Almost 20 percent of practical nurses in 1900 were Black U.S.-born workers, and foreign-born workers made up another 20 percent, immigrants from Canada, Ireland, Germany, and England in almost equal numbers. While White U.S.-born women were still the majority, large numbers of Black women were practical nurses, in contrast to their virtual absence from trained nursing. This division of labor reproduces the racialized construction of the role of the housewife as spiritual and the work of the domestic servant as menial that characterized the nineteenth century.[16]

Further down the hospital hierarchy from nurses were the positions that in early years were called generically "attendants" and that evolved into the various ranks of nursing aides and orderlies that work in modern hospitals. These jobs were as far removed from the rhetorical valorization of nurturance that had become associated with trained nursing as from the aura of authority and skill that surrounded physicians. In 1900, women represented just under 40 percent of attendants, the least sex-segregated occupational category in the hospital. By 1950, the occupation had begun a trend toward more females than males that would continue into the second half of the century, but the occupation remained much more balanced than other hospital jobs, with about 60 percent women and 40 percent men. In the early part of the century, then, while the roles of physicians and nurses were profoundly gendered, the job of hospital attendant was more gender neutral. This occupational category encompasses a wide variety of jobs, and it is likely that there was more sex segregation by specific task than is apparent in these composite numbers. But on the whole, the population of attendants was far less segregated by sex than by race-ethnicity.

While the majority of hospital attendants were White and U.S. born, the substantial numbers of foreign-born workers in 1900 and of Black workers in 1950 show some similarity to the racial-ethnic makeup of practical nurses and a distinct contrast to the racial-ethnic makeup of the trained nursing workforce. In 1900, foreign-born workers were 27 percent of hospital attendants, compared to 21 percent of the overall labor force (see figure 3.5). Paralleling the ethnic composition of domestic service, almost half the foreign-born hospital attendants in 1900 were from Ireland. By 1950, as immigration declined, only 7 percent of hospital attendants were foreign born (see figure 3.6). However, in 1950, over 18 percent of hospital attendants were Black U.S. born, while Black U.S.-born workers were less than 10 percent of the labor force as a whole. The association of the work of hospital attendants with menial labor appropriate for workers lower in the social hierarchy would continue and harden as the century progressed.

THE CONFLICTED PATH TO
PROFESSIONALIZATION FOR NURSES

Nurses, like other women in the years after World War II, became less likely to leave the paid labor force when they got married. By 1951, 47 percent of all active nurses were married, compared to less than 20 percent in 1928. That more and more nurses were married and had family lives of their own accelerated the demise of live-in hospital training schools. Although 84 percent of hospitals in 1936 included full "maintenance" (room and board) in their salary schedules, by 1946, only 10 percent still required student nurses to live in.[17]

Nursing leaders now began to pursue a goal that they hoped would achieve rewards for nurses similar to those gained by physicians. They argued that the title "professional nurse" should be reserved for nurses who had university degrees, and not awarded to those trained in the more practice-based hospital training schools. Gradually, formal degree-based nursing programs began to replace hospital training schools. In addition, mandatory licensing laws, first introduced in New York in 1938, soon became standard practice. The American Nurses Association (ANA) worked to control the occupation as the AMA had done for medicine. Nurses did succeed in drawing some boundaries around the profession, and in clearly differentiating themselves from lower-paid and less trained nurses' aides and attendants. However, despite some advances in wages and benefits, nursing never achieved the level of economic and social recognition gained by doctors. And nurses' subordination to another occupational group—physicians—limited their ability to use their professional judgment and have control over their work. Some nursing scholars have argued that this structural subordination prohibits nursing from ever becoming a profession.[18]

Attempts to professionalize nursing also met resistance from a substantial number of nurses, who saw professional identification as a loss of the essence of nursing, which many considered more a vocation than a career. While its association with the increasingly technical world of medicine had begun to give nursing some credibility as a skilled occupation, many nurses still saw themselves more as moral guardians than as technical medical personnel. The intense association of nursing with female nurturance cultivated in the early history of the occupation proved difficult to translate into a language of professionalism. While nursing leaders ultimately implemented some of the conditions for professional status, these ideological conflicts about the role of nurses—which are really also conflicts about the meaning of care—continue to complicate images and realities of nursing care today.

Susan Reverby has pointed out that it was in the hospitals' economic interest to maintain a "divided and cheap" workforce.[19] In the second half of the century, the economic driving forces of hospital business would become even more salient and have a continued and profound impact on care workers in health care across the board. But health care would remain the domain of experts, physicians trained in expert knowledge and nurses trained in technical skills and capable of feminine nurturance. The care of the ill had been redefined in content and reorganized in delivery, and the new forms of paid care would become part of the backbone of the growth of nurturant care in the twentieth century.

Caring for the "Priceless" Child

Between 1870 and 1930, as health care in the United States underwent its most dramatic transformation, a profound redefinition of childhood and what it means to care for a child was also under way. The "economically useful" child of the eighteenth century gave way to what Viviana Zelizer has called the "sacred" child, "economically useless but emotionally priceless."[20] Children, once indispensable members of the household economy and contributors to its labor, gradually came to be seen primarily as the recipients of that labor, in need of nurturance and protection. And while the domain of nineteenth-century children was often home, farm, or factory, by 1900 children's lives revolved increasingly around school.

In the early 1800s, most children attended formal schooling only sporadically if at all. The labor of maintaining a household in the eighteenth and early nineteenth centuries was arduous and time consuming, as we have seen, and required the contributions of men, women, children, and paid workers. Children learned the skills and the behavioral norms they would need to be productive working adults primarily through the family and religious organizations. By midcentury this had begun to change, and by 1876, 60 percent of school-age children were enrolled in public schools for at least some months of the year.[21]

THE COMMON SCHOOL MOVEMENT AND
THE FEMINIZATION OF TEACHING

Teachers in the eighteenth century were usually men. In fact, teaching was characterized as an occupation inappropriate for females because of the requirements of physical strength (important in controlling students through the corporal means prevalent at the time) and intellectual rigor. But around 1840, a group of activists in New England, intent on opening up a decent-paying occupation to women, began to argue that teaching was well suited to the female character. In language strikingly similar to that used later by nursing advocates, they argued that women possessed the "female qualities of emotionality, maternal love, gentleness, and moral superiority" necessary to be good teachers.[22] The language about women's appropriateness for the job implied a changed understanding of what children needed that was compatible with emergent ideologies of parenting among the growing urban middle class.

What Zelizer calls the "sacralization" of childhood had begun among these middle-class families, who no longer lived on farms where children's labor was part of family life. Prioritizing children's education as preparation for future work replaced concerns about children's immediate economic contributions.[23] The increasing ideological separation of work and family placed children clearly in the family sphere with their mothers rather than in the work sphere with their fathers. Urban middle-class children lived in an industrializing world which demanded new skills, and schools became important institutions for socializing children in preparation for the new world of work.[24] The feminization of teaching allowed schools to be viewed as an extension of the family sphere, a place where a newly sacred childhood could be preserved even as children were prepared to enter the workforce. Even though most schools resembled those of an earlier era—a drillmaster model, with a teacher who ruled through physical and verbal punishment—the rhetoric of teaching was beginning to shift.

In the 1840s, reformers interested in the expansion of public education saw that the movement to open up teaching to women presented them with an opportunity. Horace Mann and his followers in the Common School movement thought that local leaders would be more willing to open more schools if teaching had a lower price tag. All teachers were paid relatively low wages, but female teachers' wages could be as little as half those received by men.[25] Mann's movement gained a hold in New England and by the late 1800s had become a model for school reform and expansion across the country.[26] The demand for educated workers in the rapidly increasing number of service- and commercial-sector jobs helped drive the expansion.[27] As the number of schools rose, the ideal of the female teacher became entrenched, and by 1870 over two-thirds of teachers nationwide were women.[28] By 1900, women made up 75 percent of the growing teaching workforce. Male teachers remained more common in rural areas, but by the middle decades of the twentieth century, this difference had disappeared.[29] "Over the course of the nineteenth century, then," as Jo Anne Preston has observed, "teaching became women's work not only statistically but ideologically and prescriptively as well."[30] Like nursing, teaching became not only sex segregated but also gendered in its construction.

THE SACRED CHILD BECOMES THE NORM

While the economic and social dislocations that accompanied industrialization contributed to new notions of childhood and the rise of schooling for urban middle-class children, industrialization had a very different impact on working-class and immigrant children. Just as many women were excluded from the emergent ideology of domesticity by structural constraints and cultural prescriptions, many children continued throughout the nineteenth century to contribute their labor and their earnings to the family economy. The rapid pace of industrialization after 1860 created many occupations in which children could be employed, and in 1870 at least one out of every eight children was working in the paid labor market.[31] The decades between 1870 and 1930, however, would see not only the emergence of a widespread movement against child labor, but also an intensification and broadening of the cultural transformation of childhood that had begun with middle-class families.

Some have argued that the movement against child labor was driven by labor-market dynamics—an influx of immigrants offering an alternative source of low-wage labor, and fear that working children were driving down wages for adults. This was the era of campaigns for a "family wage" that would allow a workingman to earn enough to support his wife and children. This notion was a consequence of as well as reinforcement for the gendered division of labor, and again placed children squarely in the nonwork sphere. While such economic forces had an impact, the protracted and bitter battle over child labor reflected a much larger cultural struggle over the value of children and the meaning of childhood.

During the first three decades of the twentieth century, modern medical technologies drove infant and child mortality rates down dramatically. Industrialization also lowered birth rates, as children became more an economic liability than an asset. Having fewer children, along with the higher probability that they would live to adulthood, now made parents more willing to become emotionally attached to their children. The construction of children as sentimental objects of affection and nurturance thus went beyond the battle over child labor. For example, during this period a child safety movement emerged, warning parents that they should not send their children on errands unsupervised, and that they should restrict their play to protected spaces like playrooms and playgrounds. By 1930, childhood was firmly established as sacred, across class and regional boundaries. Caring for the economically useless but emotionally priceless child was a fundamentally different task from that entailed in raising and socializing children in the nineteenth century.

SCHOOLS AND TEACHERS IN THE EARLY TWENTIETH CENTURY

The sentimentalization of childhood, the expulsion of children from the labor market, and the continued need for a workforce with formal training and skills drove the growth of schools at the turn of the century. While hospitals became the primary locus of caring for the ill, schools became the central institution for socializing children between the ages of six and eighteen. By the late nineteenth century, most children spent between three to six years attending school for most of the year. The majority of those attending school were between the ages of eight and eleven; in 1890, less than 1 percent of the population had attended secondary school.[32] School attendance varied substantially by region, with the highest numbers in the Northeast where the Common School movement had begun. In 1900, more than 90 percent of students enrolled in the Northeast attended school for more than six months, while in the South the proportion was less than 40 percent.[33]

By 1920, schooling was compulsory in nearly all states, and almost 80 percent of children were enrolled. The average length of the school year had also increased significantly since the nineteenth century.[34] Between 1900

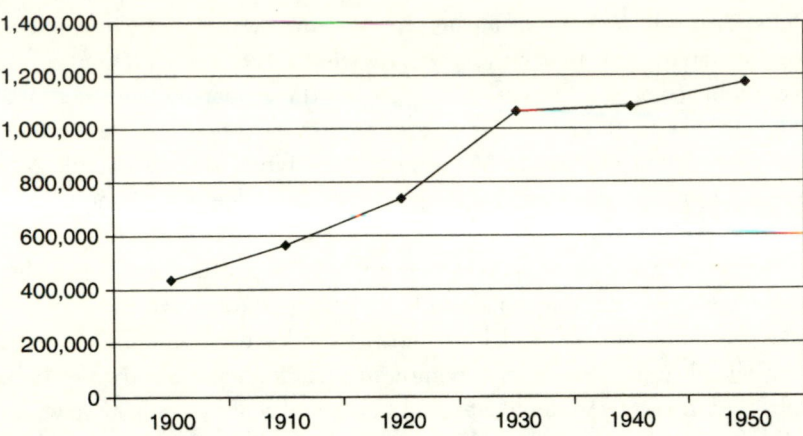

Figure 3.7. Number of teachers, 1900–1950 *Source: Calculated by author using U.S. Census data (1900–1950) available through the Integrated Public Use Microdata Series (IPUMS).*

and 1950, the number of teachers more than doubled to over 1.1 million workers (see figure 3.7). In 1950, there were more than twice as many teachers in the United States as professional nurses, and five times as many teachers as hospital attendants.

As schools became established as the central institutions to care for children and prepare them for the future, the structure of schooling itself was reorganized. Between 1890 and 1920, business and educational leaders took control of school boards and imposed on public education a business model based on scientific rationality and bureaucratic efficiency. Large cities consolidated their schools into centralized administrative systems with powerful superintendents.[35] A well-defined hierarchy was created in school systems across the country. Significantly, a perceived need for expert knowledge in the planning of education emerged along with the overall cultural trend toward dependence on specialized information. Just as significantly, it was not the (mostly female) teachers who were considered the experts, but rather the (largely male) principals, superintendents, and school board members. In 1905, over 60 percent of elementary school principals, 95 percent of high school principals, and nearly all district superintendents were men.[36] The power structure of schools was remarkably similar to that of hospitals, with male experts making decisions and females implementing them.

Some groups of teachers resisted this tightening external control of classrooms and of their work, and the period from 1900 to 1920 was one of exceptional activism: teachers organized in unions, advocated for higher salaries and job protections, and fought for more control over decisions about their own working conditions as well as school policy. Women activists also agitated for gender equality in the occupation, including equal wages.[37]

Like nurses, educational leaders pursued professionalization by tightening entry requirements to the occupation. The 1920s saw an increase in both the length of formal education required to become a teacher and the minimum passing grade on the state licensing exams. This movement toward professionalization had a negative impact on union activity and organizing in two ways. First, more working-class applicants, who were more likely to be sympathetic to unions, were excluded from teaching. Second, the culture of professionalism encouraged teachers to cooperate with administrators rather than organize in an adversarial relationship to administration. Culturally, unions were associated with manufacturing and other working-class jobs, not with professions. By 1940, these developments, as well as increasing legal suppression and a general rise in antiunion sentiment, had subdued the most radical teacher activism.[38]

Despite being one of the most common occupations for women through the beginning of the twentieth century, teaching never became as sex segregated as nursing. From 75 percent in 1900, the proportion of women in teaching reached a high of 84 percent in 1920 and then leveled off to around 75 percent again by 1940. These numbers do reflect high levels of sex segregation, if not quite as extreme as those in nursing or domestic service. Nursing and domestic service have been from their inception conceptualized as women's work, while teaching underwent a conflicted transition to a feminized occupation. Perhaps this difference at least partly explains the somewhat less extreme levels of segregation in teaching as a whole. The composite averages also mask more specific sex segregation within this large field that does reach more extreme levels.

Like nursing, the construction of teaching during this time was based on a highly gendered notion of nurturance. Teacher-training schools in the early twentieth century emphasized moral and character development for women to enable them to be the guides that children needed. As one scholar observed: "If becoming a teacher meant anything, it meant literally becoming a certain kind of person."[39] Teacher-training schools emphasized that teachers were to dress, speak, and behave in certain ways; they were subject to control and monitoring not only of their work but also of many aspects of their personal lives.[40] Norms of teacher behavior were closely linked to the ideals of middle-class femininity, and in some ways being a good teacher was equivalent to being a good woman. The image of teachers in the early twentieth century paralleled notions of spiritual womanhood, despite the realities of difficult students, tedious clerical work, and unsafe or unsanitary working conditions.[41]

The racialized as well as gendered aspects of this construction of nurturance appear in teaching as clearly as in nursing. Through the first half of the century, almost 90 percent of teachers were White and U.S. born (see figure 3.8).

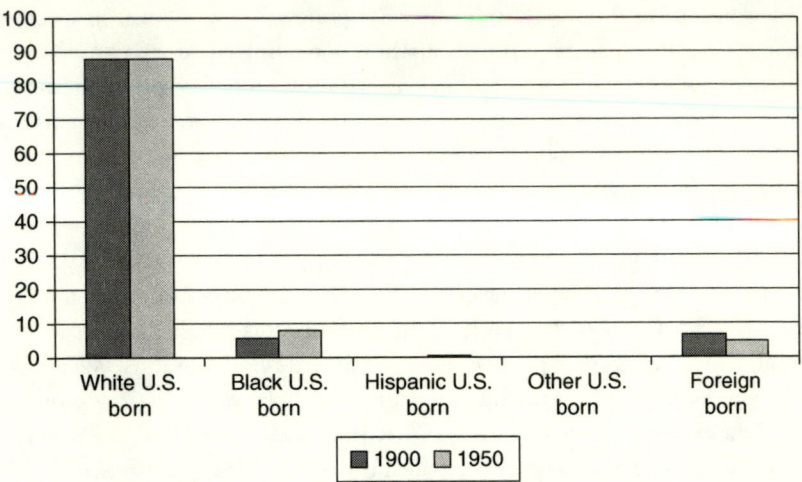

Figure 3.8. Race-ethnicity and birthplace of teachers, 1900 and 1950 (in percentages)
Source: Calculated by author using U.S. Census data (1900 and 1950) available through the Integrated Public Use Microdata Series (IPUMS).

Although foreign-born women were hired as teachers in particular regions and cities, they were underrepresented among teachers at a national level. Black women were an even smaller presence in the overall teaching workforce, concentrated primarily in the segregated schools of the South.[42] In schools, the new favored institution for the socialization of children and youth, White U.S.-born women had been chosen as the most appropriate to deliver nurturant care to the priceless child.

THE CREATION OF INFANCY

The transformation of childhood in the nineteenth century had some unique consequences for norms of care for children under six. While older children in the nineteenth century were able to contribute to the family economy by working on the farm or in the emerging factories, children in this youngest group required supervision until they grew old enough to participate. Sometimes, older siblings or other family members provided this supervision, but in the early 1800s, there were also institutions to care for very young children. Infant schools flourished, serving parents who worked in urban factories, along with day nurseries, Sunday schools, and monitorial schools. As in all schools of the era, children in these settings were subject to strict control through physical and verbal punishment.[43]

As notions of childhood changed in the mid-1800s, the idea of infancy as a special stage in which children needed extra protection and care took shape.

While schools became a significant agent of socialization for older children, the youngest children were thought to need protection from influences outside the family. Where families had once hired wet nurses, these and other strangers became suspect, and young children were increasingly seen as best taken care of within the confines of the family, and more specifically, by their mothers. As the ideology of domesticity took hold for middle-class women, the expectation that mothers alone should care for their young children helped cement the ideal of the nuclear family. As we have seen, many families hired domestic servants who helped with child care, but the importance of the mother-infant bond and of protecting the youngest children from outside influences was the rhetoric common in the voluminous advice literature for parents in the late nineteenth century, and schools and nurseries for this age group became much less common. While the nineteenth century was a time of increasing school attendance for children ages six to fourteen, the opposite was true for children under six.[44]

This ideological transformation led reformers in the late nineteenth century to frame the idea of kindergarten as an extension of domestic nurture and a family environment rather than as intellectual training for future work.[45] The proponents of "child gardening" defined its purpose in opposition to both contemporary primary schools and the infant schools of the past. Early kindergartens were not intended to prepare children for school, but rather to "inoculate children against the rigid discipline and deadening didacticism" of primary schools.[46] The youngest children came to be seen as a separate group meant to be protected from the world rather than instructed in it.

The sacralization of childhood and the distinction of infancy as a separate stage transformed the nature of caring for children in the United States. The twentieth-century expansion of education, as well as the particular framing of child care for younger children, originated during this period. As we will see, schooling continued to expand, including more children, older children, more years of attendance, and longer school years. And the care of children younger than six continued to operate in a somewhat separate sphere, subject to both the maternalist ideology that became entrenched during this era and to scientific discoveries that would again change the nature of care.

Doing Good: Charity Becomes Work

The beginning of the twentieth century was a time of profound change not only for health care and child care, but also for care of the poor, mentally ill, and other groups considered in need. In the nineteenth century, the ideal of femininity that celebrated women's domesticity was extended to the sphere of "benevolence."[47] Women's role as moral guardians was extended from the family to the wider community; middle- and upper-class women's activism and charity work reached into many arenas, including child welfare, the care of the mentally ill, and the care of unwed mothers (as well as hospital reform). Just as nursing and teaching drew upon dominant notions of femininity to describe the special fit of women in hospital and school roles, activists used the language of feminine virtue to portray benevolence as uniquely suited to the female character. Between 1870 and 1930, as science emerged as the basis for the treatment of physical illness, a strong move to use science to treat all kinds of emotional, mental, and social dysfunction would alter the nature of social services and lead to a new group of nurturant care occupations.

At the turn of the century, most individuals considered mentally ill were placed in custodial institutions where the primary goal was social control rather than treatment. Although psychoanalysis had a presence in the United States, it was an intensive type of treatment that only the wealthy could afford and only the seriously neurotic would undertake.[48] Most individuals with mental illness in 1900 were considered to comprise one of a number of groups of "dependents," a classification that also included orphaned or abandoned children and the poor. In fact, most asylums in the late 1800s were generalized institutions that housed all these groups under one roof. By midcentury, mental health care would be transformed, and mental health services would straddle the boundary between health care and social services.

THE CHARITY ORGANIZATION SOCIETY

Although women's benevolent work took many forms in the nineteenth century, the one most directly associated with modern social services, and particularly with the occupation of social work, was the Charity Organization Society (COS), founded in the 1870s explicitly to bring scientific rationality to the practice of benevolence.[49] The procedure of investigating, recording, and planning intervention for individuals that is the basis of modern casework had its origins in the COS approach. While nineteenth-century benevolent work had been largely based upon charitable impulses, the COS sought to bring the methods of scientific inquiry and systematic "treatment" to dealing with the poor and needy. By coordinating services and acting as gatekeepers and referral sources for those seeking help, COS leaders sought to make charity work more efficient and more effective.[50]

The leaders of the COS had very particular ideas about the nature of poverty and appropriate (and inappropriate) ways of helping the poor. First, the approach of the COS focused on individual faults as the cause of poverty, a philosophy rooted in the Poor Laws of England, which were based upon a view of the poor as fundamentally lazy and morally flawed. Although several contemporary reform movements had grown out of the notion that the industrial economy was largely to blame for the poverty of some members of society, COS leaders flatly rejected external causes as mainly responsible for an impoverished individual's situation. While settlement house leaders and Progressive Era reformers advocated systematic improvement of laws protecting workers and families, as well as more public support for the poor and needy, COS leaders set their sights on fixing individual deficiencies.[51]

Second, and in part because of this view, COS leaders were stridently opposed to support of the poor and needy through government programs. They believed that only private charities were capable of the individual interventions necessary. They were particularly opposed to outdoor relief, the provision of material assistance to poor families absent a requirement that they enter an institution (indoor relief). COS leaders fought against public relief, and in some cases succeeded in having it abolished or suspended. The COS put into place a system of "friendly visitors," volunteers who were trained to go into the homes of the poor to provide them with moral guidance and advice. The overall goal of the organization has been described as "the maintenance of virtuous families," and the provision of cash relief did not adequately address this purpose.[52]

THE INCOMPLETE PROFESSIONALIZATION OF SOCIAL WORK

The work of the Charity Organization Society set the stage for the professionalization of social work by defining a scientific basis for intervention with the poor and therefore a need for experts. Like doctors and nurses, social workers advocated formal education rather than practical training to distinguish professionals from charity workers, and in the first two decades of the twentieth century seventeen schools of social work were founded. Following the model of professionalization that had been pioneered by doctors, social workers in 1921 established the American Association of Social Workers (AASW), which defined standards for membership in an attempt to differentiate trained social workers from untrained charity workers.[53] Between 1900 and 1950 and particularly between 1930 and 1950, the number of social workers grew considerably (see figure 3.9). While the overall scale of expert social service workers remained small compared to workers in health care and teaching, by 1940 professional social workers outnumbered untrained religious workers.[54]

As in nursing and teaching, the emergence of this occupation can be understood as a labor-market process of professionalization connected to a particular construction of care. The COS brought the late nineteenth century's increasing respect for scientific knowledge to the problem of poverty, arguing that individual deficiencies could be discovered through systematic

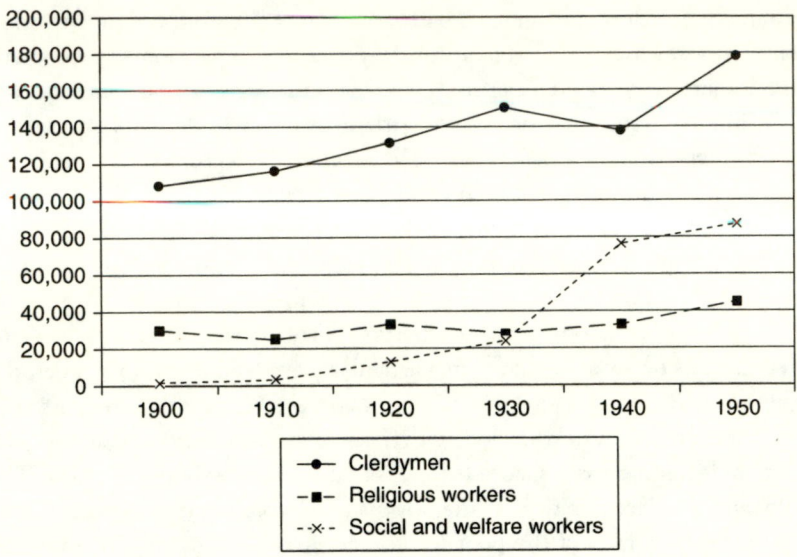

Figure 3.9. Number of workers in selected social service occupations, 1900–1950
Source: Calculated by author using U.S. Census data (1900 and 1950) available through the Integrated Public Use Microdata Series (IPUMS). Note: The 1950 Census occupational titles use the category "clergymen," reflecting contemporary gendered assumptions about the makeup of the clergy.

investigation. Understanding poverty through this lens created the need for expert workers trained in investigation and treatment methods.

The role of gender in the case of social work is particularly interesting, as early leaders deliberately shunned the feminine image of charity work. Trained social workers were presented as skilled individuals who were objective and rational, in contrast to the sentimentality of untrained charity workers. The language of professional authority had become associated with the masculine sphere, and social work leaders embraced the language of scientific neutrality, rejecting the aura of morality and relationality that had characterized female benevolence. Social work leaders recognized the gendered piece of this process and attempted to attract men to the field as a way to raise its status.[55]

While leaders did succeed in establishing some of the basic conditions for professional status, social work for the most part failed to attain either the social and economic recognition or the authority of a profession. Attempts to attract more men and to distance social work from its female-identified roots were also not successful. In 1930, 75 percent of social workers were female (see figure 3.10). While the proportion of men had increased somewhat by 1950, the occupation remained distinctly female dominated.

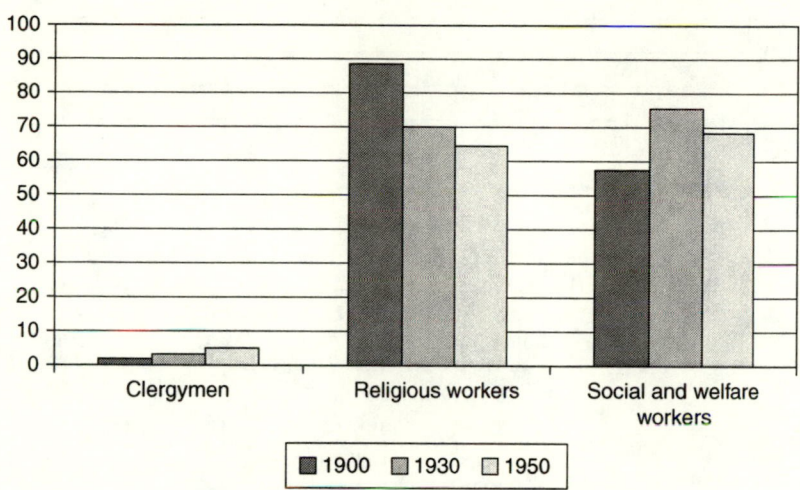

Figure 3.10. Women in selected social service occupations, 1900–1950 (in percentages) *Source: Calculated by author using U.S. Census data (1900–1950) available through the Integrated Public Use Microdata Series (IPUMS). Note: The 1950 Census occupational titles use the category "clergymen," reflecting contemporary gendered assumptions about the makeup of the clergy.*

In 1900, the emerging occupation of social work, along with religious and charity work, had a high proportion of foreign-born workers compared to other nurturant care occupations (see figure 3.11). Among social workers, these immigrants came exclusively from Europe and overwhelmingly from Ireland (80 percent of foreign-born social workers in 1900 were from Ireland). Over 40 percent of the much larger group of religious workers were also Irish born, with smaller groups from Germany and Canada. With decreases in immigration, all these social service occupations experienced declining numbers of foreign-born workers by 1950. As social work moved toward professionalization, it became dominated by White workers; by 1950, social work was 85 percent White and U.S. born, and had joined nursing and teaching as one of the preferred occupations for White women entering the paid labor force (see figure 3.12).

Black women's underrepresentation among professional social workers contrasted with their long history of social activism and community involvement. In the late nineteenth and early twentieth centuries, Black women created a network of Black women's clubs. Initially organized in support of the antilynching campaign of Ida B. Wells, these networks became hubs for "educating and aiding poor African-American girls and women," as well as for

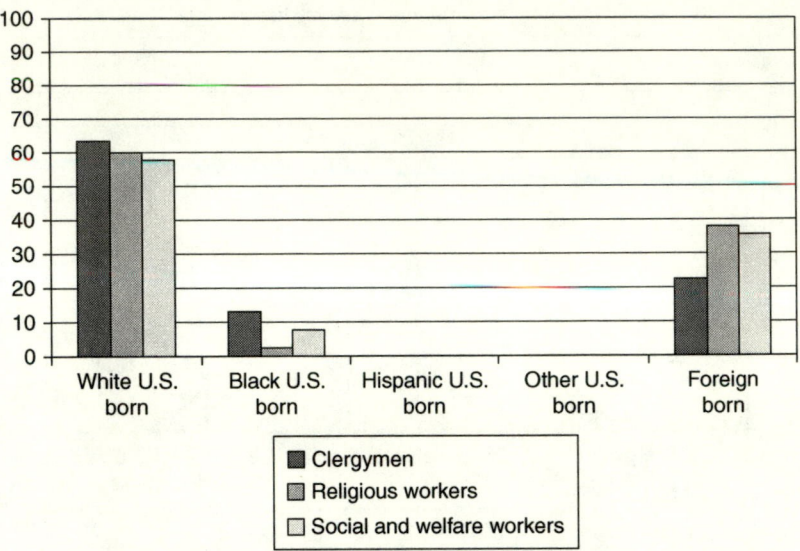

Figure 3.11. Selected social service workers by race-ethnicity and birthplace, 1900 (in percentages) *Source: Calculated by author using U.S. Census data (1900) available through the Integrated Public Use Microdata Series (IPUMS). Note: The 1950 Census occupational titles use the category "clergymen," reflecting contemporary gendered assumptions about the makeup of the clergy.*

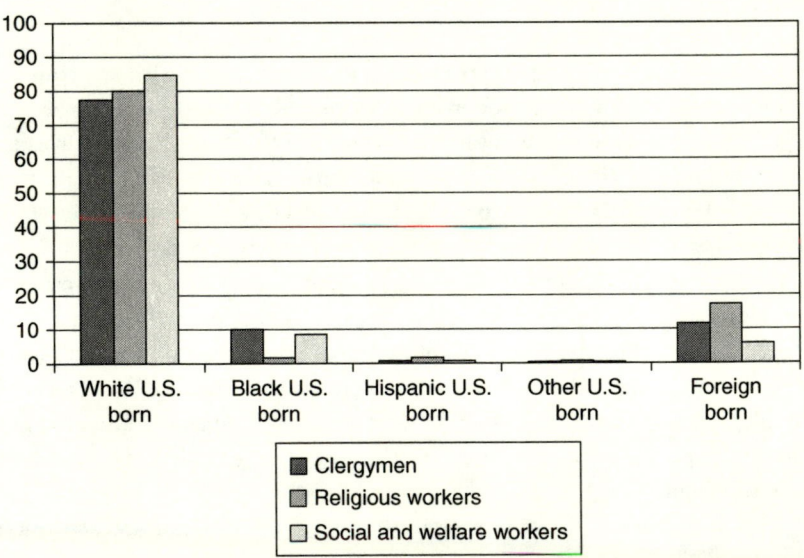

Figure 3.12. Selected social service workers by race-ethnicity and birthplace, 1950 (in percentages) *Source: Calculated by author using U.S. Census data (1950) available through the Integrated Public Use Microdata Series (IPUMS). Note: The 1950 Census occupational titles use the category "clergymen," reflecting contemporary gendered assumptions about the makeup of the clergy.*

antiracist and feminist activism.[56] Black women also created settlement houses and associations to address the abuse of Black working women. For the first half of the century, these clubs operated parallel to similar networks of benevolence among White women, whose organizations often actively resisted Black women's participation. Professional social work emerged from White women's charity organizations in this segregated environment, and it was only later in the century that Black women would enter social work in significant numbers.

FROM MENTAL ILLNESS TO MENTAL HEALTH

In the late 1800s, the catchall model of the almshouse for orphans, the mentally ill, and the poor was the target of a number of reform movements. Both child-welfare and more general mental health reformers advocated for a shift from custodial care to active treatment, and by the early twentieth century, specialized systems and expert workers in these areas had begun to emerge. Only after World War II, however, would the scope of mental health services expand dramatically, addressing not just serious mental illness but the mental health of all Americans.

Nineteenth-century child-welfare advocates urged states to set up child-welfare systems and to move children out of almshouses, focusing on foster care and the prevention of abuse and neglect in families.[57] These efforts grew in part out of the cultural move toward recognizing childhood as a sacred time to be protected, and states took an increasingly active role in ensuring the welfare of children. While Progressive Era child savers worked for social reform such as child-labor laws and safety regulations, by the 1920s the child-welfare movement had largely turned to the model of individual intervention in the tradition of the COS and early social work.[58] Through a growing number of state child-welfare agencies and juvenile court systems, experts intervened in families and with children and youth. In the 1920s, there was a growth in models that focused on prevention of problems like delinquency through individual intervention with children at risk. A system of child-guidance clinics was instituted whose mission was to deal with the "everyday problems of the everyday child," and child psychology became a subfield of a growing discipline.[59]

The emergence of child-guidance clinics was linked to a larger mental hygiene movement. Reformers like Dorothea Dix led a move in the 1800s to change the way the seriously mentally ill were cared for. Dix advocated the creation of specialized institutions to treat mental illness in contrast to the almshouse, which primarily served as a warehouse. Although reformers saw many state mental hospitals built, at the beginning of the twentieth century, conditions at most of these institutions remained little better than those at the poorhouses Dix had condemned.[60] Nevertheless, these institutions at least paid lip service to a model focused on treatment led by expert psychiatrists and psychologists. In addition, Freudian psychoanalysis began to find more adherents in the United States among those who could afford its intensive time demand and high cost.[61] In the 1920s, social welfare reformers began a move toward "preventative mental hygiene," based on emergent public health strategies; advocates argued that the wider application of expert mental health assessment and intervention would prevent some individuals from becoming more seriously impaired and contributing to larger social problems. This push led to the expansion of mental health care to a broader U.S. audience.[62]

These trends toward understanding mental health as a care need of large numbers of Americans rather than limited to the seriously mentally impaired gained significant traction during and after World War II. Psychiatrists gained prominence and public recognition for performing mental health screening of military recruits on a much larger scale than had ever been carried out before. After the war, psychotherapy came to be seen as of benefit not only to soldiers recovering from trauma, but also to the many other individuals who had suffered trauma or disruptions because of the war. In addition, postwar prosperity allowed Americans to spend more time and money focusing on their well-being. New models of treatment were less intensive than traditional psychoanalysis, and occupations like psychiatry and psychology entered a period of unprecedented growth.

Regina Kunzel has argued that the growing prominence of psychotherapy led to a shift in strategy for social work leaders. A new specialty of psychiatric social work gained prominence, as social workers aimed to boost their own claims to expertise by aligning themselves with the growing cultural authority of psychiatry. However, leaders had a hard time articulating what made social work unique. One leader, speaking in 1951, argued that "social work is something in its own right, and not just a poor substitute for, or an adjunct to, psychiatry; . . . common sense, readiness to help, warmth, and efficiency are qualities not to be ashamed of. Social workers should not aim at becoming third-rate therapists."[63] Ironically, in their attempts to differentiate social work from psychiatry and psychology—both then predominantly male occupations—leaders reclaimed the relational skills they had once shunned.

Like health care and the care and education of children, the broadly connected fields of social services and mental health underwent a dramatic transformation early in the twentieth century. A broad focus on individual intervention for children, families, the seriously mentally ill, and those with everyday worries led to the expansion and redefinition of the role of a range of expert nurturant care workers. Despite attempts by social work leaders to distance themselves from the tradition of female benevolence, social work remained a female-dominated occupation both practically and ideologically. In the second half of the century, more women would enter the male-dominated field of psychology, putting the mental health of all Americans increasingly in female hands.

A Hierarchy of Care

In all these arenas, the evolution of nurturant care in the first half of the twentieth century was not just a shift in who is doing the work of care or in where it is happening but a transformation in the very nature of the activity of care. Technological developments in health care, the emergence of the sacred child, the rise of a scientific model of intervention with the poor, and an expanded definition of mental health changed expectations of what care should mean. The development of a cadre of expert nurturant care workers is intimately linked to these shifting definitions of care, as well as to larger cultural trends of specialization. By midcentury, a hierarchy of care had emerged, linking particular aspects of the new nurturant care with certain groups of workers.

PROFESSIONALS AND MANAGERS: EXPERT JUDGMENT

In the realm of nurturant care, physicians were the only occupational group that achieved true professional status, along with the recognized expertise that made their judgment paramount in the growing field of health care. For the first fifty years of the twentieth century, the occupation was almost exclusively male, and doctors retained a high level of control over their own work, decisions about patient care, and the labor of their subordinates. As patients and their families relied more and more on experts in the increasingly complex world of medical care, doctors were seen as possessing the specialized technical skills and the high level of knowledge to diagnose illnesses and prescribe treatments.

While expert judgment became highly prized in education as well, no single occupational group emerged as controlling the educational enterprise. Rather, expert judgment often sat with bureaucrats and school board members (again, often male). In the emergent field of mental health, authority rested most clearly with psychiatrists and increasingly with psychologists (largely men). Social workers were partially successful in staking a claim to specialized knowledge and expert control in the social service sector, but their work was often still controlled by managers and they lacked the level of professional authority enjoyed by physicians.

Across the nurturant care sector, the early twentieth century was an era of the rising importance of specialized knowledge and expert judgment, which tended to be concentrated among a small group of mostly male professionals and managers. In health care, expert judgment sat clearly with physicians, while in other arenas it was with a less differentiated occupational group of managers and supervisors.

NURSES, TEACHERS, AND SOCIAL WORKERS: RELATIONAL CARE

Two of the largest groups of workers in this sector in the early twentieth century—nurses and teachers—played a unique role in nurturant care. Nurses and teachers claimed expert status based on formal education, specialized knowledge, and, especially in the case of nurses, technical skill, but they also staked a special claim to the relational skills that were becoming increasingly important as modern-day nurturant care took shape. I use "relational" here broadly to capture a range of aspects of care included not as part of formal knowledge or technical skills, but in relationships—things like warmth, moral guidance, and empathy. Early training in both nursing and teaching empha- sized character and the development of these relational talents as much as or more than the technical and knowledge-based aspects of the jobs. And, of course, these relational pieces were most closely associated with the feminine. While the rhetoric of the early professionalization of social work shunned some of these more sentimental aspects, they were firmly entrenched in the female tradition of benevolence with which social work remained associated despite leaders' efforts to the contrary. Ruth Schwartz Cowan has argued that while technological innovations reduced the time spent in certain household tasks for women in the late nineteenth and early twentieth century, there was a concurrent expectation that women would be increasingly emotionally and relationally available to their husbands and children.[64] This expectation became part of the ideal of femininity that was linked to nursing, teaching, and benevolent work.

This linkage did allow nursing and teaching to become job opportunities that many White middle-class women found far preferable to factory work or private household service. It also was a source of tension within these occu- pations at times, as the relational aspect of nurturant care was perceived to conflict with the technical and scientific aspects. Some nurses thus resisted professionalization and the requirement of formal education because they feared the relational aspects of their jobs would get lost. Conversely, social workers, in their quest for professionalization, deliberately (and unsuccessfully) tried to distance themselves from feminine relationality in favor of professional (and masculinized) objectivity. But despite the tensions, leaders in these occupations at different historical moments proudly claimed the relational aspects of care as important components of their jobs, and as skills that were critical to being a good nurse, teacher, or social worker. Even though they emphasized character, early nursing and teacher-training programs saw character itself as something to be molded through instruction and practice, in a sense giving women the relational skills they needed for the job. On the one hand, then, feminine relationality was posed in opposition to technical skill and professional knowledge. On the other hand, relationality was presented as a skill to be developed and valued. This tension in the construction of the female-dominated jobs that constituted the core of the expansion of nurturant care became both a source of richness and a source of profound conflict as these occupations developed.

The sex segregation of these occupations in the first fifty years of the twentieth century was matched by racial-ethnic segregation. Black women were barely visible in nursing, teaching, or social work, and while there were sizable minorities of foreign-born women who were nurses and social workers in 1900, by 1950, these too were gone. In 1950, the occupations of nursing, teaching, and social work were all well over 80 percent White and U.S. born. The dominance of White women in the most relational occupations of nurturant care was well established by 1950.

HOSPITAL ATTENDANTS: MENIAL CARE

Of all of the occupations included in this discussion of nurturant care, only one was more than 10 percent Black U.S. born in 1950: attendants in hospitals and other institutions. In 1900, 20 percent of practical nurses were Black U.S. born, and 20 percent foreign born. By 1950, as even "practical" nurses became "licensed practical nurses," the proportion of White U.S.-born practical nurses had increased to almost 80 percent. In the more generic "attendants" category, about 70 percent were White U.S. born in 1900, and the majority of the rest were foreign born. By 1950 the makeup had shifted to include over 18 percent Black U.S.-born workers.

The pattern of racial-ethnic segregation and sex segregation of hospital attendants is unique in the nurturant care sector. While most nurturant care occupations were highly gendered, in 1950 this category remained relatively mixed. And in a sector dominated by White workers, this is the one occupation with meaningful numbers of Black workers. This pattern parallels the makeup of the cooking and cleaning occupations that are the more menial parts of reproductive labor. The work of hospital attendants was defined as menial in part because these jobs did not require formal education or licensing and were seen as unskilled. But, importantly, they were also seen as menial because they involved the execution of routine tasks and did not require the exercise of relational skills. As the century progressed, the construction of nursing aide jobs as menial would also become conflicted, as workers contested the definition of their labor as unskilled by staking a claim particularly to the relational skills necessary for their work.

The beginning of the twentieth century was a time of profound transformation for care work, and ideological and economic shifts drove the redefinition and reorganization of nurturance. What emerged was a hierarchical structure that reflected both gender and racial-ethnic stratification in its construction of care. Nurturant care had become the domain of experts, professionals with specialized knowledge and White U.S.-born women with both technical and relational skills. In 1950, Black, Hispanic, and foreign-born women are notable in nurturant care primarily for their absence. Although there would be some shifts in that pattern over the second half of the century, the historical roots of nurturant care occupations show how intertwined the development of these occupations was with the construction of the nature of care and of gender and racial-ethnic identities.

Chapter 4

Managing Nurturant Care in the New Economy

By THE MIDDLE OF the twentieth century, the notion of expert care was well established, and a range of occupational roles had been defined (or redefined) to provide that care. In the second half of the century, population growth and demographic trends continued to expand the demand for care services, and paid care grew exponentially. Paid nurturant care work is not only crucial for meeting the needs of contemporary society in the United States, but also a vital part of the economic engine of the country. Nevertheless, nurturant care workers at the dawn of the twenty-first century operate largely in a context of constraints. Since the 1980s, economic restructuring and political retrenchment have once again redefined the boundaries of paid care, limiting the autonomy and control workers are able to exercise as well as squeezing out the relational aspects of their jobs. In the process, related gender, racial-ethnic, and class hierarchies have both persisted in recognizable patterns and taken on new shapes.

The Market, the State, and Care

During the course of the twentieth century there have been a number of watershed moments in U.S. economic and political life. The Great Depression of the 1930s and the subsequent expansion of social welfare policies as the New Deal increased the government's responsibility to protect workers and provide them with a safety net. The social movements of the 1960s opened the door to legal rights and expanded material opportunities for Blacks, women, and other disenfranchised groups. And in the 1980s the Reagan revolution proscribed the role of government in social welfare and business, extolling free markets and an ethic of individualism.

Ronald Reagan's philosophy was part of a global phenomenon of which Margaret Thatcher was another vocal advocate. Sometimes referred to as "neoliberalism," it is an approach premised on the primacy of individual responsibility and the undermining of collective identification. In fact, Thatcher is famously reported to have said that there "is no such thing as society."[1] In practice, Reagan and Thatcher followed similar paths, cutting government spending on social welfare and deregulating business (including loosening government protections of workers), in addition to implementing large tax cuts. In the neoliberal worldview, the free market was to be as unfettered by government interference as possible. The consequences for workers in this new economy were the loss of regulatory protection and an undermining of union organizing by the emphasis on individualism (among other forces working against unionism). For care workers, the impact of neoliberalism on their work environments was exacerbated by the direct cuts to publicly funded care enterprises—public schools, health care (through Medicare and Medicaid), and publicly provided social services.

The combination of funding cuts, declining worker protections, and an ideological commitment to proscribing the limits of public responsibility for care changed the landscape of paid care. An increase in bureaucratic and managerial control that has eroded the autonomy of many groups of nurturant care workers is part of an overall process of routinization and deskilling. As Ilene Philipson interprets Harry Braverman's classic analysis, deskilling is "the process by which work requiring the exercise of conceptual and judgmental abilities is separated off from that requiring only routine execution."[2] In manufacturing industries, mechanization and automation had facilitated the process of turning many jobs into the performance of a series of routine tasks, a shift that allowed employers to hire unskilled workers at lower wage rates. For workers, this shift meant a considerable loss of autonomy and control over the labor process. In the context of neoliberal economic restructuring, the burgeoning service sector also became vulnerable to deskilling.

Scholars who have critiqued Braverman's use of the concept have argued that the very notion of skill is socially constructed and historically tied to the status of the primary group of workers in an occupation.[3] If skill is considered a measure of the complexity of the demands of a job, occupations require different levels of a range of skill sets—cognitive, manual, social, verbal, visual, or emotional. Advocates of comparable worth have demonstrated that the skills most usually associated with female-dominated jobs are less recognized and less well compensated than those associated with male-dominated jobs.[4] Numerous studies of male occupations that have become female dominated, including teaching and clerical work, demonstrate that as the gender composition of an occupation changes, the language used to describe its skills shifts.[5] Seen through this lens, deskilling is as much a cultural process of redefinition as an objective process of changing labor-market and workplace conditions.

In the context of nurturant care work, deskilling involves redefining the boundaries of care itself. Separating the conceptual from the routine is complicated in care settings, where technical knowledge and relational competence are both important and can overlap considerably. Nurses may chat with patients about their pain level while taking their blood pressure, or teachers may have a conversation with a child about their feelings about their parents' divorce after a math lesson. Breaking care work down into a series of tasks that can be routinized means defining the tasks that constitute care. And in an environment of cost cutting, the tendency has been to draw those tasks' boundaries narrowly. On the one hand, many nurturant care workers who had achieved professional or semiprofessional status have experienced some increase in the routinization and external control of their jobs. On the other, deskilling in some care industries has translated into more low-wage workers performing tasks once assigned to more highly trained groups. Again, the definition of the roles of care workers and the construction of the nature of care work are inextricably intertwined processes. The domain of the expert care worker established by early twentieth-century transformations got smaller and smaller as the century ended.

This process of defining the boundaries of care is driven not only by cost-cutting pressures and other economic aspects of neoliberalism, but also by the political process that enforces the limits of public support for care.[6] Medicare will pay for "medically necessary care" but not for "custodial care," and the program for home care specifically states it is not intended to replace family care.[7] Although these limits and the many others set by government programs are in line with a cost-cutting paradigm, they send a larger message about who is responsible for care. And, despite the exodus of certain kinds of care work from the domestic labor of the home, in the United States the responsibility for providing care still rests with the individual and the family. In addition to the economic process, this political ideology has helped redefine and subdivide care work in the late twentieth century.

The Big Picture: Nurturant Care at the Dawn of the Twenty-first Century

Considered broadly, the occupations of nurturant care experienced unprecedented growth in the last half of the twentieth century. Based on a measure of occupations that reflects 1990 categories, the number of nurturant care

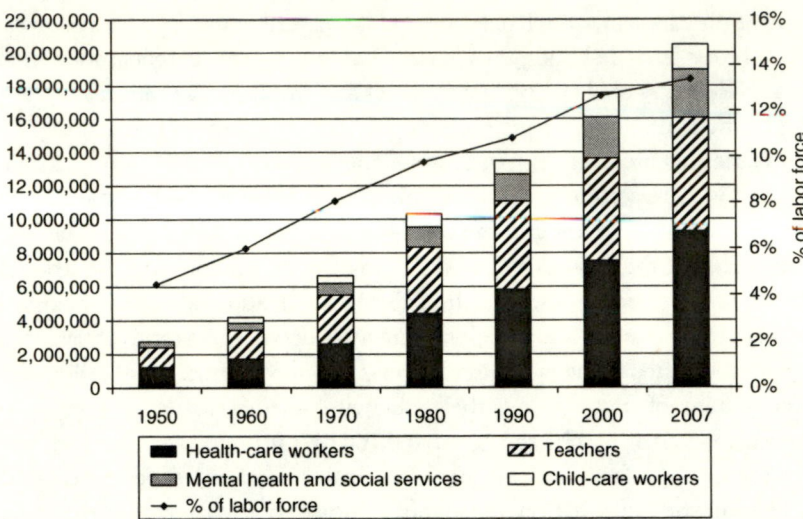

Figure 4.1. Number of nurturant care workers by occupational group, 1950–2007 *Source: Calculated by author using data from the U.S. Census (1950–2000) and the American Community Survey (2007) available through the Integrated Public Use Microdata Series (IPUMS).*

workers grew sixfold between 1950 and 2007, reaching just over 20 million workers—more than 13 percent of the labor force (see figure 4.1).[8] These increases far outpaced rates of expansion of the labor force as a whole, which doubled during the same period.

Given the highly gendered and racialized origins of many nurturant care occupations, the development of new categories of nurturant care inevitably involved gendered and racialized constructions of value. The increasing feminization of the nurturant care workforce evident in the first half of the century continued into the second. In 1900, only 55 percent of nurturant care workers overall were female. By 1950 that percentage had grown to 65 percent, and by 2007, to almost 80 percent. While the association of nurturant care work with women is often considered a relic of the past, it is clear that its increasing dominance by women reflects a complex and contemporary trend.

As we will see, the occupations firmly linked to ideals of femininity in their early stages of growth—nursing, teaching, and social work—remained female dominated throughout the century. As these occupations expanded, the number of female nurturant care workers expanded as well, and very few men entered these growing fields. By contrast, between 1960 and 2007, women made significant inroads into some of the nurturant care occupations that had been male-dominated through the first half of the century—notably

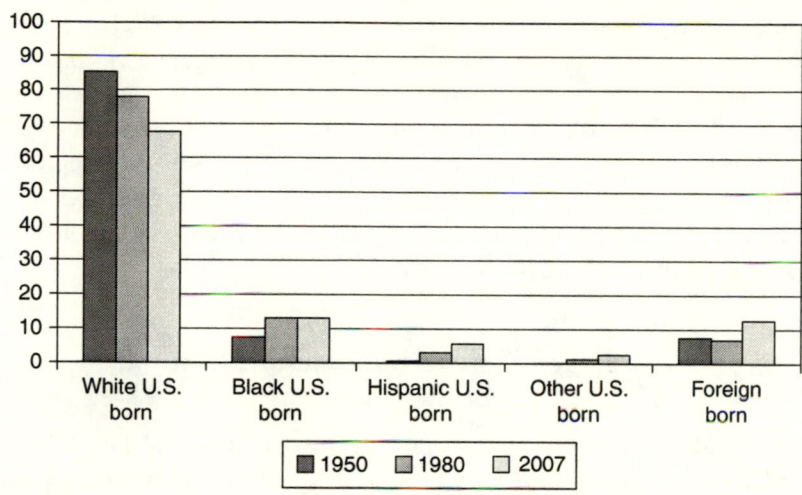

Figure 4.2. Nurturant care workers by race-ethnicity and birthplace, 1950–2007 (in percentages) *Source: Calculated by author using data from the U.S. Census (1950 and 1980) and the American Community Survey (2007) available through the Integrated Public Use Microdata Series (IPUMS).*

physicians, psychologists, and hospital attendants. The result has been that, as Philipson observed, "the well-being of the elderly, animals, the mentally ill and the emotionally injured" (as well as the physically ill and children and young people) rests increasingly on women's shoulders alone.[9]

In 1950, White U.S.-born workers made up 85 percent of the nurturant care workforce, a proportion that decreased to just over 65 percent by 2007 as the labor force became more diverse and the structure of the nurturant care workforce again underwent substantial change. With the exception of physicians, most nurturant care occupations followed the trend of the overall labor force, becoming proportionately more U.S. born between 1900 and 1950. In the second half of the century, as immigration laws were once again relaxed, immigrants were less likely than their nineteenth-century counterparts to be from Europe or Canada and more likely to be from Latin America or Asia. By 2007, foreign-born workers made up almost 17 percent of the labor force, still lower than the levels of immigration in 1900, but considerably increased from 1950. The presence of foreign-born workers in the nurturant care sector as a whole had also increased somewhat to 13 percent in 2007, with high concentrations in particular nurturant care occupations (see figure 4.2).

The shifting demographics of nurturant care in the late twentieth century included larger numbers of Black and Hispanic women than in previous decades, although both groups still make up relatively small proportions of the sector as a whole. Between 1950 and 1980, the proportion of Black U.S.-born workers in nurturant care rose from 7 to 12 percent (see figure 4.2), compared to a relatively steady representation of just under 10 percent of the labor force. Hispanic U.S.-born workers, barely visible in the nurturant care workforce in 1950, made up about 5 percent of it in 2007, just under their level of representation in the labor force as a whole. Like foreign-born workers, U.S.-born Black and Hispanic workers in the nurturant care sector are concentrated in a relatively small number of occupational groups.

From Expert Care to Bureaucratic Control: Health Care at the End of the Century

The second half of the twentieth century witnessed substantial growth in the number of workers in health-care occupations, especially registered nurses and nurses' aides, whose numbers between 1950 and 2007 grew eightfold to a combined total of over 5.5 million workers (see figure 4.3). Relatively speaking, the number of physicians grew at a considerably slower pace and at an overall smaller scale, quadrupling during this period to just over 825,000 workers. Rates of expansion in all areas of health care outpaced that of the overall labor force, which barely doubled between 1950 and 2007. Some of this expansion can be understood as a continuation of the forces of specialization and increasing

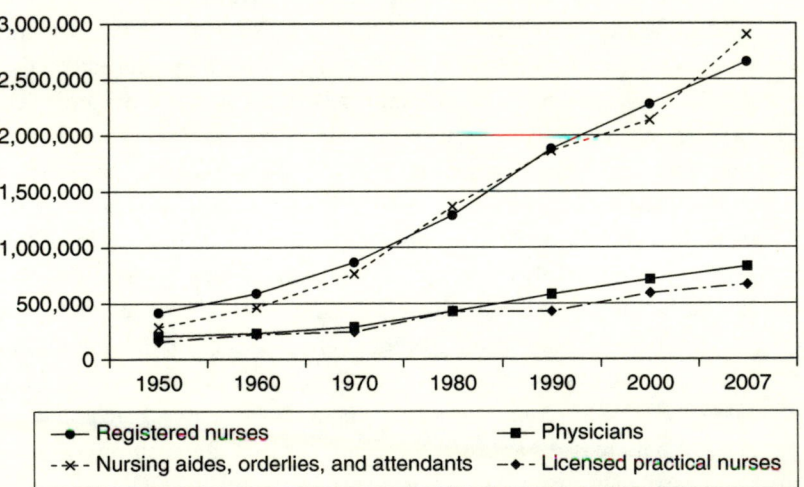

Figure 4.3. Number of workers in selected health-care occupations, 1950–2007 *Source: Calculated by author using data from the U.S. Census (1950–2000) and the American Community Survey (2007) available through the Integrated Public Use Microdata Series (IPUMS).*

technological complexity that helped catalyze the early growth of modern health care. However, the specific shape of health care—in particular the construction of nurturance, the working conditions of care workers, and the stratification of the health-care workforce—can be understood only in the context of the cost-containment and political retrenchment that came to dominate health care in the latter decades of the century. In addition, the nature of care has been profoundly changed once again by the demographic trends wrought in large part by advances in medical care that allow people to live much longer and in a much more sick condition than at the turn of the century.

In 1900, average life expectancy at birth in the United States was forty-seven years. By 1950, this had increased to sixty-eight years, and by 2004, to seventy-eight years.[10] Because of the massive health-care structure put in place in the first half of the century, as well as improvements in living conditions, hygiene, and public health, more and more U.S. residents began to live longer and longer lives. This aging of the population again changed the face of care, as the range of care needs that face the elderly can be quite different from the curing of acute illness that had been the focus of hospitals for the first half of the century. In addition, medical technology allows us to save many more lives than was ever before possible—premature babies, people injured in accidents, people with life-threatening conditions, people who have massive heart attacks and strokes. In some cases, individuals who survive a crisis illness or disabling injury require ongoing care. In the second half of the century, care of chronic conditions, along with long-term care of the frail elderly and the disabled, has become much more prominent in the health-care landscape.

Health care has also been affected in multiple ways by the overarching economic and political movements of the late twentieth century. The creation of Medicare and Medicaid in the 1960s expanded the role of the federal government in paying for health care. With the advent of the Reagan years, these budgets (like all social welfare spending) were cut substantially, putting pressure on health-care organizations to cut their own costs. Health-care costs had mushroomed, the result of a combination of the rising price tag for technological innovations, inefficiencies in the system of health-care delivery and payment, the emergence of for-profit health-care companies, and the high cost of new test procedures and pharmaceutical treatments.[11] Cost containment became the mantra of health-care reform with the introduction of health maintenance organizations (HMOs) in the 1970s and the ascendance of managed care as the primary model for financing and delivering private health care.[12] While the driving force behind the implementation of HMOs was cost containment (a goal yet to be achieved), the impact of this organizational shift for health-care workers was more far-reaching than could have been predicted.

PRIMARY NURSING: A MODEL OF RELATIONALITY

Although the American Nurses Association (ANA) remained committed to a path of professionalization for nurses, the emergence of a number of nursing unions in the middle of the century put pressure on nursing leaders that led to considerable innovation in nursing practice. There had been substantial resistance among nurses as early as the 1930s to organizing attempts by the American Federation of Labor (AFL) and the Congress of Industrial Organizations (CIO); many saw unionization and the accompanying demands for better wages and working conditions as in opposition to nursing's "spirit of service and humanitarian dedication."[13] The ANA also directly opposed union organizing among nurses, which leaders argued was not compatible with nurses' increasingly professional identity (university degrees had already become a norm). Despite these obstacles, in the 1940s and 1950s, a small but vocal number of nurses pursued union organizing as an alternative to professionalization.

Although nursing unions did not immediately achieve significant wage gains, the emergence of an alternative organizing structure put substantial pressure on the ANA. Criticized at times for being driven by the agenda of nursing managers and educators rather than by the concerns of staff nurses working at bedsides, nursing leaders in the 1960s and 1970s raised the profile of the staff nurse in their advocacy and innovation.[14] Journals and nursing textbooks began to emphasize "total patient care," and a new model, primary nursing, emerged at some of the nation's top hospitals.[15] Primary nursing matched each patient with a single nurse for the duration of the patient's hospital stay; each nurse had primary responsibility for a certain number of patients and was charged with coordinating their care.

Primary nurses had more substantive input into patient care. Integrated to varying degrees into health-care teams, they were counted on to provide important information and insight into patient-care planning. Although final authority remained in the hands of physicians, primary nurses had an increased voice in decision making. Importantly, nurses' claim to expertise and authority rested as much or more on their knowledge of each patient as on general technical knowledge. Primary nursing elevated the relational skills of nurses, framing them as complementary to, not opposed to, their technical skills. The combination of medical knowledge and consistent relationships with patients gave primary care nurses a unique position in the hospital hierarchy. While primary care was not the norm in nursing practice in the 1970s, it was rapidly expanding and heralded as the future of nursing. However, as the next decades unfolded, even this model, once at the forefront of nursing practice, changed beyond recognition.

THE RISE OF BUREAUCRATIC AUTHORITY AND
THE RECONFIGURATION OF HEALTH CARE

One of the most significant consequences for health-care workers of the reorganization of medical care in a neoliberal environment has been a substantial loss of autonomy and control over their own labor. Since early in the century, physicians had enjoyed the autonomy that is a hallmark of professional status. Most physicians not only operated independently rather than as employees of hospitals, but also retained almost exclusive power over patient diagnosis and treatment decisions. In the increasingly scientific and technical world of medicine, doctors were the experts, and their judgment was paramount. However, with the advent of cost containment, HMO managers, hospital executives, and government administrators have asserted more and more control over diagnostic and treatment decisions. Doctors are increasingly constrained by regulations and payment limits put in place by insurance companies and government programs that dictate everything from length of hospital stay to allowable test procedures to covered drugs. In the service of cutting costs, administrative regulation and systematic rationalization of medical care have gradually eroded the role of professional medical judgment.[16]

Some scholars have argued that the increasing presence of women among the ranks of physicians is related to this loss of professional autonomy. As late as 1960, women made up only 6 percent of all physicians. In the 1970s, that figure began to rise, and by 2007, almost one-third of U.S. physicians were women (see figure 4.4). Undoubtedly, some of this increase is due to the impact of the women's movement and an environment of increasing gender equality. Women have entered a wide range of professions in the past thirty years that were once all but closed to them. However, in "Women's Recent Progress in the Professions, or Women Get a Ticket to Ride after the Gravy Train Has Left the Station," Michael Carter and Susan Carter point out that these professions have opened up to women largely in the wake of occupational transformations that undermined the autonomy characteristic of professional stature.[17] To make a similar argument, Barbara Reskin and Patricia Roos have used the notion of "job queues." They suggest that those occupations that are the most desirable are dominated by White men, and that it is only as those jobs become less desirable that other groups of workers further down the gender or racial-ethnic queue have access to them.[18]

Queuing theory is not uncontested, and Jerry Jacobs and Ann Boulis contend that the increase in the number of women doctors is driven more by women's changing roles in society than by the decline of the profession.[19] Putting this debate to one side, here I consider the growing feminization of medicine within the context of the larger transformation of nurturant care at

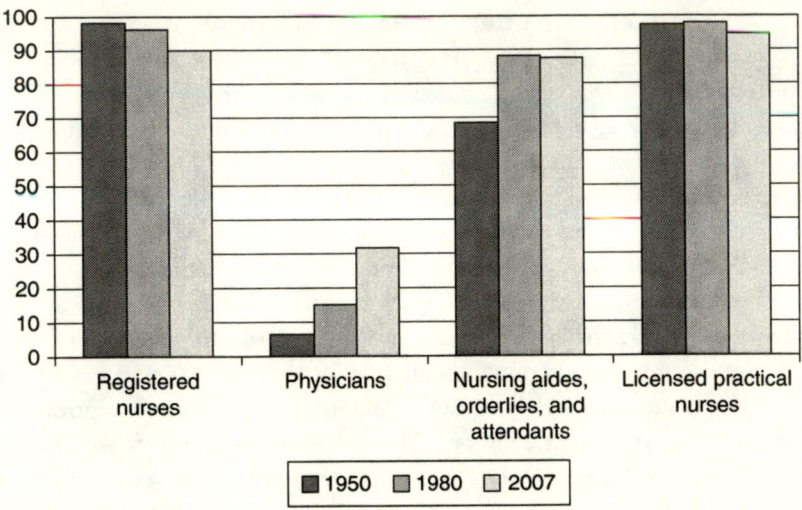

Figure 4.4. Women in selected health-care occupations, 1950–2007 (in percentages)
Source: Calculated by author using data from the U.S. Census (1950 and 1980) and the American Community Survey (2007) available through the Integrated Public Use Microdata Series (IPUMS).

the end of the twentieth century. In recent decades, nurturant care as a whole has become more feminized and nurturant care workers across the board have experienced a loss of autonomy and increased bureaucratic control of their labor. The increase in women doctors is no doubt linked to shifting gender roles, and medicine remains a relatively high-status profession in the United States. However, like other nurturant care workers, doctors have seen shifts in the cultural construction of their labor and in the structural constraints of their work simultaneous with the growing presence of women in the profession. And this process has been quite distinct from the feminization of nursing and teaching earlier in the century.

The latter half of the twentieth century has also seen an ongoing rise in the number of foreign-born doctors practicing in the United States. Between 1950 and 2007, the proportion of U.S. doctors who are foreign born doubled, reaching almost 30 percent of the total number of physicians (see figures 4.5 and 4.6). The countries of origin of these immigrant doctors have shifted over the century; the largest number now come from India, with substantial numbers from China and other Asian countries, and a significant minority from Europe.

For nurses, cost cutting stopped in its tracks any movement toward greater professional authority that had been achieved in the 1970s and early 1980s.

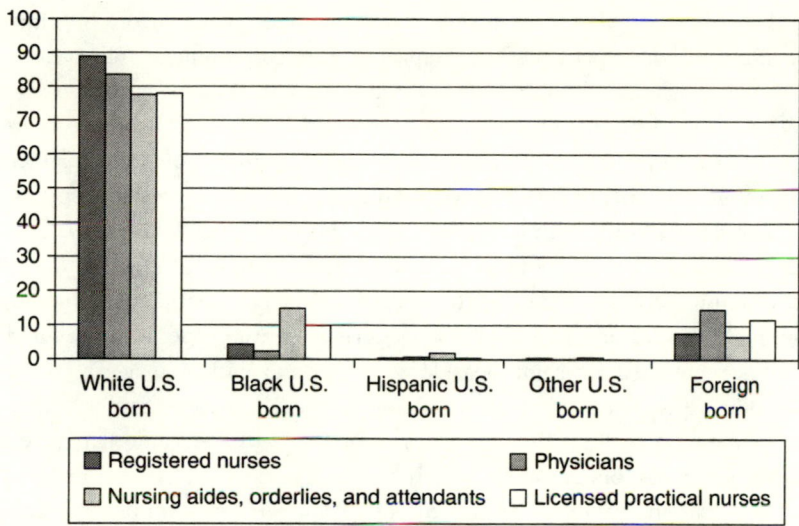

Figure 4.5. Selected health-care workers by race-ethnicity and birthplace, 1950 (in percentages) *Source: Calculated by author using U.S. Census data (1950) available through the Integrated Public Use Microdata Series (IPUMS).*

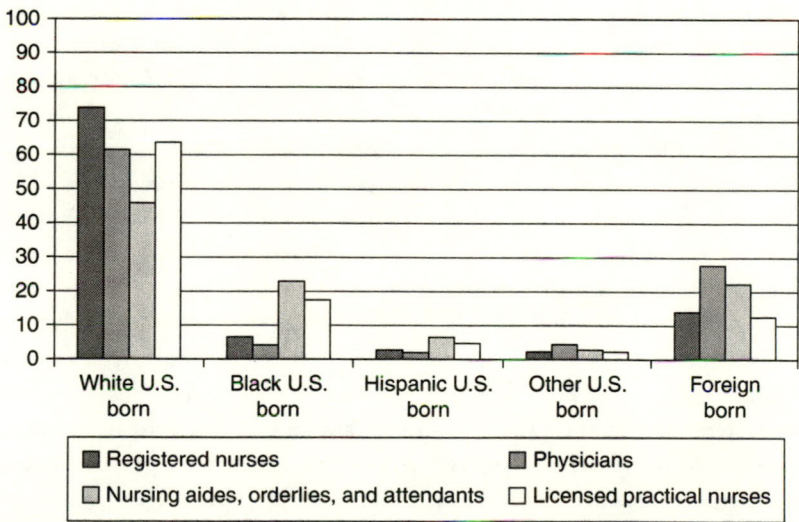

Figure 4.6. Selected health-care workers by race-ethnicity and birthplace, 2007 (in percentages) *Source: Calculated by author using American Community Survey data (2007) available through the Integrated Public Use Microdata Series (IPUMS).*

By the end of the 1980s, even hospitals that had once been beacons of primary nursing care had experienced the impact of cost containment and routinization.[20] For nurses, deskilling meant not only the loss of many gains in authority, but also the transfer of some tasks to lower-paid aides. So, while registered nurses have never achieved professional-level recognition of their judgment, they retain authority over the growing ranks of auxiliary workers in hospitals— aides, orderlies, and attendants, as well as licensed practical nurses. These workers perform a range of tasks considered menial enough to require little to no training, or routine enough to necessitate merely technical know-how. Registered nurses at the end of the twentieth century operate in a middle ground, removed from some bedside activities and with managerial control over nursing assistants, but with no real authority over patient care.

Some scholars have linked a renewed union movement among registered nurses to this loss of autonomy, which has undermined the professional identity of nurses and therefore weakened one of the barriers to union organizing. Union membership among registered nurses increased from 16.6 percent in 1990 to 19.4 percent in 2007, making it one of a minute number of occupations that have experienced union growth during these decades.[21] Philip Dine has pointed out that recent organizing campaigns among nurses have addressed not just wages and working conditions but staffing cuts and policies that lead to nurses having "less time and flexibility to care for their patients and attend to their specific needs and requests."[22] In this way, some nurses' unions have directly challenged the squeezing out of the relational element of their jobs that has accompanied increased bureaucratization and external control of their work.

As the roles of nursing aides and attendants have come to include more tasks that were once performed by registered nurses, these occupations have become more feminized. For the first half of the century, the workers in the more general category "attendants" were primarily male. By midcentury, women outnumbered men in these roles. And by 2007, almost 90 percent of nursing aides, orderlies and attendants were women (see figure 4.4). While the dynamics behind this change are undoubtedly different from the reasons for the increasing numbers of female physicians, both trends reflect the ever-greater representation of women in nurturant care, in contrast to the much smaller increases of men among registered nurses and licensed practical nurses.

As they expanded numerically, these auxiliary health-care occupations also became the site of heavy concentrations of Black, Hispanic, and foreign-born workers (see figures 4.5 and 4.6). Although White U.S.-born workers still held almost 80 percent of nursing aide, orderly, and attendant jobs in 1950, Black U.S.-born workers were overrepresented; Black U.S.-born workers made up just under 15 percent of nursing aides, and under 10 percent of the labor force as a whole. By 2007, White U.S.-born workers were a minority in this occupational group. Despite Black U.S.-born workers remaining just under 10 percent of the labor force, they represented almost one-quarter of auxiliary nursing workers. Foreign-born workers made up 22 percent of this occupational group (compared to 16 percent of the labor force). Fully one-quarter of foreign-born nursing aides in 2007 were from the West Indies, with substantial numbers from Mexico, Central America, and the Philippines. The racial-ethnic segregation that had always to some extent characterized this menial labor in health care thus intensified dramatically at the end of the twentieth century. A similar if less extreme pattern exists among licensed practical nurses. These growing low-wage health-care occupations were some of the alternatives open to Black women leaving domestic service.

Black women also made some inroads into registered nursing. Barely visible among professional nurses throughout the century, by 2007 Black U.S.-born workers made up almost 7 percent of registered nurses. Foreign-born women are even more of a presence in the nursing workforce, making up 14 percent of registered nurses (compared to under 10 percent in 1950). Over 30 percent of foreign-born nurses are from the Philippines, and substantial numbers also come from the West Indies. Suzanne Gordon has attributed the rising numbers of foreign-born nurses to the decreasing appeal of nursing to White U.S.-born women in light of deteriorating working conditions and the opening up of more attractive employment options.[23] Yet, despite these demographic shifts, White U.S.-born women continue to be disproportionately represented in nursing.

MANAGING RELATIONALITY

The reconfiguration of health-care work in a cost-cutting environment has not only shifted the boundaries of authority of groups of health-care workers, but also redefined the role of relationality in health care. For example, nursing practice at Beth Israel Hospital in Boston, once a beacon of primary nursing care, has been transformed in the wake of a controversial merger and the intensification of cost cutting in the early 1990s. According to Dana Beth Weinberg, in the period before the merger, "primary nursing elevated the professional status of nurses by defining even mundane tasks as part of a complicated process of evaluating patients, planning and implementing their nursing care, coordinating that care with other members of the care team, and continually reassessing the efficacy of interventions." This formulation of the role of nurses integrated technical, relational, and even "menial" tasks into a single intertwined labor process. After the merger, as cost-cutting imperatives began to drive the design of nursing practice, nurses' relationships with patients were no longer considered a critical part of their care work, but rather a "luxury" the hospital could not afford.[24]

This separation and devaluation of the relational element of care allowed hospitals to justify labeling certain tasks "menial," and therefore suitable for lower-paid, less skilled workers. Once tasks like making beds, drawing blood, changing dressings, positioning patients, and inserting catheters were removed from the larger context of developing a relationship with patients and learning about their needs, workers other than RNs could perform them.[25] Not only did this process change the jobs of nurses, but also it clearly demarcated the roles of the auxiliary hospital workers to whom these tasks were assigned. Their jobs were defined as requiring less skill than those of nurses, and as primarily manual and largely absent any relational component.

While not all hospitals had implemented the model of primary nursing in the way the newly merged Beth Israel Deaconness Medical Center had, the approach epitomized the ideal of total patient care emphasized in the textbooks and nursing journals of the time. Now, without an emphasis on relationality, nurses at Beth Israel, as at many other hospitals, were no longer assigned to particular patients through the duration of their stay. In fact, nurses were not even given regularly scheduled shifts but were asked to operate on flexible shifts based on the number of beds filled in the hospital on a given day. Additionally, nurses were to float from unit to unit, further disrupting relational continuity and predictability. Shrinking limits on patient stays imposed by insurance companies and government programs also meant that patients were in the hospital for fewer days and needed more acute care during their stays. These developments combined with staffing decreases led to a general speedup of the work of RNs, further limiting their time for relating to patients.[26]

Other health-care workers have also experienced the diminution of the relational aspects of care. While relational skills have never been emphasized among doctors to the extent they have among nurses, doctors have also experienced a speedup that has constrained whatever relationship with patients they might have developed. The work of lower-paid health-care workers, as noted earlier, was specifically defined as menial and nonrelational. Among certified nursing assistants (CNAs) in nursing homes, Timothy Diamond describes the work of CNAs as routinized to the point that "if it is not charted it didn't happen." The result is to make the relational labor of CNAs literally invisible. While the chart may say the CNA gave a resident a bath, it says nothing of the fact that she also listened to the resident talk about her loneliness. The chart may say that the CNA fed a resident breakfast but says nothing of the way the CNA has learned to coax that particular elderly woman to eat. Diamond describes a work schedule that neither provides time for nor acknowledgment of these relational elements of care, and he argues that both the working conditions for workers and the quality of care suffer as a result.[27]

While these workers operate in an environment in which their ability to exercise relational skills is severely constrained, relationality continues to be valorized in training rhetoric and often is valued highly by the workers themselves.[28] A recent nursing textbook describes the "explosion of clinical narratives, reflective practice, and theoretical work on caring" since the 1990s as a return to valuing the "essence" of nursing.[29] And Diamond describes an instructor in a CNA training course who emphasizes to her students the need to use their "mother wit" to connect with their patients.[30] At best, the dissonance between workers' identification and training to value the relational aspects of care and their inability to follow that model in the workplace leads to conflicts for workers. At worst, it becomes a mechanism for exploitation and the extraction of additional labor from care workers.

Lisa Dodson and Rebekah Zincavage have found that the explicit comparison of care work in nursing homes to family relationships is widespread both among managers and workers. Managers often evoked kinship metaphors to describe the environments in their nursing homes, as well as to define the ideal CNA. Many expressed a desire that CNAs would treat residents as they would their mothers. Many CNAs also defined their work in kinlike terms, comparing their relationships with residents to that with their own grandmother and saying that they came to love some of the residents like family. But, importantly, according to managers, the expressions of that relational connection were to occur *on workers' own time* in activities like bringing in birthday cakes for residents or going shopping. That is, while relationality receives lip service from managers, it is not built into the structure of the labor of CNAs; managers expect that relational obligations will compel CNAs to go above and beyond their defined duties. Just as the relational context has made it difficult for domestic servants to enforce boundaries around work demands, expectations of relational connection for health-care workers can lead to expanding obligations within a highly constrained workplace structure.[31]

BACK TO THE HOME?

While hospitals in the latter half of the twentieth century became increasingly focused on acute care, the long-term care and chronic care needs of an aging population continued to increase. Institutional care in nursing homes and other residential facilities became more common and was defined as qualitatively different from hospital care.[32] Institutions like rehabilitation centers and some nursing homes offered post-acute care after a hospitalization until an individual was ready to return home. And nursing homes also offered long-term care to the frail elderly, assisting them with the tasks of daily living. Interestingly, as early as the 1960s, there was a push to provide care not provided in hospitals in private homes rather than in institutions. Home care was heralded as an alternative to meeting the chronic and long-term needs of the elderly in particular, with little recognition of how recently in history "home care" had been the norm.[33]

In contrast to the first decades of the twentieth century, when caring for patients in private homes was the labor of the most highly trained nurses, home care was defined in its new iteration as low-skilled work that could be lower paid than skilled nursing care. In the 1970s, one of the main arguments for such home care was cost savings, a motivation strengthened by the budget cuts and constraints of the Reagan era. A general move toward deinstitutionalization of the frail elderly, the mentally ill, and individuals with disabilities was driven by an ideological commitment to the home and community as a preferred site for care. Preserving the supremacy of the hospital in providing acute care to the ill necessitated delineating which kinds of care were appropriate for the home. After all, it had not been that long ago that nursing leaders and medical associations had campaigned to convince the public that hospitals should be the preferred site for medical care.

Home care was defined in two specific ways. First, home care might be provided after a hospitalization to contribute to recovery through nursing services, physical therapy, or other assistance considered medical in nature. The federal Medicare program, which funded health care for the elderly, defined which home-care benefits it would cover through this medicalized model. Second, home care for "functionally disabled elderly adults" would assist them with the activities of daily living, such as bathing, dressing, preparing and eating meals, and toileting. This model was adopted by Medicaid, which funded benefits to the poor.[34] The roles of various groups of workers in these two models were clearly delineated as well. Post-acute skilled care was to be provided by RNs and other professionals like physical therapists and occupational therapists. The menial tasks of bathing, feeding, and assisting patients with toileting either during post-acute episodes or over longer periods were delegated to home-care aides or personal care attendants.

These home-care aides and personal care attendants are at the bottom of a hospital hierarchy with so little opportunity for mobility that it has been called segmented.[35] The development of this rigid hierarchy within hospitals, as well as among home-care workers, is not just a consequence of cost cutting but at least partly a product of professionalization efforts by registered nurses.

To preserve their own authority and recognition as skilled workers, nurses pushed to limit the technical tasks that hospital nursing aides and home-care aides could perform, defining the role of these other health-care workers as unskilled in part to reinforce their own position.[36]

A number of scholars have begun to analyze the more recent trend toward assigning technical and complex medical tasks to home-care workers or friends and family members as an extension of the deskilling of nursing. Some of the technical and medical tasks deliberately constructed during the professionalization of nursing as requiring skill and training—giving injections, setting up intravenous drips, and so on—are now portrayed as jobs easily done by unskilled workers or family members with minimal instruction from an RN. Nancy Guberman and her colleagues have called this process the "trivialization" of medical care, another strategy to shift more labor from RNs to lower-wage (or unpaid) workers.[37] Again, this process involves a recharacterization of the work, not just a redistribution of tasks.

For paid home-care workers and personal care attendants, the expectation of relationality in their labor is profoundly conflicted. On the one hand, their work is often defined as a series of manual tasks—bathing, lifting, toileting, feeding—a description that leaves many home-care workers feeling constrained regarding the relational aspects of their work.[38] Importantly, even when the agency or home-care workers themselves recognize relational aspects of the work, these are specifically excluded from coverage by federal programs as well as by most insurance carriers. So, while workers from one home-care agency record their activities on a chart that includes a section labeled "companionship," Medicaid specifically states that "companionship" services are not covered.[39] Any social responsibility for care is to be limited and certainly not to include care that has been defined as primarily social and relational rather than medical. The labor that is recognized is reduced to a series of manual tasks.

Yet home-care aides and personal care attendants have been legally identified as providing "companionship" services and therefore excluded from basic labor protections under the Fair Labor Standards Act (FLSA) and other legal frameworks. Even when private household workers were finally brought under the auspices of the FLSA in 1974, home-care workers were excluded, categorized as more similar to casual babysitters than to domestic workers.[40] The exclusion of home-care workers from basic labor protections like minimum wage, maximum hours, and overtime compensation was upheld by the Supreme Court as recently as 2007.[41] The exclusion is based upon a definition of companionship services as services that provide "fellowship, care, and protection" for those who cannot care for themselves.[42] Companionship services under this definition can include such tasks as meal preparation, laundry, and housecleaning as well as intimate tasks like bathing, if the primary purpose of the job is considered to be custodial rather than medical. Custodial care has therefore been defined as falling even lower in the hierarchy of care than unskilled menial care, and viewed both socially and legally as something other than real work.

Caring and Competence: Teachers and Child-Care Workers

In the years following World War II, children in the United States were the "healthiest, best-fed, best-clothed, and best-housed generation the nation had seen."[43] While poor families and children were left out of the postwar prosperity, large numbers of children enjoyed unprecedented material privilege. In the second half of the twentieth century, formal schooling became the norm for children ages six and older across the country. Increasing demands for social and emotional nurturance and a simultaneous movement toward rigid control and standardization of curricula combined to put contradictory pressures on teachers. These contradictions emerged in a different way in the field of care for the youngest children, where competing visions of appropriate models of care created a range of child-care and early education occupations. Although some of the historical causes may have been different, like nurses and other health-care workers, teachers experienced a loss of professional autonomy and increased bureaucratization during this time period, and teachers and child-care workers also find themselves struggling with conflicting structural constraints and cultural messages about the role of relationality in their work.

TEACHING IN A CHILD-CENTERED AGE

The second half of the twentieth century was a time of dramatic growth for schools in the United States. The postwar baby boom strained the capacity of the public school system in the 1950s and, despite the expanding number of teachers, demand outstripped supply.[44] After the 1957 launch of *Sputnik* by the Soviet Union, the educational system was widely blamed for the humiliating loss in the space race, and education received an infusion of federal funding.[45] As the demand for workers with formal education continued to increase, rates of school attendance became more comparable across regions, and school became the norm nationwide for a growing number of children.[46] Between 1950 and 2007, the number of primary and secondary school teachers in the United States grew fivefold, more than twice the rate of overall labor-force growth (see figure 4.7).[47]

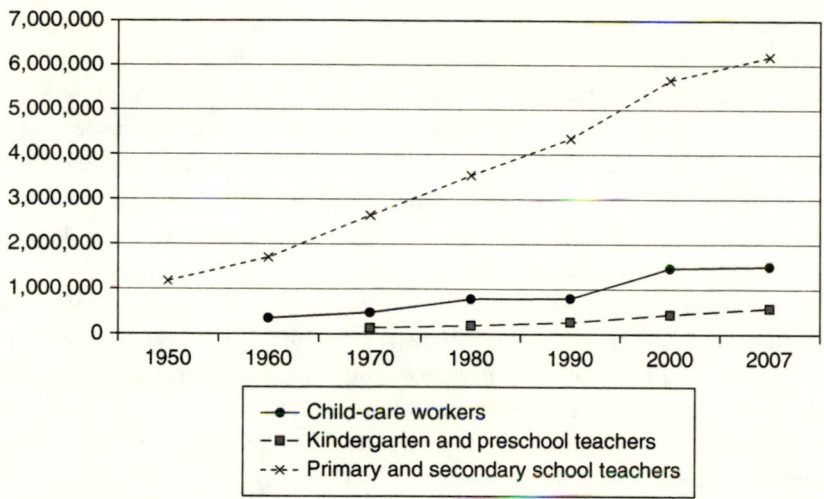

Figure 4.7. Number of teachers and child-care workers, 1950–2007 *Source: Calculated by author using data from the U.S. Census (1950–2000) and the American Community Survey (2007) available through the Integrated Public Use Microdata Series (IPUMS).*

In 1946 Dr. Benjamin Spock published *The Common Sense Book of Baby and Child Care*, which became emblematic of the child-rearing ethos of the time. The book remained popular for many decades, and by 1979 it had sold more than 28 million copies, making it the second best-selling book of the century after the Bible.[48] The child-centered approach advocated by Spock and adopted at least in part by many parents demanded a lot of time and energy of parents, especially of mothers. Parents in the postwar period "chose large families and then placed the welfare of the children at the center of family life."[49] For middle-class families, the care of the sacred child had become a central driving force. Before 1945, Urie Bronfenbrenner has suggested, middle-class mothers were more severe than working-class mothers in their demands of their children; with the rise of the child-centered family, working-class mothers were generally more strict than the "permissive" parents of the middle class.[50] The new child-centered environment increased demands on teachers of middle-class children to focus on the individual child's needs across a range of emotional, social, and behavioral dimensions in addition to their academic charge.

For teachers in poor and working-class neighborhoods, social and behavioral intervention had been part of the job for several decades. Midcentury educators had inherited the legacy of a social welfare mission associated with schools as early as the 1920s, when the predominant view linked poverty to individual deficiencies, a notion compatible with the emerging emphasis of social workers.[51] School was seen as the ideal place to intervene in these perceived deficiencies before they became entrenched into patterns of dependency. By midcentury, teachers were increasingly expected to nurture and protect vulnerable children from cultural or family influences perceived as negative. In a child-centered age, teachers of children of whatever class background were expected to deal with substantial social and behavioral dimensions of socializing children.

The rising expectation of social and behavioral work by teachers was not accompanied by decreasing expectations of academic rigor. Quite the contrary. In the wake of the national humiliation at losing the space race, the educational system was placed under ever greater scrutiny. The approach to fixing the educational system was not to increase the skills of teachers, but to standardize curriculum content so that the teacher became merely an intermediary in education, not a central figure. In the 1950s, university-based researchers developed "teacher-proof" curricula by which students were certain to reach the objectives, even with a minimally competent teacher.[52] Standardized testing emerged as a way to judge the performance not only of students, but also of teachers. Reform during this period was top-down, imposing ever-greater control on teachers. Like nurses, teachers had never achieved a high level of professional autonomy, but this era marked the beginning for public school teachers of further control via a system of standardized inputs and quantifiable outputs.

Teaching largely continued to be constructed as women's work, although between 1950 and 1970 the proportion of teachers who were women declined from 75 percent to 70 percent. The increasing presence of men among the teaching workforce is largely attributable to the rising importance of secondary schools, which remained much less female dominated. In 1960 and 1970, men constituted more than 50 percent of secondary school teachers and only 15 percent of primary school teachers. Nonetheless, in 1970, over half the female college graduates who were in the labor force were employed as elementary and secondary school teachers.[53]

Patterns of racial-ethnic segregation among teachers also changed little during the middle decades of the century. In 1970, over 85 percent of primary and secondary school teachers were White and U.S. born (see figure 4.8). There had been some increase in the number of Black primary school teachers since earlier in the century, as the civil rights movement had increased pressure on school districts to hire Black teachers and on colleges to admit more Black students.[54] However, by 1970 Black U.S.-born teachers were still only 9 percent of primary school teachers, and only 7 percent of secondary school teachers (lower proportions than in the labor force as a whole).

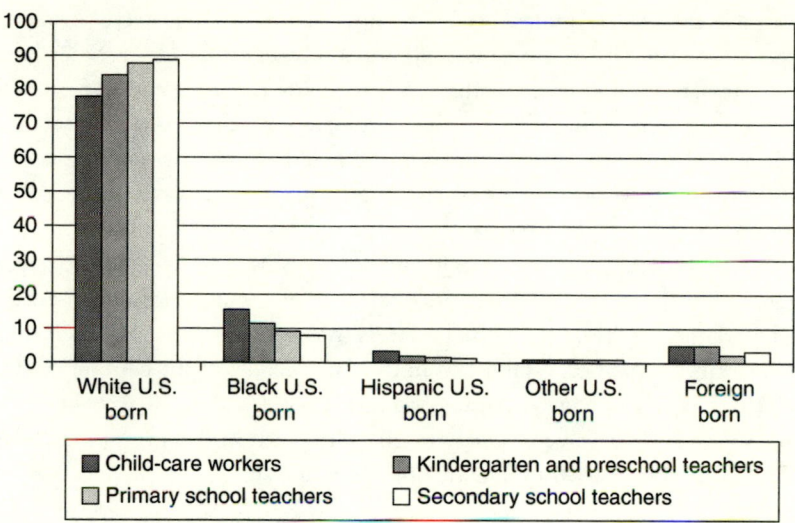

Figure 4.8. Selected education and child-care workers by race-ethnicity and birth-place, 1970 (in percentages) *Source: Calculated by author using U.S. Census data (1970) available through the Integrated Public Use Microdata Series (IPUMS).*

While the gender and racial-ethnic makeup of the teaching workforce remained relatively stable in the middle of the twentieth century, other demographic areas saw considerable change. By the 1950s, the legal and cultural prohibitions against married women teachers that had been so entrenched in the early century were being eroded, and more teachers were married and looking to teaching as a career rather than a short-term activity. In 1900 only 4 percent of female teachers were married; by 1940, the proportion had reached 26 percent. The next twenty years saw a substantial rise in the number of married female teachers, and by 1960 fully 60 percent of primary and secondary school teachers were married. As more women began to work after marriage, the teaching workforce aged. The average age of female teachers in 1900 was twenty-eight; by 1940, it was thirty-six; and in 1960, it had climbed to forty-three.[55]

Some scholars have argued that the shifting demographic makeup of the teaching workforce is one of the factors that led to increased labor activism among teachers in the 1960s and 1970s, contending that older teachers were more motivated to fight for long-term gains for the occupation. The prominence of teacher organizing during this period also reflected the relative success of labor unions in other industries, as well as the general social tenor of the time.[56] In addition, the teacher shortage created by the baby boom and the opening of more occupational alternatives to women gave teachers increased leverage.[57]

Like the ANA, professional associations for teachers were stridently opposed to union organizing, and, like nurses, teachers faced substantial cultural pressure against union affiliation. Especially controversial were strikes, which were seen as in conflict with the image of teachers as public servants dedicated to their students.[58] Although the external trappings of professionalism were in place for teachers by the 1950s, teachers had not succeeded in attaining either the degree of authority or the economic and social rewards gained by professions like law and medicine. Most teachers had four-year degrees, and licensing requirements were in place, but wages remained low and working conditions difficult. Teachers in the 1940s and 1950s built upon the organizing tradition established in the first decades of the century, and by the 1960s teachers had established powerful national unions that began to push wages up.[59] A wave of teacher strikes followed in the 1960s and 1970s, most focused on salary issues, many of them successful.[60]

RISING STAKES, LESSENING CONTROL

The 1980s saw an intensification of the movement for educational reform through standardizing curriculum content and measuring quality through testing. Ronald Reagan's ascension to office meant deep budget cuts for education as well as for health care, but federal attention to and control over schools heightened. The 1983 report *A Nation at Risk* was an urgent call to action to raise standards in education, and set the precedent of federal demands without concomitant increases in funding.[61] The 2002 passage of the No Child Left Behind Act (NCLB) mandated standardized testing as the benchmark for judging individual students, as well as teacher and school performance, raising the stakes again for teachers. Under the pressure of NCLB, teachers found their work more controlled than ever by external forces, as the content of the tests defined the substance of their courses and anxious administrators sought ever-increasing top-down control of classrooms.

The movement toward standardization and high-stakes testing simultaneously increased the routinization of teachers' work and narrowed the definition of their role in the education and care of children and youth. In the early part of the twentieth century, teacher-training programs emphasized "both broad social education and technical proficiency," educating teachers to meet the range of social, behavioral, and academic demands they would face in schools.[62] Many contemporary teacher-training programs also emphasize the social and behavioral dimensions of child development, as well as the content of academic subjects, and Nel Noddings has argued that such programs should approach caring and competence as intimately connected aspects of good teaching. According to Noddings, relational skills are essential not only to the social and behavioral aspects of teaching, but also to the effective delivery of academic content.[63] However, the NCLB defines highly qualified teachers largely in terms of content knowledge, determined by their responses to a standardized subject test, a narrow definition of competence that contradicts the model of most schools of education. One teacher noted upon leaving a teacher-training program that the "push for us to treat each child as an individual and to create safe, diverse learning experiences seems to be at direct odds with mass, mandatory, silent, nationwide testing."[64]

Like this graduate, along with nurses and other health-care workers, many teachers experience a contradiction between what they are trained to do (and often what they most value about their work) and the way their jobs are currently structured. Recent issues of *Education Digest* include articles titled "Teaching to Survive NCLB," "Preparing Teachers to Beat the Agonies of No Child Left Behind," and "Nurturing Teachers in the Famine of NCLB."[65] In some ways paralleling health care, teaching in the late twentieth century came to be characterized by a squeezing out of relationality and an increase in bureaucratic control.

Also paralleling the shifting gender composition of health care, teaching has become more female dominated since 1970. Between 1970 and 2007, the proportion of teachers who are female rose from 70 to 76 percent.[66] The pattern underlying this increase parallels that in health care, with the occupations that have been female dominated shifting only slightly, and those that have been male dominated shifting more substantially. In 2007, 80 percent of primary school teachers were women, compared to 84 percent in 1970; by contrast, the proportion of female secondary school teachers rose from 49 to 59 percent. Again, the female-dominated occupations show remarkable resistance to gender integration, while male-dominated occupations within the overall field of care have become gender integrated simultaneous with an undermining of professional autonomy. At the same time, the feminized discourse of caring remains an important part of the rhetoric of teaching in both teacher training and in teachers' descriptions of their work.

The proportion of primary school teachers who were Black and U.S. born actually decreased between 1970 and 2007, from 9 to under 8 percent (see figure 4.9). While in 1970, fewer Black teachers taught at the secondary school level, by 2007, the proportion of secondary school teachers who were Black U.S. born was about equal to that among primary school teachers. Between 1970 and 2007, the number of foreign-born primary and secondary school teachers also increased somewhat, though still at rates lower than the representation of immigrant workers in the overall labor force. Although there has been some diversification of the teaching workforce, educating and

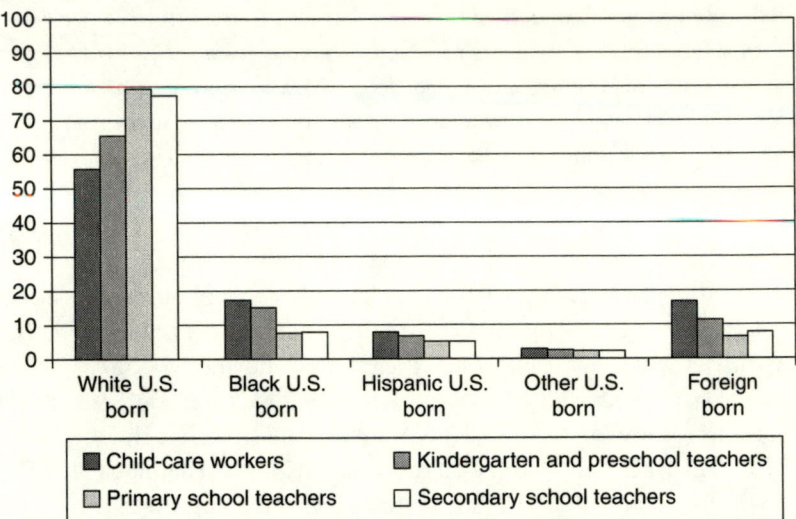

Figure 4.9. Selected education and child-care workers by race-ethnicity and birth-place, 2007 (in percentages) *Source: Calculated by author using American Community Survey data (2007) available through the Integrated Public Use Microdata Series (IPUMS).*

socializing school-age children thus remains disproportionately the work of White U.S.-born women.

Rates of unionization remain relatively high among teachers compared to many other occupations, although unions on the whole experienced a decline in the last decades of the twentieth century. In 2007, almost 50 percent of elementary school teachers and 54 percent of secondary school teachers were members of a union, rates that reach considerably higher levels among public school teachers.[67] Nonetheless, these rates represent a decline from earlier decades, and surveys show that younger teachers are less likely to regard the union positively.[68] While unions have been an important force in winning job security, benefits, and wage increases for teachers, they have been less effective in addressing working conditions and professional autonomy.[69]

MOTHERS AND OTHERS CARING FOR THE VERY YOUNG

If belief in the importance of schooling for children over age six has become a dominant norm in the second half of the twentieth century, ideas about the care of very young children have perhaps never varied more. The idealization of the mother-child bond during the earliest years of childhood that emerged in the nineteenth century continued to wield profound influence in the twentieth. The development of a range of paid child-care options must be understood against a backdrop of a strong cultural attachment to exclusive maternal care and in the context of a number of parallel historical trends.

Midcentury kindergarten advocates continued to argue that young children needed an environment qualitatively different from school that would nurture their growth and joyful development before they entered the more rigid world of primary schooling.[70] For poor children, child care was also seen as a way to remediate perceived deficits in poor families.[71] Further, the second half of the twentieth century has witnessed an explosion of research showing the critical importance to adult learning and functioning of the development of the brain during the first six years of life, creating a new sense of urgency to provide stimulating environments in early childhood.[72] Meanwhile, as increasing numbers of women entered the paid labor force, some advocates began to support the need for day-care options to allow more mothers to work outside the home. Finally, pressures on school performance put the burden of school readiness on preschool and kindergarten programs.

The confluence of these forces has created not only a wide range of paid settings in which the care of young children happens but also a wide range of beliefs about the goals of that care. Workers who take care of children may be employed in a child-care center, for a school, as a nanny in a private home, or as a family day-care provider. Even providers who work in similar structural settings may have very different philosophical approaches. Lynet Uttal has suggested that child-care providers be assigned different titles—such as "edu-carer," "co-childrearer," or "preschool teacher"—to give parents information about their underlying approach to care.[73] These labels highlight some of the dimensions along which child-care providers and parents can vary in their beliefs about what the care of young children means and who should provide which elements of that care. For example, some providers and parents may see education as at least part of the goal for the time a child spends with a provider. Others may follow in the path of early kindergarten advocates, emphasizing the ways in which these settings are distinct from schools for older children. Many parents see the primary qualifications for paid child-care workers as their ability to provide warmth and nurturance rather than as their having specific training. Others want their children to learn particular skills during their time in paid child care. In some child-care settings, the parents clearly play the role of expert; in others, paid workers lay claim to certain areas of expertise and may give guidance or advice to parents.

Given the range of ways in which child care is organized as well as conceptualized, it is striking how monolithically female the child-care labor force is. Since the U.S. Census started separately identifying the categories "child-care workers" and "kindergarten and preschool teachers," both occupations

have been consistently over 90 percent female. The strength of the association of the care of very young children with mothering appears to override any
other philosophical or structural variation in child-care arrangements. The
proportion of women in child-care occupations is far higher than that among
teachers of school-age children, and more closely matches the female domination of private household service and nursing.

The racial-ethnic makeup of the child-care workforce is also very different from patterns among teachers of children over six, and the segments of
child care are somewhat distinct from each other as well. Of the almost
500,000 people reported as child-care workers in 1970, 15 percent were Black
U.S. born, an overrepresentation compared to the proportion of Black U.S.-
born workers in the overall labor force (see figure 4.8). By 2007, despite relatively steady labor-force representation, the proportion of Black U.S.-born
child-care workers had risen to 17 percent (see figure 4.9). In addition, despite
making up less than 3 percent of child-care workers in 1970, Hispanic U.S.-
born child-care workers were 8 percent of the total by 2007 (compared to 6
percent of the labor force). Increasing concentrations of foreign-born workers
among child-care workers reflected larger labor-market trends during this
period, and almost 17 percent were foreign born in 2007 (compared to 16 percent of the labor force). As a result of these converging demographic shifts, in
2007, White U.S.-born workers made up about 65 percent of the labor force,
but only 56 percent of child-care workers.

Among those identified as teachers of kindergarten and preschool, the
racial-ethnic composition lies between the dominance of White U.S.-born
women among primary and secondary school teachers and their underrepresentation among child-care workers. In 2007 these teachers of the youngest
children were 66 percent White U.S. born, 14 percent Black U.S. born, 7 percent Hispanic U.S. born, and 11 percent foreign born (see figure 4.9). While
the proportion of foreign-born kindergarten and preschool teachers was
higher than that among primary and secondary school teachers, it was still
lower than the labor force proportion of 16 percent. By contrast, among private household child-care workers, only 6 percent in 2007 were Black U.S.
born, but fully 27 percent were foreign born.[74] So, while White U.S.-born
women still make up the majority of workers who care for very young children,
there are significant concentrations of Black women (particularly among family day-care providers and child-care center workers), and of foreign-born
women (particularly among private household nannies).

In her study of family day-care providers, Mary Tuominen observes the
frustration these child-care workers experience because of the lack of respect
and societal value afforded their work. One provider she interviewed spoke of

the problems with family day care as an occupation: "Well, low pay. That's probably the main thing. And then also there's somewhat of a—not a stigma; that isn't the word. Some people don't consider it work when you're at home working with day care. I mean, they sort of do. But not really."[75] As is the case for domestic workers, the labor of family day-care providers becomes invisible both due to its association with a supposed natural feminine role and because of its location in the home.

The title of Tuominen's book—*We Are Not Babysitters*—reflects the insistence of many family day-care providers she interviewed that their work is labor and also that it is valuable. Interestingly, the most common way they articulated this value was by claiming that the work was more than custodial care. Babysitters are the archetype of custodial care, both culturally and legally. Most recently, home-care workers' legal status was defined as outside the bounds of labor protection laws because of their similarity to "casual babysitters." The family day-care providers Tuominen spoke with resisted being perceived as "just babysitters," articulating the view that child care was more than a series of tasks and responsibilities—that the whole of caring for a child is more than the sum of its parts.[76] Explaining what quality care for young children *is* seems to be more difficult than articulating what it is *not*.

Providers are not the only ones who struggle with defining care for young children. In her study of parents making child-care choices, Uttal found that "although parents articulated their interest in educational opportunities, it was not entirely clear if they were actually expressing their preferences or if they were limited by lack of language to describe what they really believed constituted quality care."[77] While neither the providers in Tuominen's study nor the parents in Uttal's study were always able to express exactly what they valued in child care, there was strong agreement in both groups that the relationship between the provider and the child is key. Providers talked about their relationships with children as one of the main rewards of their jobs, and of nurturing those relationships as part of the work, inseparable from the tasks of daily care. And the parents Uttal interviewed wanted care providers to be nurturing or—her word—"maternal."[78]

The link between the emphasis on maternal nurturance and the overwhelming dominance of women in these occupations is perhaps obvious. The more complex problem is understanding how the patterns of racial-ethnic representation among child-care workers reflect cultural norms about maternal care. Researchers have found that parents want to find in a child-care provider a "mother substitute," and so cultural stereotypes may influence their choices. For example, Uttal found that some mothers expressed a preference for women who had emigrated from a Latin American country, perceiving them as more naturally maternal and good with children.[79] Other mothers chose child-care providers who were similar to themselves culturally in an effort to find someone likely to share their philosophical approach to child rearing.[80] Race-ethnicity can therefore signal different meanings in the quest to find a maternal substitute.[81]

While many parents want to find warm and nurturing care for their children, there is also cultural pressure on mothers to live up to the ideal that intensive mothering is necessary for infants and very young children. Julia Wrigley found that certain groups of mothers used the social distance created by racial-ethnic or class dissimilarity to reinforce the ideological boundary between spiritual parenting (reserved for the mother) and menial child care (delegated to the employee).[82] By delegating only the routine tasks and physical maintenance of child care to paid workers, these mothers seek to maintain their identity as the primary nurturers.[83] And, in a dynamic similar to the relationship between employing women and their domestic servants, the dirty work of child care is relegated to racial-ethnic women and poor women, preserving the ideal of intensive motherhood for upper- and middle-class women.

In the feminized world of child-care, not only are the majority of the paid workers women, but also women—mothers—are often the primary link to the employing family. Given the primacy of maternal ideology, both mothers and child-care workers are often constantly negotiating the boundaries of their relationships with the children in question. On the one hand, relationality is conceptualized as one of the primary jobs of a child-care worker and one of the most important qualifications for the role. Child-care workers have to demonstrate that they can be nurturing and warm and are able to connect with the children in their care. On the other hand, mothers and child-care workers police the boundaries of the relationship between child-care workers and children to be sure it does not infringe upon maternal territory. Cameron Macdonald has described the emotional labor that nannies must engage in to maintain this careful balance, showing affection to children enough to prove themselves as nurturers, but at the same time minimizing or denying their connections when mothers feel they are being displaced. Margaret Nelson has called this practice among family day-care providers "detached attachment."[84]

In the second half of the twentieth century, the overall rise in child-centered values among middle-class families has manifested in a new ideological construction of parenting that Annette Lareau has called "concerted cultivation." Lareau's concept is similar in some ways to the "child gardening" concept espoused by early kindergarten advocates, except the middle-class parents Lareau interviews sees the parent-gardener as engaging in a large number of focused cultivation activities to nurture the growth of the child. Parents at

home engage with their children in reading or other types of play or enrichment activities; they sign their children up for music or drama or sports activities and then they stay engaged with those activities as spectators, supporters,
and mediators; and they interface with schools regularly, communicating with
teachers and administrators about their children's progress and problems.[85]
This commitment to concerted cultivation appears to extend to younger children of the middle class, who are enrolled in Mommy and Me enrichment
classes and provided with Baby Einstein videos and toys.

For the paid workers caring for these middle-class children, concerted cultivation may mean demands that they provide even greater active nurturance
and enrichment. That is, concerted cultivation calls for fundamentally relational skills. At the same time, the level of investment and involvement
demanded of parents by a concerted cultivation model also raises the stakes for
mothers. Intensive mothering has grown into helicopter parenting—mothers
must be not only physically present for children but also emotionally and
intellectually involved in every aspect of their lives. For child-care workers,
this may mean more direct involvement from mothers as well as a more vigor-
ous defense of the maternal role as primary gardener. The rise of concerted
cultivation has therefore exacerbated the tensions in paid child-care work,
requiring higher levels of emotional labor from workers to create the balance
of detached attachment.

While most child-care workers are not employed in large bureaucratic
institutions like the health-care system and the public education system, the
end of the twentieth century saw increasing pressures on all these workers to
manage relationality. In health care and public education, externally imposed
systems of control have limited the opportunities for the practice of relationality despite its increased rhetorical value. For child-care workers, the necessity to manage the relational aspects of their jobs is imposed not by an
institution, but by the structural conditions of their jobs as well as the cultural
prescriptions of intensive motherhood. Like the nursing home workers who
were expected to treat the residents like their own mothers—and yet were not
supposed to grieve them when they died—child-care workers must navigate
the boundaries of care as part of their labor. And although most child-care
providers are not subject to the rigid guidelines of medical charts or standardized tests, in some ways the boundaries of their work are even more intensely
guarded.

Although these tensions around relationality exist for all child-care workers, the dynamics of paid care for poor children differ in important ways from
care for children of families steeped in concerted cultivation. At least since
the initiation of Head Start, care for very young children has been perceived

as a vehicle to compensate for deficits in poor families. The ideological assumptions embedded in our culture about middle-class mothers and poor mothers are quite distinct.[86] Policies that target poor mothers have often at least implicitly assumed that paid care in these cases was *better* than maternal care, and welfare reform efforts' emphasis on mothers working has increased the socially perceived desirability of poor children being cared for by someone other than the mother. An editorial cartoon in the 1990s that depicted a circle of women holding children in their laps was captioned: "Welfare reform: Hand your baby and $6 an hour to the woman on your left." Enabling poor women to work in the paid labor force required only the most basic form of custodial care, which was devalued in this formulation at the same time as it was held up as a solution.

In fact, low pay and lack of societal value for their labor are perhaps the only common factors among all these groups of child-care workers. These workers have to date not achieved even the semiprofessional status of elementary and secondary school teachers, and as a group remain among the lowest paid workers in the labor force. Organized efforts to professionalize child-care work have been hampered by both structural barriers and cultural resistance. The lack of an overarching institutional structure for child care has made creating consensus on raising entry requirements and other exclusionary paths to professionalization challenging. And, as in the early stages of the professionalization of nursing, some resistance comes from the sense that child care should be a vocation rather than a career, chosen out of a more spiritual and lofty motivation than professional gain.

In addition, for child-care workers, the most obvious route to professional status is to claim their status as educators, an occupation already recognized as having some authority. However, some providers and parents resist "the professionalization of child-care work if it mean[s] simply dropping the existing educational system for older children down into the arena of early care."[87] So while some child-care workers embrace the label "early childhood educator," some actively resist this definition of their work, following the historical tradition of defining the care of the very young as distinctly different from school. As one advocate for child-care workers explains: "When we start dropping off the word 'care' we're just saying that's a whole part of it that isn't really valuable. And that that's not part of the paycheck; it isn't about the caring part. The paycheck is about the educating part."[88] So far, efforts to professionalize child care as an occupation have been largely ineffective, although there are some examples of local victories.

Unionizing child-care workers has also been challenging. Like private household workers and other nurturant care workers, child-care workers are vulnerable to work expansion because of the relational context of their labor. Tuominen found that even family day-care providers with contracts often provided additional unpaid or lower-paid care and worked extra hours or failed to observe other contractual conditions.[89] The sense of relational obligation not only makes workers more vulnerable to exploitation, but also may lead them to resist unionization and other forms of worker organizing. While such resistance was an obstacle for organizers of nurses and teachers as well, these occupations each had an alternate way of defining their labor—as medical/technical skill and as content expertise. In addition, child-care providers work in dispersed locations and most do not share a common employer or common work setting, creating logistical barriers to traditional organizing. While there have been some successful efforts to organize child-care workers, these efforts are localized and have not had much impact on the occupation as a whole to date.

The Rise and Fall of Relationality: The Evolution of the Helping Professions

The expansion of mental health services that began after World War II continued into the second half of the century. The decades between 1960 and 1990 saw unprecedented expansion in psychology, social work, and related therapeutic helping occupations, although social workers and psychologists remained relatively fewer than health-care workers or teachers (see figure 4.10).[90] By 1990, there were more than 650,000 social workers and almost 200,000 psychologists.[91] However, the budget cuts and cost cutting that transformed health care beginning in the 1980s also affected mental health and social services; after 1990 their expansion slowed, in some occupations reaching the point of reversal. The last decades of the twentieth century also saw a reversal in the gender balance of psychotherapy as a whole, as social work became even more feminized, and psychology transformed from a male-dominated occupation to a solidly female-dominated one.

While psychiatrists had played a leading role in the post–World War II growth of psychotherapy (broadly defined), the changing environment had important impacts on other occupations in the field of mental health and social services. To differentiate themselves from psychiatrists, social workers now began to emphasize the importance of warmth and relational skills.[92] The definition of preventative mental health services and of the role of mental health professionals expanded to take in a much broader population than the seriously mentally ill. The paradigm of psychology was shifting, but in 1960, as psychologists began to gain recognition as a result of the increasing stature of psychiatry, psychology was 70 percent male (see figure 4.11).

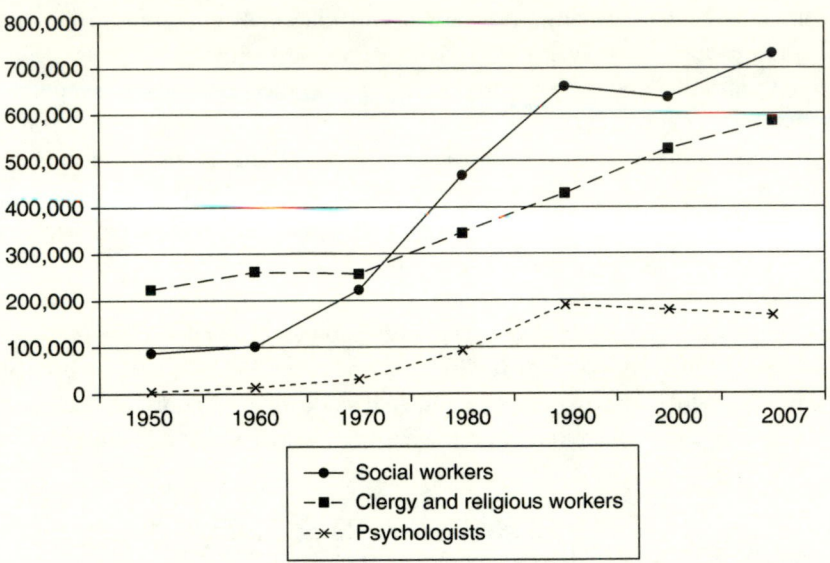

Figure 4.10. Number of workers in mental health and social service occupations, 1950–2007 *Source: Calculated by author using data from the U.S. Census (1950–2000) and the American Community Survey (2007) available through the Integrated Public Use Microdata Series (IPUMS).*

In the next two decades, psychotherapy in the United States moved away from a traditional psychoanalytic model toward what Ilene Philipson has called a "relational" model.[93] Traditional Freudian psychoanalysis had emphasized detached objectivity and interpretation, and psychology in the middle of the century was an occupation based in academic institutions and dominated by men. Talk therapy emphasizes empathy in the context of an interpersonal relationship between therapist and client. This flexible relational approach was more compatible with the expanded vision of mental health during this period, and more amenable to serving larger numbers of people with everyday problems in contrast to a focus on those with severe mental illness. The shift toward a more relational model in psychology coincided with an increase in the number of women entering the field. By 1980, over 45 percent of psychologists were women. Philipson has argued that the cultural reconstruction of psychotherapy as "professional motherhood" was intimately linked to this change.

Philipson also points to structural changes in the occupation as important factors in the process of feminization. As demand for psychologists continued to grow, professional schools of psychology began to emerge outside traditional

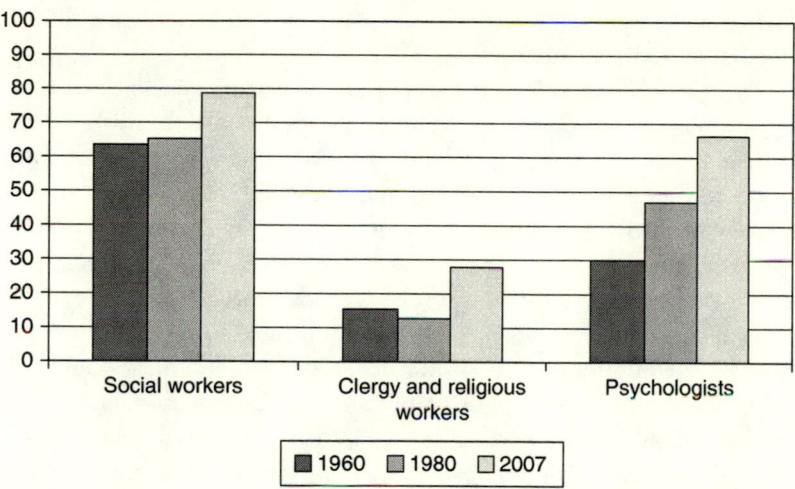

Figure 4.11. Women in selected mental health and social service occupations, 1960–2007 (in percentages) *Source: Calculated by author using data from the U.S. Census (1960 and 1980) and the American Community Survey (2007) available through the Integrated Public Use Microdata Series (IPUMS).*

academic structures. While the more flexible and aggressive recruiting and admissions procedures at these professional training schools may have increased access for women, this shift also contributed to what Philipson calls the "degrading" of the occupation. Perceived as less exclusive than university programs, professional training programs downgraded the status of psychology. (This process was the reverse of what happened in nursing, which increased in status when university-based degree programs replaced independent training programs in hospitals.) As mental health services expanded to accommodate everyone, mental health occupations admitted a broader population as well.

The budget cuts in mental health services and rise of managed care in the 1980s presented further constraints and challenges for mental health workers. Despite continued increases in demand, the number of psychologists and social workers had flattened out by 1990 (see figure 4.10). Managed care also tightened external controls on the labor of mental health workers. Regulations that limited outpatient visits with psychotherapists and restricted inpatient treatment to crisis management undermined the professional authority of mental health workers, who were no longer free to determine the appropriate course of treatment for their patients. In addition to the loss of autonomy, managed care changed the nature of the labor of mental health workers. Like nurses, these workers found themselves increasingly restricted to doing similar short-term interventions over and over again, rather than using the full spectrum of their tools and abilities.

By 2007, more than 65 percent of psychologists and almost 80 percent of social workers were women (see figure 4.11). Philipson links this intensified feminization of psychotherapy during the last decades of the twentieth century to the "deskilling, declassing, and degrading" of the occupation in a complex intertwining of structural transformation, cultural redefinition, and demographic redistribution. The result was the relegation of psychology to the status of many other nurturant care jobs as a women's occupation.

Like child care, the work of therapists is defined by a reliance on interpersonal and nurturing skills. However, as for doctors, nurses, and other health-care workers, the imposition of more restrictive external controls on psychologists and social workers has reduced the time and opportunity for relationship building. For example, by imposing limits on the number of times a therapist may see a client, insurance companies and government agencies cut short opportunities for sustained relational connections. Relationality remains the central defining characteristic of therapeutic work, yet that relationship is devalued and constrained by bureaucratic controls.

At the same time, the field has seen the introduction of a wide range of new drug treatments for mental illness, including many for common ailments like depression and anxiety.[94] The growing emphasis on biological explanations and chemical treatment is not only a consequence of new drug research and availability, but also compatible with a cost-cutting philosophy, as drug treatment is often cheaper than extensive relational therapy. Importantly, drug treatment is the province of psychiatrists rather than of psychologists or social workers. The increasing prominence of biological approaches further marginalizes the relational work of these therapists.[95]

While some similar forces have affected the fields of social work and psychology in the second half of the twentieth century, these two occupations have developed along distinctive paths, most strikingly in their racial-ethnic composition. As social work was professionalized in the early part of the century, it evolved from a charity workforce that included many foreign-born workers to an occupation dominated by White U.S.-born women. By 1950, almost 85 percent of social and welfare workers were White and U.S. born (see figure 4.12). The second half of the century saw another shift, as social work became a much more racially-ethnically diverse occupation. By 1970, over 16 percent of social workers were Black U.S. born, and by 2007 that proportion had reached almost 20 percent (see figures 4.12 and 4.13). This increase occurred as the overall proportion of Black U.S.-born workers in the labor force remained relatively steady, reflecting a shift in the proportion of Black

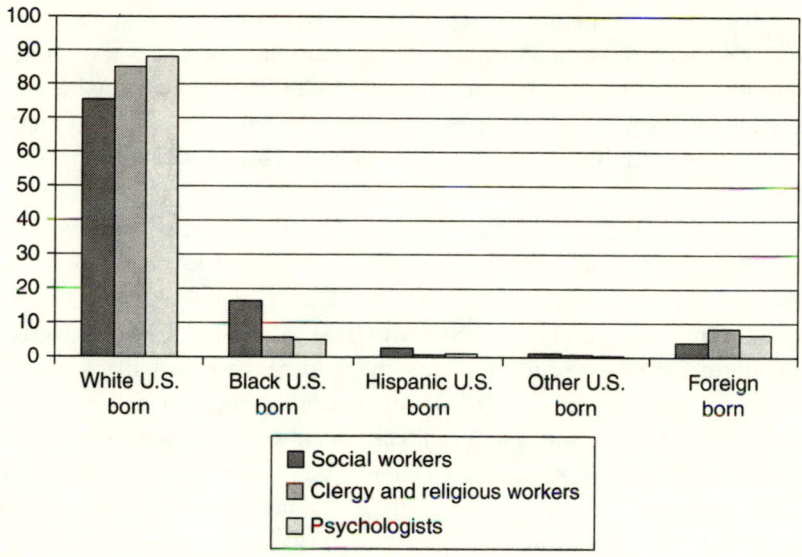

Figure 4.12. Selected mental health and social service workers by race-ethnicity and birthplace, 1970 (in percentages) *Source: Calculated by author using U.S. Census data (1970) available through the Integrated Public Use Microdata Series (IPUMS).*

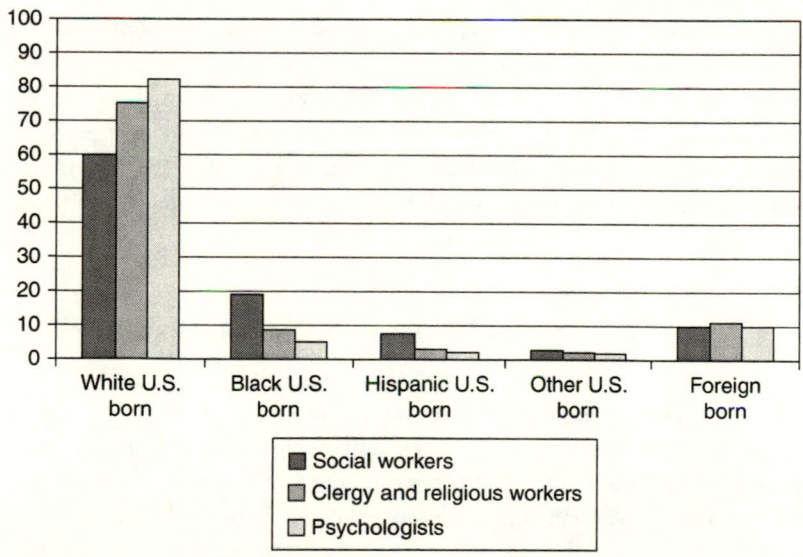

Figure 4.13. Selected mental health and social service workers by race-ethnicity and birthplace, 2007 (in percentages) *Source: Calculated by author using American Community Survey data (2007) available through the Integrated Public Use Microdata Series (IPUMS).*

U.S.-born women entering social work rather than their influx into the labor force. Overall changes in labor-force composition at the end of the century, however, also affected social work. By 2007, over 7 percent of social workers were Hispanic and over 10 percent were foreign born. The combined impact of these shifts was that by 2007, only 60 percent of social workers were White U.S. born.

The increasing concentration of Black women in social work has been accompanied by analyses of the role of early Black social work "pioneers," recognizing as important contributors to the field the same activists who were excluded from the organizations from which professional social work emerged. Importantly, in retrospective accounts, the work of these early Black activists is differentiated from the work of White charity organizations in a number of ways. Iris Carlton-LeNay describes Black social work pioneers as bringing a "race lens" to their work that was lacking among many White social workers, and as approaching the work holistically; she argues that these early activists used an Afrocentric paradigm that "emphasizes a collective conceptualization of human beings and their group survival." Carlton-LeNay goes on to demonstrate how these elements of practice should be maintained in contemporary settings when working with Black families and communities, a framing that echoes the association of child care with particular racial-ethnic groups in part because of cultural fit.[96]

In contrast to the demographics of social work, although psychology underwent a reversal in sex composition toward the end of the twentieth century, it remained the province of White U.S.-born workers. In 2007, just over 82 percent of psychologists were White U.S. born, down slightly from 88 percent in 1970 (see figures 4.12 and 4.13). Black, Hispanic, and foreign-born workers have all been consistently underrepresented in the field, despite some slight increases during these decades.

Value, Virtue, and Vulnerability: Nurturant Care Workers in the Twenty-first Century

The emergence of expert care and more recent economic and cultural processes have shaped contemporary gender and racial hierarchies in the nurturant care labor force. To say that paid nurturant care is overwhelmingly performed by women will come as no surprise to anyone. However, an examination of the intertwining histories of the range of nurturant care occupations reveals that this feminization is not a straightforward phenomenon, but rather the result of a complex set of social, economic, and cultural forces. Each occupational trajectory is unique, yet strong thematic similarities emerge that tell a story about the development of paid nurturant care work as a whole during the twentieth century. Importantly, while the association of paid nurturant care with the feminine has deep historical roots, the domination of these jobs by women is not simply a relic of the past. Rather, the end of the twentieth century has been a time of steadily increasing feminization of paid nurturant care overall, as new forces exacerbate feminization and once again shift both the cultural construction and the structural conditions of paid nurturant care.

We have seen how in the 1800s teaching came to be women's work in part because of a conscious attempt by activists to rhetorically align the goals of teaching with supposed feminine virtues to open up respectable jobs for women. This cultural reconstruction of the work of teaching, however, coincided with a desire by school reformers to expand education—and to pay lower wages to female teachers to achieve that goal sooner.[97] Over one hundred years later, the feminization of psychology also involved an ideological redefinition of care work. As the field of mental health expanded, relationality became central to the very work of healing and therapeutic support. The shift to a relational model was linked to the feminization of psychotherapy, as the nurturant skills required by the new approach were associated with femininity. Philipson, as we have seen, has argued that the feminization of psychotherapy was also a consequence of the "deskilling, declassing, and degrading" of the occupation.[98] Again, a cultural reconstruction of care combined with changing structural conditions are linked to an overall trend toward feminization.

These two examples, a century apart, demonstrate the intersections of cultural and economic forces in the shift from male-dominated to female-dominated occupations. According to queuing theory, male-dominated occupations transition through an integrated phase to female-dominated jobs when they simultaneously become less attractive to men 'and more desirable and accessible to women.[99] In the second half of the twentieth century, several expert care occupations lost some degree of professional autonomy and judgment. Psychotherapy is the most extreme example, as it transitioned from a male-dominated occupation to a female-dominated one. But a similar trend can be seen in the increasing presence of women among physicians, for example.

Late in the twentieth century, the semiprofessional roles that had been established firmly as women's work in the early twentieth century—nursing and teaching—also saw an increase in external control and a decrease in autonomy. Nursing, dominated by women from its origins, remained consistently over 90 percent female throughout the century. On balance, even more teachers are female at the end of the century than at midcentury, as more women teachers join the faculties of secondary schools. Although the female dominance of nursing and teaching has deep historical roots, we see through the lens of queuing that contemporary forces of deskilling have contributed to the persistence of sex segregation in these occupations. Despite efforts at professionalization and unionization, these jobs have over time become less attractive options for workers with other choices. Perhaps the most striking evidence of this is the recurring worker shortages in both nursing and teaching over the course of many decades. To college-educated White U.S.-born women, once the mainstay of both occupations, deteriorating working conditions in teaching and nursing have made these jobs less attractive, especially in light of expanding alternative opportunities. Attracting college-educated White U.S.-born men to these occupations has become even less likely. And while there has been some increase in the number of Black and foreign-born teachers and nurses, structural barriers and persistent cultural associations have limited the scope of this diversification on a national scale.[100]

Ironically, even as paid nurturant care has become more numerically female, tighter control and cost-cutting pressures often allow less time for the work's relational aspects, which are so often the basis of the rhetorical association with the feminine. Registered nurses have less time at the bedside, teachers have less time to support their students socially and emotionally, and psychotherapists have less room for relational therapy in light of managed-care rules and drug treatment. The expectations of relationship clash with the demands to speed up and with increased bureaucratic rigidity to make many nurturant care jobs increasingly difficult for workers to manage.

In health care, the occupations of hospital attendant, CNA, and other workers identified with so-called menial care are also proportionately more female than at the beginning of the century. But the concentration of racial-ethnic and foreign-born women that began early intensified as these jobs expanded exponentially in the cost-cutting environment of recent decades. These jobs have been on the receiving end of deskilling, absorbing the pieces of the labor labeled unskilled and therefore shunned by or taken away from skilled workers. Within nurturant care, these are some of the jobs relegated to larger numbers of racial-ethnic women.

The division of nurturant care work in hospitals is where we begin to see most clearly the replication of the pattern of the racialized hierarchy of spiritual and menial labor identified in domestic service. However, as we see in the next chapter, this hierarchy is only the tip of the iceberg, and to see patterns of racial-ethnic inequalities in care work more clearly requires looking at workers who would not even be included in a nurturant definition of care.

Chapter 5   Doing the Dirty Work

BECAUSE RACIAL-ETHNIC DIVISIONS in paid reproductive labor have been organized in part along a spiritual-menial continuum, focusing only on nurturant care leaves out the jobs at the menial end, where racial-ethnic workers are most concentrated. Cleaning, food, and laundry workers are important to a complete picture of racial-ethnic stratification in paid care.[1] These nonnurturant reproductive labor occupations also contrast with the overwhelmingly female-dominated arena of nurturant care. Although cleaning in the domestic sphere is associated with women, cleaning jobs in nondomestic settings have evolved as more gender-integrated occupations, as have food preparation and service jobs, suggesting that the association of nurturant care with women is historically contingent rather than inevitable. In the absence of strong associations with feminine qualities and relationality, strategies for raising wages and recognition for these workers have focused on class solidarity and social justice, important discourses too often ignored in discussions of nurturant care work.

Completing the Picture: Menial Labor, Changing Times

Housecleaning, preparing and serving food, and doing laundry, core tasks of reproductive labor, were once a substantial part of the labor of domestic servants. In contemporary settings, paid private household workers often perform some cleaning, cooking, and laundry tasks, even when their job is defined primarily as child-care provider.[2] Those employed to care for the elderly or disabled in their homes often also perform such tasks, as well as personal or medical care tasks. In addition, a range of new organizational structures has emerged for providing cleaning and laundry services to private households, from workers who do day work for multiple clients to multistate corporations that hire cadres of "merry maids" to go into households and clean.

Food preparation and service has evolved differently, as fewer households have paid workers assisting with these tasks within the home (outside of feeding a child or an elderly or disabled client). However, the twentieth century has seen the emergence of an enormous restaurant and prepared-food industry. Families increasingly rely on the labor of restaurant and food workers to provide at least some of the food they eat, either bringing it into their homes already prepared or eating in restaurants, venues that also employ cleaners and generate laundry. While one hundred years ago, a private household cook or a general maid might have helped with food preparation, today workers who prepare and serve food are much more likely to be employed outside private homes.

The institutions of nurturant care that have increased so rapidly during the twentieth century—hospitals, schools, and nursing homes—also require an enormous number of workers to clean buildings and rooms, do laundry, and feed those being cared for. In order for doctors, nurses, teachers, and nursing assistants to do their jobs, janitors, cafeteria workers, and laundry workers have to do theirs. Theirs are the quintessential backroom jobs that Evelyn Nakano Glenn has argued are relegated to racial-ethnic women, perpetuating the racialized spiritual-menial hierarchy that characterized domestic service in the early century.[3]

The racial-ethnic composition of workers in cleaning, food, and laundry jobs in fact more closely parallels patterns in domestic service than in nurturant care (see figure 5.1). In 1900, of the few workers in cleaning, food, and laundry outside private households, only slightly over 30 percent were White and U.S. born. In comparison, White U.S.-born workers were almost 45 percent of domestic servants and 85 percent of nurturant care workers. By midcentury, although Black U.S.-born women had become a majority among private household workers, their representation among these more public cleaning and food workers had declined from 37 to 23 percent. In 1950, cleaning and food work was less dominated by racial-ethnic women than private household work—but still considerably more so than nurturant care, which remained almost 80 percent White and U.S. born.

In the twenty-first century, foreign-born workers have again become a much more important presence among cleaning, food, and laundry workers. In 2007, over 25 percent of these workers were foreign born, 7 percent were Hispanic U.S. born, and 13 percent were Black U.S. born, still well over the level of Black representation in the labor force as a whole. Only 50 percent of those who perform the labor of cooking, cleaning, and laundry are White U.S.

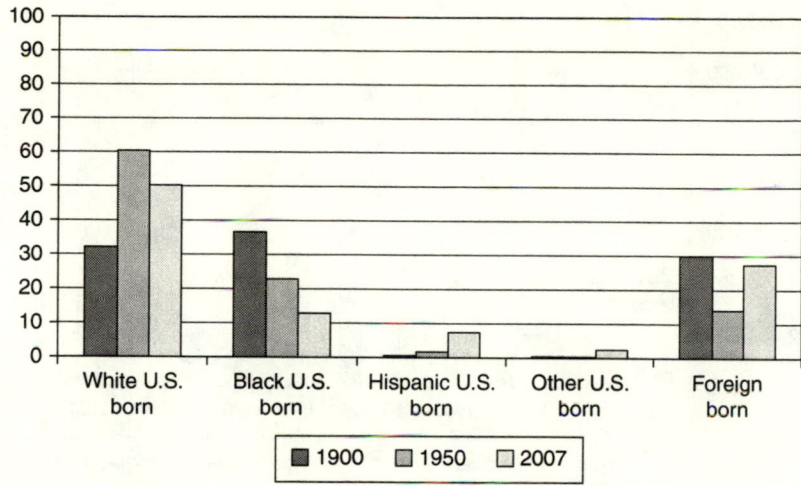

Figure 5.1. Cleaning, food, and laundry workers by race-ethnicity and birthplace, 1900–2007 (in percentages) *Source: Calculated by author using data from the U.S. Census (1900 and 1950) and the American Community Survey (2007) available through the Integrated Public Use Microdata Series (IPUMS).*

born. By contrast, 67 percent of nurturant care workers are White U.S. born. Although racialized hierarchies exist within nurturant care, we must look at occupations excluded by those using a nurturance lens to fully appreciate the ways in which gender and race-ethnicity intersect with the intimate labors of social reproduction.

In 1900, when 1.4 million domestic servants were doing cooking and cleaning labor, the number of workers engaged in these tasks outside private households was under 600,000 (see figure 5.2).[4] Most of these workers were janitors in apartment houses and public buildings, or sextons who were in charge of cleaning and maintaining churches. With the growth of restaurants and the rapid increase of schools and hospitals, cleaning and food preparation and service jobs became much more numerous, increasing from under one million workers in 1920 to over six million workers in 1970 (about the same number as in nurturant care overall in that year). Since 1970, the number of workers in nurturant care occupations has continued to increase at a rate that has outpaced overall labor-force growth, while the number of cleaning, food, and laundry workers has remained close to 8 percent of the labor force. Nonetheless, by 2007, more than twelve million workers were engaged in cleaning, food, and laundry occupations, including a large number working in public buildings, apartment complexes, and restaurants. The other institutions in which these

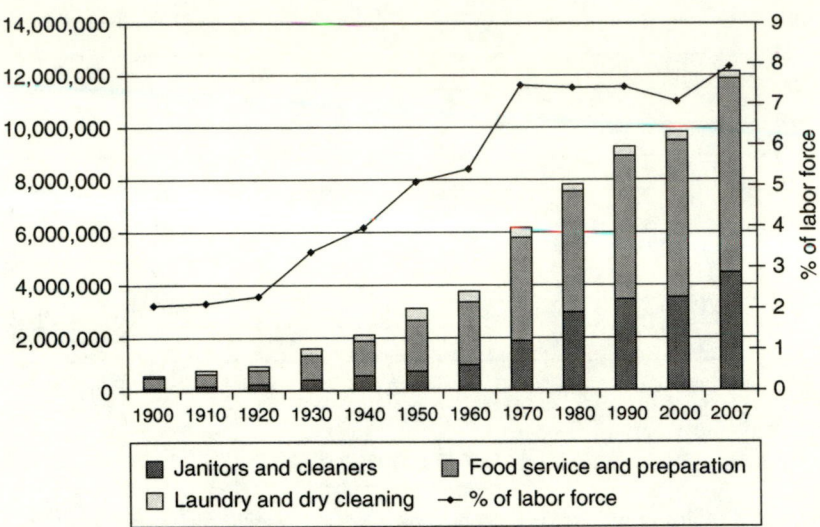

Figure 5.2. Number of cleaning, food, and laundry workers, 1900–2007 *Source: Calculated by author using data from the U.S. Census (1900–2000) and the American Community Survey (2007) available through the Integrated Public Use Microdata Series (IPUMS).*

workers are concentrated are hotels and motels, schools, hospitals, and nursing homes.[5] The rise in the number of workers engaged in cleaning, food, and laundry occupations outside private homes closely parallels the decline in the number of those identified as private household workers.

Cleaning, food, and laundry tasks are overwhelmingly associated with women when performed in private households, whether by family members or by paid workers. When these same tasks are performed in nondomestic settings, the jobs are not overwhelmingly female. In contrast both to the consistent dominance of women among private household workers and to their increasing presence in nurturant care jobs, cleaning, food, and laundry jobs have been fairly evenly distributed between men and women throughout the century. Only in 1960 did this group of occupations exceed 57 percent female—the proportion then reached 63 percent—and in some decades males were the majority. This broad view certainly masks sex segregation by occupation or by industrial location within this overall group, as we will see, but that is true of nurturant care as well. Yet, as a sector, nurturant care has been overwhelmingly and increasingly female, while the cleaning, food, and laundry sector has not.

Within individual occupations or occupational groups among these jobs, changes in sex composition have been characterized more by fluctuation than by the unidirectional trends found in the development of nurturant care occupations. For example, women made up only 24 percent of janitors and cleaners in 1900, a proportion which fluctuated within 10 percentage points of that range until 1970, when it began a steady rise, reaching 52 percent in 2007. Within food service occupations, the occupation that has shown the clearest trend toward feminization is that of waiter and waitress. In 1900, only 40 percent of waiters and waitresses were women, a percentage that gradually increased, reaching a high of 89 percent women in 1970 and then reversing; by 2007, the proportion of waiters and waitresses who were female had decreased to 73 percent. By contrast, the proportion of cooks who are women began the century around 47 percent in 1910, fluctuated to as high as 64 percent women in 1960, and ended the century with representation almost the same as in 1910.[6]

Although a detailed analysis of the historical development of this wide range of occupations is beyond the scope of this chapter, I here explore two threads that illuminate the complex relationships between inequalities and care work. First, I examine how gender and race-ethnicity have been intertwined in the evolution of cleaning work. There are some very interesting overlaps with the patterns in nurturant care, and also some important differences. Second, I explore the role of cleaning, food, and laundry workers within hospitals, one of the institutions that has become a prominent part of the nurturant care landscape in the twenty-first century.

Wives, Cleaning Ladies, and Janitors

A student once told me about a scenario she observed at the service station where her husband works. As she stood in the shop, several of the mechanics and waiting customers laughed and made comments to the man who emptied trashcans and cleaned the bathrooms:

"He would make someone a great wife, don't you think?"
"Look at how good he cleans!"
"Wanna come clean my house?"

When she asked her husband about it, he told her that the man was a mechanic at the shop who had asked the boss if he could take over the work of the recently fired "cleaning lady" to make some extra money.

This short anecdote reflects many of the contradictions and complexities that characterize cleaning work at the dawn of the twenty-first century. Despite the large numbers of men employed in cleaning occupations, scrubbing bathrooms and other cleaning tasks are still fundamentally seen as women's work in many contexts. And despite the fact that most of those who work in cleaning services are not working in private homes, the association of cleaning with the domestic chores of housework also persists. Contemporary U.S. Census occupational categories embody these contradictions as well, capturing cleaning workers in two different categories, "janitors and building cleaners" and "maids and housekeeping cleaners."[7] A closer examination of these categories illustrates the ways in which cleaning work has been constructed as the number of workers engaged in cleaning tasks has grown.

According to the U.S. Census 2000 Classified Index of Occupations, the duties of "janitors and building cleaners" (an occupational category that was 68 percent male in 2007) are these: "Keep buildings in clean and orderly condition. Perform heavy cleaning duties, such as cleaning floors, shampooing rugs, washing walls and glass, and removing rubbish. Duties may include tending furnace and boiler, performing routine maintenance activities, notifying management of need for repairs, and cleaning snow or debris from sidewalk." The same index explains the duties of "maids and housekeeping cleaners" (89 percent female in 2007) as including the following: "Perform any combination of light cleaning duties to maintain private households or commercial establishments, such as hotels, restaurants, and hospitals, in a clean and orderly manner. Duties include making beds, replenishing linens, cleaning rooms and halls, and vacuuming."[8]

Although the goal of both jobs is to maintain cleanliness and order, these descriptions differ on two dimensions. First, the work of mostly male janitors is described as "heavy" cleaning, and the work of mostly female maids is described as "light." Second, the location of the work of the two groups appears to be different. While janitors are described rather generically as working in "buildings," maids and housekeeping cleaners work in private homes or in establishments such as hotels, hospitals, and restaurants.

Descriptions of the labor of those identified as housekeepers belie its characterization as light work. Barbara Ehrenreich found during her time working for a housecleaning service in Maine that scrubbing floors on hands and knees and vacuuming with a strap-on backpack vacuum, all under intense pressure to move quickly, is heavy physical labor: "this form of exercise is totally symmetrical, brutally repetitive, and as likely to destroy the musculoskeletal structure as to strengthen it."[9] Studies of hotel housekeepers have found that the labor of moving around a hotel with a heavy cart of supplies, lifting mattresses to make beds, pushing vacuums, and scrubbing tubs is a highly physical job that puts its workers at significantly elevated risk for occupation-related pain and injury.[10] Cleaning workers in hospitals and nursing homes also experience backbreaking conditions, and similarly high injury risk.[11] The experience of making beds all day as a hotel or hospital housekeeper bears little resemblance to the experience of a child making her bed in the mornings. All of these workers clean floors, remove garbage, and wash glass and walls. And while maintaining furnaces and performing routine maintenance—tasks attributed to janitors—are certainly more gender-typed tasks, it is difficult to argue that this work is inherently heavier than the labor of maids and housekeeping cleaners. Like the characterization of skill in some gender-typed occupations, the distinction between janitorial work and housekeeping work on the basis of physical demands seems largely to be socially constructed along gender lines.

The term "housekeeping" implies that there is something more domestic about this role than the job of a janitor, and in fact maids and housekeeping cleaners are reported to work primarily in private homes or in establishments such as hotels, restaurants, and hospitals that have stronger domestic associations than do other buildings. While the nature of the tasks involved in cleaning an office building, apartment house, hotel, hospital, or school are similar in many ways, these jobs are constructed quite differently based on their location. By contrast, many nurturant care occupations are strongly feminized whether that labor takes place in a private home or in a public institution. For example, child care is numerically dominated by women and culturally associated with the feminine whether it occurs in a private home, in a family day-care setting, or in a more institutional child-care center or school. While there are gender-typed differences in cleaning tasks, the most visible differences are based on context rather than on the content of the labor. Again, this is in contrast to nurturant care, where the nature of the work itself is reified and linked inextricably with the feminine.

THE BUREAUCRATIZATION OF HOUSECLEANING
In the first half of the twentieth century, myriad technological advances—from indoor plumbing to washing machines to vacuum cleaners—fundamentally changed what cleaning entails, as we have seen. The second half has seen important changes in the social organization of cleaning work. Within private households, the most notable change has been an increase in the number of homes that employ cleaning services rather than a single domestic employee. These businesses range from small mom-and-pop operations that clean multiple homes weekly to national franchises that deploy large numbers of cleaning teams every day. Ehrenreich wrote in 2001 that nationwide and international cleaning services like Merry Maids controlled 20 to 25 percent of the housecleaning business, and that their share of this market continues to rise.[12]

Given that the personal nature of the employment relationship for domestic servants made them vulnerable to exploitation, it is reasonable to ask what the impact of this shift to more formal organizational structures has been on cleaning workers. Mary Romero has argued that private housecleaning services run by individual women or groups of women represent the "modernization" of domestic work, and she and other researchers have documented that workers prefer this arrangement to live-in or live-out domestic work because of higher wages, more control over work hours, and more autonomy.[13] Working with multiple clients limits the impact of any single personal relationship on their livelihoods, and most report more distance between themselves and employing families than domestics that work for a single family. Of course, the work is still physically demanding and stigmatized. One housecleaner interviewed by Pierrette Hondagneu-Sotelo, when asked what she liked least about housecleaning, replied: "Well, that you have to clean."[14] Breaking into the market as an independent housecleaner also requires access to social networks to build a client base, something that may be impossible for newly arrived immigrants in particular.

Corporate cleaning services offer an alternative to workers with fewer resources—at a substantially lower wage rate than privately owned housecleaning services provide. These tightly controlled bureaucracies are at the opposite end of the organizational spectrum from the individualized employer-employee relationships in domestic service, so workers in these companies are not vulnerable to the same kinds of pressures as domestic servants from relational entanglements with employers. In fact, many housecleaning workers never even see the homeowners face-to-face, and receive instructions through a central office. But the cost of this personal distance for workers is being subject to a highly regulated work environment. Cleaners are trained to follow specific rules that dictate everything from the amount of water used to clean a floor to the direction to move while dusting a room to the twenty-two steps to clean a bathroom. Held to strict time constraints, workers must move quickly through the standardized procedures, which are designed to produce a consistent impression of cleanliness.[15] Parallel to the work of nurturant care workers in the late twentieth century, the work of housecleaners in these corporate arrangements has become so routine that they have none of the autonomy that may exist for housecleaners running their own businesses.

Paradoxically, the appeal to individualized relationships is still prominent in this hyperstandardized workplace. Jennifer Bickham-Mendez has found that corporate cleaning services use what she calls "strategic personalism" to control employees in an environment that does not allow for consistent direct supervision. The first aspect of this approach is that workers are told to demonstrate that they "care" by paying attention to the client's special requests and engaging in personable interactions with clients when they are present (all the while keeping to the cleaning regimen). One training video gives the example of a worker who saw a note a client had left a child to take the chicken out of the freezer and took it out herself. The simultaneous demand by employers to follow rigidly standardized protocols and to treat clients with a personal touch (which often requires extra labor on the part of the worker) is a common strategy in the service industry, intended to provide an image to consumers and potential consumers of a reliable, predictable, but professional and personalized service product.[16]

The second aspect of strategic personalism that Bickham-Mendez documents, also widely used throughout the service sector, is reminiscent of the patronlike attitude that has often characterized the relationships between domestic servants and their employers. Managers in the housecleaning service Bickham-Mendez studied referred to the "Helping Hands Housecleaners family" (a fictitious name). The managers demonstrate their "care" for their employees by bringing doughnuts to the office in the morning and throwing birthday parties for them, and explicitly state that being part of this "family" is more important to their workers than higher pay or benefits. Thus, despite the changes in the context of cleaning work for some at the end of the twenty-first century, personalism is still used as a tool to exploit and control the labor of workers. While workers in nurturant care occupations have been subject to the exploitative as well as the rewarding potential of the relational nature of their jobs, these essentially nonrelational workers have not escaped some version of the paradox of personalism.

On the surface, these bureaucratized organizations allow both employers and employees to escape the discomfort of a master-servant relationship increasingly seen as incompatible with the egalitarian ideologies of the twentieth century and beyond. Many clients choose corporate cleaning services and particularly request the workers come when they are not home to avoid being face-to-face with the uncomfortable reality of inequality.[17] Yet most of these franchises have the word "maid" in their title, evoking the very servile relationship both workers and employers claim to want to avoid. Many advertise proudly that their maids clean the floors on their hands and knees, the epitome of a servile pose.[18] The work of housecleaning in the twenty-first century presents a set of contradictions that both mirrors and conflicts with the patterns of early domestic service, as well as with the evolution of nurturant care.

JUSTICE FOR JANITORS; OR, HOW THE OTHER HALF LIVES
What about the large cleaning industry that has emerged connected to hotels, hospitals, schools, office buildings, and other nonhousehold locations? How has the labor of these much more gender-mixed groups of workers evolved?

The neoliberal turn in the economy since the 1980s has also affected building cleaners. To cut costs, building owners and managers have increasingly subcontracted out cleaning work to cleaning services as opposed to hiring employees with access to benefits and higher levels of protection. Cleaning services also tended to be nonunionized, and so this shift also represented a movement away from unionized janitorial workers, who had made some gains in wages and working conditions in the post–World War II era.[19]

Restructuring had consequences for both the demographics of the janitorial workforce and the conditions of work for janitors. As nonunion contractors replaced unionized workers, wages and working conditions for the janitors who had been organized declined. Building services workers were also impacted by the general workforce trends of speedup and cost cutting. Like housecleaners, they were increasingly expected to perform a large number of predetermined tasks in a short amount of time. One of the cleaning workers interviewed by Cynthia Cranford describes the work this way: "They gave you an area to clean. They gave me an area for 4 hours. But I saw that this area was for, like, 6 hours. And I had to finish the work as quick as I could, and I had to leave it finished. And they never paid me one minute more. . . . She would send me to dust the legs of the desks and the bottom of the toilets. . . . Five minutes before I would enter work I would get a headache."[20] Building-cleaning work therefore had much in common with bureaucratized housecleaning work in the wake of restructuring.

Importantly, the move to nonunionized subcontractors led to a shift in the racial-ethnic and gender composition of the cleaning workforce. In areas with large populations of Hispanic immigrants, nonunionized workers newly arrived from Mexico and Central America, often without legal documentation, gradually took over the unionized janitorial jobs previously held disproportionately by Blacks.[21] In addition, employers had traditionally divided tasks between male janitors and female maids, as described earlier. The mandates of speedup and cost cutting led nonunion contractors to assign both Latina women and Latino men to the whole range of gender-typed tasks, breaking down the gendered division of cleaning labor within these organizations.[22]

In Southern California, scholars have connected these demographic shifts to a revitalized union movement in the janitorial industry. The Justice for Janitors campaign launched by the Service Employees International Union (SEIU) in the 1990s has met with considerable success in a number of locations and has been extensively studied as an example of renewed union strategies in a changed economic context. Scholars attribute some of the success of the group's most visible campaigns in Southern California to the prevalence of class consciousness among the Mexican and Central American immigrants in the janitorial industry in that region.[23] In contrast to a professionalization model based on distinguishing an occupation by emphasizing skills and setting entry requirements, Justice for Janitors drew on workers' class consciousness to mobilize support for wage increases and improvements in working conditions on the basis of worker rights and social justice. As one scholar has noted, the campaign was purposively called "Justice for Janitors," not "Compensation for Custodians."[24]

Since its celebrated victory in Los Angeles (memorialized in the film *Bread and Roses*), Justice for Janitors has met with mixed success. But it remains an important model, which the SEIU has built upon in organizing other groups of workers, including child-care workers, personal care attendants, and home-health aides. It is notable that the unionization of janitorial workers was driven by class and racial-ethnic identity in a gender-integrated environment, and was relatively free from the kinds of conflicts around either relationality or professionalization that have been part of unionization efforts in nurturant care occupations.

In many ways, the development of cleaning occupations over the course of the twentieth century offers a telling contrast to the story of nurturant care. In the absence of women's advocates staking a claim to cleaning work, the labor of cleaning was not overwhelmingly linked to purported feminine qualities. Gendered associations developed based on the location of the work rather than on the process of the labor. Where efforts to improve wages and working conditions among nurturant care occupations were often entangled in the sometimes competing discourse of professionalization and essentialized notions of feminine caring, gender-integrated janitorial unions united workers on the basis of class (and to some extent racial-ethnic identity) and drew on ideals of social justice and rights to make their case. These contrasts highlight, first, that the gendered construction of care work is the product of a particular history rather than a foregone conclusion; and second, that the cultural construction as well as the demographic makeup of an occupation influences the rhetorical and organizational strategy used to argue for its value.

The history of cleaning work also shows surprising continuities with the development of nurturant care. Among housecleaners, as among other service-sector workers, the language of care is popular. This language, which evokes relational embeddedness and obligation, can be aimed at extracting labor from workers even when their jobs do not appear to have much relational content. Exploring how the unique relational context of nurturant care work is connected to worker exploitation requires acknowledging the larger labor market environment in which this practice is a common strategy. In addition, nurturant care scholarship may prove useful to understanding this practice across the service sector more broadly.

The Underbelly of Nurturant Care

As nurturant care was transformed in the early twentieth century, the sites of the delivery of health care and education—hospitals, doctors' offices, and schools—mushroomed. The later decades of the century also saw a rise in the number of institutions like nursing homes and long-term care facilities. Each of these organizations employs cleaning, food, and laundry workers, without whom the work of these institutions would grind to a halt. The intimate labors of such workers, defined as almost entirely manual, often are ignored in discussions of care work, which focus on nurturant care as a group of occupations bound by their essentially relational nature. If nursing aides are considered menial laborers compared to nurses, then cleaning, kitchen, and laundry workers are considered even more menial. Their jobs have no formal relational component.

Because it has been widely studied, I focus here on the hospital workforce. An examination of the racial-ethnic and gendered hierarchies within hospitals not only reinforces the argument that an exclusive focus on nurturant care occupations obscures a critical piece of the puzzle of racial-ethnic inequalities and care work but also adds another dimension to understanding the role of relationality in that puzzle. We have noted that some scholars argue that nurturant care occupations are seen as less valuable—as less like work—at least in part because of their relational content and the construction of relationality as a natural female trait. But for some workers at the bottom of the hospital hierarchy—cleaning, food, and laundry workers among them—a claim for recognition as skilled and valuable labor is based precisely on the recognition of their work as relational.

HOLDING UP HEALTH CARE

During the years that hospitals were consolidating as primary sites of health-care delivery, nurses provided the majority of the labor necessary to run them. In 1920, trained nurses and nurses in training made up 45 percent of the hospital workforce.[25] Early nursing labor, as we have seen, involved not only a growing repertoire of technical and medical tasks but also changing bedpans, washing operating room floors, and laundering and changing linens on hospital beds. As the century progressed, the role of trained nurses became more narrowly defined, and some of these duties were shifted onto less trained (and lower-paid) attendants and aides or redistributed among specialized cleaning, food, and laundry workers employed within hospital walls.

The hospital workforce has become so rigidly hierarchical that Nona Glazer has called it "segmented" rather than stratified due to the unscalable barriers to vertical mobility for workers in the lowest positions.[26] Nursing's battle for professionalization has contributed to this trend. As nursing leaders in the early century struggled to define nursing skill as worthy of recognition, as we have seen, part of their strategy was to redistribute tasks seen as unskilled to less trained workers. But the segmentation of the hospital workforce is also a consequence of larger economic trends in the second half of the twentieth century—the rise of neoliberalism as an approach to both government policy and corporate organization. The push for cost control in the health-care sector has put extra pressure on hospitals to shift labor from more highly trained workers (like nurses) to low-wage workers (like aides, cleaning workers, etc.).

This hierarchy has been not only gendered but also racialized in the structural divisions between jobs, as well as in the cultural constructions of the work, as we have seen. The racial-ethnic makeup of various categories of workers within hospitals is shown in figure 5.3.[27] The concentration of racial-ethnic workers in cleaning, food, and laundry jobs is even more extreme than the racial-ethnic stratification among registered nurses, licensed practical nurses, and nursing aides discussed earlier. Among cleaning workers in hospitals, fully 30 percent are Black and U.S. born; just under 25 percent are foreign born. Hispanic workers are also overrepresented, and White U.S.-born workers make

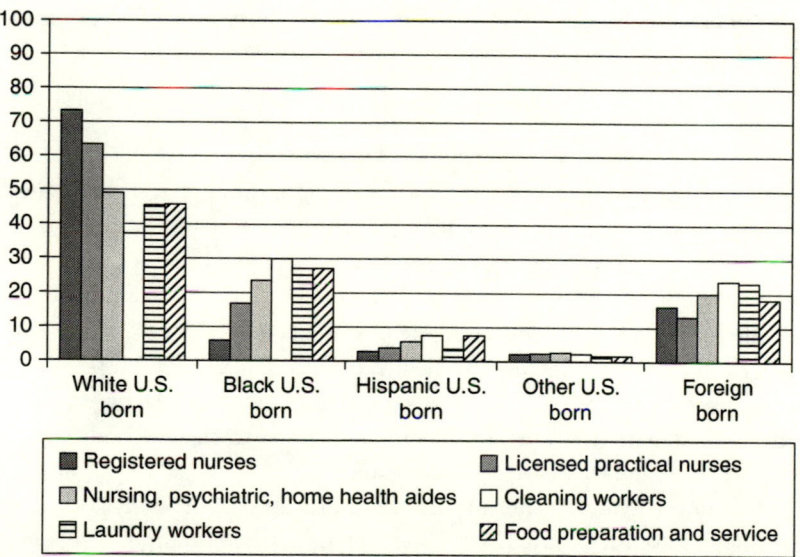

Figure 5.3. Selected hospital workers by race-ethnicity and birthplace, 2007 (in percentages) *Source: Calculated by author using American Community Survey data (2007) available through the Integrated Public Use Microdata Series (IPUMS).*

up only 38 percent of the hospital-cleaning workforce (compared to 65 percent of the overall labor force). Similar if less striking patterns exist among laundry and food workers in hospitals. Interestingly, the proportion of Black U.S.-born cleaning, food, and laundry workers in hospitals is much higher than in other industries: 30 percent in hospitals compared to 15 percent elsewhere. Other industries have a higher concentration of foreign-born cleaning workers compared to hospitals (32 percent compared to 23 percent in hospitals). The pattern among food and laundry workers is similar. If the division between spiritual labor, assumed to be skilled, and menial labor, assumed to be unskilled, is a major axis of racial-ethnic stratification, a view that includes only nurturant care workers eliminates some of the very occupations where racial-ethnic workers are most concentrated.

Looking outside the bounds of nurturance also illuminates contrasts in the gendered construction of care work. While the racial-ethnic makeup of nursing and practical nursing are somewhat different, both occupations have been consistently over 90 percent female. The more heavily racialized category of nursing aides, somewhat less female dominated, is still over 80 percent women. By contrast, occupations that are the least associated with relationality are far less female dominated: fewer than 70 percent of laundry and food preparation and service workers are women, and among cleaning workers only 60 percent are women. While women are still the majority of these categories of hospital workers, many more men are doing the dirty work of hospitals than are engaged in the relational work of nursing and the intermediate work of nursing aides.

CRITICAL TO CARE

Some scholars and activists suggest that doing cleaning, food, and laundry jobs in a hospital context fundamentally changes the nature of the jobs. Pat Armstrong and her colleagues, for example, have argued that workers usually labeled "ancillary" in hospitals—not only cleaning, food, and laundry workers but also secretaries and other clerical workers—should be recognized as engaged in the important work of health care. In contrast to the portrayal of these jobs as unskilled and therefore comparable to other low-wage jobs, the authors hold that "there is considerable evidence to suggest both that the work is skilled and that it is specific to care."[28]

Part of the evidence the authors present focuses on the increased hazards and higher stakes of cleaning, food, and laundry work in hospitals compared to similar work in other settings. With the growing recognition of the importance of cleanliness for health, hospitals instituted strict protocols for cleaning workers to minimize the transmission of illness and disease. The workers are also themselves vulnerable to infection from airborne germs, surfaces tainted by various bodily fluids, and needles and other hazards. The authors describe laundry workers who must separate laundry not in terms of colors and fabrics, but in terms of diseases and patients, and who must approach all items with caution to be sure they do not contain biohazards. Food preparation and service workers must correctly prepare food for patients with a whole range of specific dietary needs—in an environment where the consequences of a mistake could be deadly. Armstrong and her colleagues argue that because of these higher stakes, working in a health-care setting requires specific skill sets and creates more difficult working conditions than for other cleaning, food and laundry workers.

Importantly, the other characteristic the authors claim makes these jobs in health care unique is the inherently relational nature of their jobs. Although relating to patients directly may not be in the job descriptions of ancillary workers, it is inevitably part of their work. "Those needing care seldom know who is assigned to what and simply want care now," the authors point out. A housekeeper cleaning a patient's room may find herself asked to get the patient a cup of water, or a food service worker may learn while delivering trays of food that she needs to remove the plastic wrap for a particular resident or the resident will eat it. One cleaning worker describes part of her job this way: "There's the families that are so happy to see you because they know that you chat with the patient in bed and you help them and, you know, they become part of your day."[29] Armstrong and her colleagues invoke the invisible relational content of these jobs to lay a claim for skill and differentiate these workers from other low-wage unskilled workers in the labor market.[30] Part of the argument used by advocates and scholars is that the complex relational interactions and negotiations required of care workers like personal care attendants and nursing aides in nursing homes make them skilled workers.

Here the paradox of care and relationality comes full circle. Nurturant care scholars argue that society does not value the care work of nurses and teachers and child-care workers enough in part because of its association with the purported feminine character of relationship. Conversely, scholars focus on making visible the relational aspects of the work of hospital aides and cleaners in order to make a claim that theirs is skilled labor. For the latter workers, being labeled a "care worker" is something to be pursued, something seen as reflecting and conferring value. Failing to look beyond the boundaries of nurturant care leaves this paradox—and its implications for organizing and social change—hidden from view.

Theoretically, an analysis of care work that rests exclusively on nurturant care distorts the links between gender and care, truncates our view of racial-ethnic stratification, and obfuscates some of the complex ways in which relationality is intertwined with the value of labor. Nurturant care theorists have asked some critical questions and have provided invaluable insight into some of the problematics of paid care work. The challenge now is to broaden our view by integrating these theoretical contributions with other important analyses of labor-market inequalities, an intellectual endeavor intimately connected to the project of building a movement to address the care crisis.

Chapter 6   Making Care Count

A COLLEAGUE ONCE COMMENTED to me during a discussion about care: "You know, all these years feminists were trying to convince us that care was *work*—then care theorists started trying to convince us that care was something unique and entirely distinct. Maybe we had it right the first time." Many care scholars share the same goal: to raise public recognition of and societal rewards for care work and untangle the web of gender, racial-ethnic, and class inequalities in which our approach to care is currently enmeshed. How do we make care count? What are the implications of different conceptualizations of care for the project of social change? And how can the lessons we learn from history inform our strategy for the future?

Addressing the contemporary care crisis requires scholarship and advocacy that bridge three discourses. First, nurturant care theory has brought into focus the importance of interdependence and relationship in care work, a critical contribution to understanding the history of care and its connections to gender inequalities. Moving forward, care scholars must focus on creating a framework that integrates relationality with the other skills and labor required of nurturant care workers rather than places these in opposition to each other. Second, care scholars and advocates must engage with a larger discourse of class and economic inequalities. Any approach to solving the problems of the low-wage care workforce that does not address the fundamental inequalities in our economy will prove inadequate. And finally, it is critical to understand care work as a foundational pillar in any economy and any society, and to argue for social responsibility for and public investment in care based upon this unique position. The ideas developed by scholars interested in reproductive labor remind us to pay attention not only to the labor process of care work but also to its social and economic position.

Learning from the Past

History shows that the evolution of paid care, of its gendered construction, and of its racialized hierarchies has been a far more complex process than popular narratives of care would have us believe. In some ways today's landscape of paid care is less different from the past than the story of marketization implies—both paid care work and the gender and racial-ethnic hierarchies associated with paid care work have a long history. However, the framing of a transfer of care work from family to market also understates the transformation in the cultural expectations and material realities of care work during the twentieth century.

LEAVE IT TO BEAVER?

In the popular imagination, the care crisis of today is a sharp contrast to an idealized past in which families took care of their own rather than paying others to take care of them. Conservative political discourse that has woven a narrative about the decline of the family in modern times has been quick to adopt this interpretation of the evolution of care in the twentieth century. The implication is that families today care less than did families of yesterday—both in the emotional sense of caring about other family members and in the concrete sense of doing less care work themselves (and contracting more of it out). While most care scholars would not adhere to this interpretation explicitly, many reflect the same assumptions in their assertion that the movement of care work from family to market is one of the dominant themes of the twentieth century. Scholars who focus on trends toward marketization or commodification imply that the primary fact about care in the twenty-first century is that it is provided for money rather than love, in the market rather than in the family.

There is no question that there have been dramatic changes in the landscape of paid care in the past one hundred years and that more care workers are employed in schools, hospitals, doctors' offices, nursing homes, and childcare centers than ever before. But the story is not simply one of movement from family to market. First, the domestic servants who performed the substantial tasks of cleaning turn-of-the-century homes, tending to children, and sitting with the sick were as much a part of a market for paid care as are contemporary care workers. The context of the market exchange has changed, as has the structure of the economy as a whole, but families who can afford to have been exchanging money for care for centuries, belying the notion that the marketization of care work is a new phenomenon. This point, though perhaps an obvious one, is too often overlooked in the hand wringing over the decline of the family and the impact of monetary exchange on care. Second, in the twentieth century both family care providers and paid care workers faced ever-intensifying expectations of what it means to care. We must understand the expansion and restructuring of the paid care labor force not primarily as a transfer of labor, but as a response to changing cultural norms and material realities of care.

A close look at history shows that a system which relied on family members and hired help to face one set of care challenges has been transformed into a system that combines family care and expert workers to address the radically different care challenges of today. And it is difficult to argue that this new configuration is less caring. We invest more time and money and energy into keeping people alive than we ever have before. We believe it critically important to spend time with children, both actively engaged with them as well as supervising them closely. And we consider those with even severe mental illness as deserving of treatment. This is not to minimize the real and urgent problems in the care sector today, but to point out that nostalgia for the past is misplaced and leads to misguided policy prescriptions to address today's problems.

Among the catalysts for the transformation of care into the realm of expert labor were the ascendance of scientific thinking and the rapid pace of technological change. Perhaps nowhere has technology had a more obvious impact than in health care. The complex medical procedures and drugs that exist today to treat illness were unimaginable one hundred years ago, and the work of caring for sick people today bears little resemblance to the care provided by families and hired help at the turn of the last century. The enormous expansion of modern health care, with its cadres of paid health-care workers, is directly linked to the emergence of medical care as an area of enterprise with a strong scientific base and the perceived need for expert knowledge and specialized care settings. As a result, health-care work is not substituting for the care once provided within private homes. Rather, health-care workers are engaged in a largely new set of care tasks—from performing surgery and caring for patients in its aftermath to injecting chemicals into people's bodies to kill cancer cells to teaching people how to walk with a prosthetic limb. In fact, the difference between what hospitals and doctors' offices do now and what family members and hired help did one hundred years ago is so obvious that few suggest that the movement of health care out of the home reflects a decline.

By contrast, the work of nursing homes, residential care facilities, and home-care aides has been the focus of much attention. The happy family caring for the elders within its midst in the past in contrast to the cold family of today shipping the elder off to a nursing home is perhaps the emblematic image for those who bemoan the decline of care in the twentieth century. The scale of the rise in institutional care of the elderly is often overstated, as research shows that just over 1 percent of the population is living in institutions (not including correctional facilities and the military), a proportion that has remained relatively constant since 1950.[1] True, more of that 1 percent are in nursing homes and residential care facilities and fewer are in mental hospitals, but there has not been a wholesale move toward institutionalization.

The care work in these institutions, as well as that performed by expanding ranks of home-care workers, is fundamentally different from the care of the elderly one hundred years ago. As Robert Moroney points out, most families in the past did not face the kinds of institutionalization decisions families face today, because many more people today survive to old age.[2] The notion of long-term care is relatively new, meaningful only because large numbers of people are now surviving for longer periods with more complex medical conditions. The needs of an older population with more chronic illnesses and long-term disabilities are more intense and more complicated than those of a hundred or even fifty years ago; the shifting configurations of paid care thus reflect changes in the meaning of care itself. Caring for a ninety-year-old parent who needs help toileting and walking is profoundly different from having a grandmother in her sixties living in a spare room with the extended family. Families still carry the bulk of such care work and have absorbed the most significant impact of these changes, but a group of paid care workers has also emerged to respond to these expanding needs.

Notions of care for children and youth have also changed radically in the past one hundred years. As an eight-year-old growing up in the years after World War II, my mother regularly rode the trolley by herself for half an hour each way to take piano lessons. In 2008, a mother was publicly castigated and threatened with child-abuse charges for letting her nine-year-old son ride the subway home from a store.[3] This simple contrast illustrates the enormity of the shift in child-rearing practices during the course of a generation or two. Whatever the causes of this shift, and however one judges it, the expectations of what it means to take care of a child today are very different from those of previous decades.

Of course, caring for children has always involved work. But the twentieth-century sacralization of childhood and the emergence of ideologies of concerted cultivation among the middle class have changed the landscape of parenting, as well as that of paid child care. When most children were cultivated less closely, caring for them required a different level of attention from both parents and paid workers. Particularly for children who are not infants, the child-rearing practices of the twenty-first century demand more constant and careful supervision and more active engagement than those of earlier generations. As a consequence, both the demand for paid child care and the expectations for the care paid workers will provide have been ratcheted up considerably—whether in schools, child-care centers, or family day-care homes.

In the arena of mental health, the general trend of the twentieth century has been away from institutional care. In contrast to the growth of hospitals, schools, and nursing homes, the last decades of the twentieth century saw the closing of many large state-run mental hospitals and similar institutions. A model of treatment for those with mental illness replaced an approach that was essentially custodial. The growth of mental health as an arena of scientific inquiry and expert knowledge led to the expansion of treatment options for those who are seriously mentally ill, as well as to increased attention to the mental health needs of the general population. The premise of training for mental health and social service occupations is that workers offer something distinct from the kind of support provided by friends and family. Again, the expansion of paid care in mental health is not a substitute for family care but a response to new developments in the field.

The notion that the same care work that happened in family homes yesterday is happening in institutions today is deeply flawed. A range of economic and cultural forces have fundamentally transformed the nature of the work, so that a different set of expectations and realities shape the labor of care today. The *what* of care has been revolutionized, a change much more elemental than any related changes in the *who* and the *where* of care.

MOTHER KNOWS BEST?

Contained in the marketization narrative is a story about why paid care work is associated with the feminine and done predominantly by women. The assumption is that as care work moved from family to market, it retained its association with the female domestic sphere. Setting aside the problems of the marketization frame itself, the link between the tasks of care and women is assumed to have carried over almost automatically from unpaid housewives to paid nurses, teachers, housekeepers, nannies, and home-care aides. If this were the case, then it would follow that after decades of feminist activism criticizing the gendered division of labor and the ideology of separate spheres, care work would have become less female dominated. The opposite is true. In the twentieth century, paid nurturant care as a whole became increasingly more female, reaching almost 80 percent women in 2007 (compared to only 55 percent in 1900 and 65 percent in 1950). Far from a seamless and automatic process, the feminization of nurturant care has been the consequence of a confluence of women's activism and powerful economic interests.

As the nurturant care occupations of the twentieth century emerged, they were linked to the feminine both by female activists intent on opening up work opportunities for women in a constrained labor market and by men who had a stake in keeping costs down by hiring women at lower wages. In the late nineteenth century, female activists were central in advocating for the opening up of teaching to women by arguing that women were naturally suited to the role, and the primarily male activists of the Common School movement saw an opportunity to capitalize on women's entrance into teaching to more rapidly expand schooling. At the beginning of the twentieth century, nursing advocates likewise explicitly linked the job to purported feminine character traits to stake a claim to the emerging occupation for women—a development congruent with the interests of hospitals in maintaining a cheap labor force. Later, social work activists also used the supposed feminine trait of relational warmth to distinguish themselves from the growing fields of psychiatry and psychology. Thus, all these nurturant care occupations were deliberately constructed as women's work in the quest to carve out specific occupational niches, and hiring women at lower wages met the business goals of schools and hospitals. (By contrast, the labor of cleaning, certainly heavily associated with the domestic labor of women, did not maintain its feminine association as cleaning work in public buildings expanded.) The feminization of nurturant care work therefore was by no means automatic or inevitable, but the result of specific historical processes and the overlapping interests of feminist activists, reformers, and businesses.

As the century progressed and nurturant care expanded, some of these occupations became slightly more open to men, but as a whole nurturant care became even more dominated by women. During the later decades of the twentieth century, women made significant inroads into several of the nurturant care occupations that had once been the domain of men—medicine, psychology, and secondary school teaching. As with earlier processes of feminization, the entrance of women into these occupations has been the result of linked socioeconomic and cultural processes of redefinition and shifting structural conditions. The profession of medicine has been opened up to women just as doctors are losing a degree of autonomy and control over their own labor process in the wake of the reorganization of health care into health maintenance organizations (HMOs). Psychology has been transformed from a male-dominated profession to a female-dominated one as the rise of a relational model has been linked to supposed feminine character traits and as psychologists have experienced a loss of professional autonomy due to the constraints of HMOs and growing competition with a biological model of mental health. And secondary school teachers increasingly match the rest of the teaching labor force, mostly women, in an environment of ever-tightening top-down control. The female dominance of nurturant care work that was established early in the century has not faded as the century progressed and new opportunities and more egalitarian gender ideologies expanded. Rather, contemporary economic trends have been linked with expanding feminization.

UPSTAIRS, DOWNSTAIRS?

Mona Harrington's warning that we are creating a "new low-wage servant class" of paid care workers—and that this low-wage workforce is made up largely of racial-ethnic women—sounds an important note of caution to feminists who analyze the relationship between gender and care work without paying attention to race-ethnicity and class.[4] However, the "serfdom saved the women's movement" story line is an extension of the narrative of marketization, and shares some of the same problems. The notion that White middle- and upper-class women have transferred their care work onto the backs of racial-ethnic and immigrant women is contradicted by the fact that this racial-ethnic division of reproductive labor existed long before the large-scale entrance of women into the paid labor force. Perhaps even more importantly, this formulation obscures the interrelationships and hierarchies *among* paid care work occupations. Far from being a unidimensional servant class, the paid care labor force is a multilayered interconnecting sector of the economy. And the existence of a low-wage group of care workers, along with the racial-ethnic inequalities found among them, are as much a result of the interactions within that care sector as of larger economic and cultural forces.

Building on the work of Nakano Glenn and Roberts, my historical analysis illustrates that some of the racial-ethnic hierarchies in the care labor market today represent continuities with the divisions that characterized domestic labor in the past.[5] Many of the jobs in which racial-ethnic and immigrant women are most concentrated—nursing aides and orderlies, cleaning, food service, and laundry—are backroom jobs that parallel the work of domestic servants. The concentration of racial-ethnic workers in low-wage care jobs that Harrington highlights has a long history, despite the transformations in the structure of the paid care market. A view that focuses exclusively on nurturant care obscures some of these inequalities, as a perspective that focuses primarily on relationality does not include many of these jobs in an examination of care work. A broad historical view reveals the continuities in patterns of racial-ethnic inequalities between the old servant class and the new one. Like paying for care, exploiting certain groups of racial-ethnic and immigrant women in low-wage paid care occupations is not a new phenomenon.

Exploitation is of course no less problematic because it has a long history, but it certainly must be understood in a different context.

Not all care workers are low-wage workers, and a broad view of paid care illuminates the connections among the histories of a range of care roles. While the assertion that our society does not value care is perhaps an accurate assessment as a general frame, understanding the dynamics of low-wage care work in particular requires a much more nuanced set of tools. As expert care has become the norm, the workers who have made a claim to that expertise have done so largely by placing themselves on one side of a number of dichotomous constructions—skilled versus unskilled, professional versus laborer, spiritual versus menial. The implication is that other workers are doing the unskilled menial labor. And those are the workers who have been placed squarely into the low-wage labor market. While the lived experience of care work does not fit neatly into any of these boxes, these ideological divisions have been reified and linked to material conditions.

Scholars of domestic service have shown that White women who employed domestic servants relied on them to do some of the dirty work of the household. This division of labor preserved White women's femininity, and the distribution of tasks based on race-ethnicity and citizenship was integral to upholding the gendered division of labor.[6] White women employers could be clean, pure, and gentle paragons of domesticity and sexuality only if someone else was scrubbing the floors and emptying the chamber pots.[7] The division between spiritual and menial labor in hospitals and schools reflects similar dynamics. In the early twentieth century, teachers and nurses were constructed as the moral guardians of care, a spiritual role dependent on a particular definition of femininity that was not especially compatible with some of the physical and, for nurses, often gory tasks involved in the work. As the century progressed, cadres of nursing assistants and orderlies took over some of these tasks in the hospital, preserving the role of the nurse as the relational hand of nursing. The auxiliary workers, large numbers of whom were Black and foreign born, were considered to be engaged in the menial labor of health care. In schools, White U.S.-born women dominated the relational role of educating and guiding children. The moral transcendence of the teacher was preserved by relegating to other workers the tasks of feeding the young charges and providing them with clean environments. School janitors and cafeteria workers are also much more likely than teachers to be Black or foreign born. The feminization of certain occupations within paid care has depended on the simultaneous distribution of the "menial" tasks to racial-ethnic workers.

The professionalization of nursing, teaching, and social work also depended on the simultaneous definition of other groups of workers as, respectively, unskilled health-care aides, teaching assistants, and charity workers. Advocates in the fights for recognition of these professions emphasized the ways in which nurses, teachers, and social workers were trained workers with specialized technical, educational, or social science knowledge and skills. Sometimes explicitly and sometimes as an unintended consequence, other workers were the foils for these claims. Susan Reverby is blunt in her assessment of this process in nursing: "The ring of protection drawn around nursing, and the hospital's need for a divided and cheap work force, kept . . . aides from such advancement. Nursing's 'success' in its quest for greater control was built on the limiting and degrading of others."[8] Reverby's description points out two key elements in this process. First, these divisions were drawn deliberately by those working to professionalize nursing. And, second, the creation of a separate unskilled category served the interests of hospitals looking for ways to divide tasks and hire low-wage workers.

The history of paid care demonstrates the need for examining race-ethnicity and citizenship and their interaction with gender. But the data also remind us that we need to combine these analyses with an examination of class. There is no question that racial-ethnic and immigrant women are highly overrepresented among certain occupational groups within the care sector—nannies and housekeepers, auxiliary health-care workers, child-care workers, and cleaning, food, and laundry workers chief among them. And considering the causes and consequences of these concentrations is critical to untangling the care crisis. However, even among these occupations, White U.S.-born workers make up large proportions—45 percent of private household workers; 45 percent of nursing aides, orderlies, and attendants; 55 percent of child-care workers; and 50 percent of cleaning, food, and laundry workers.[9] And within nurturant care work as a whole, White U.S.-born workers are the clear majority. We cannot explain the hierarchies within the care sector and the composition of paid care work by examining only the impact of race-ethnicity and citizenship; our analysis must include socioeconomic inequality as well.

Looking to the Future

Scholars and activists advocating for change in the care sector need to build on nurturant care theory to articulate the labor of care and integrate relationality with other aspects of care work. Further, we must use a class analysis to make a case for economic justice more broadly. Finally, to effectively demonstrate that care should be a social responsibility that requires substantial public investment, scholars need to draw on the idea of reproductive labor to show how important care work is to the continued functioning of society as a whole.

ARTICULATING THE LABOR OF CARE

One of the most important things scholars and activists can do to address the care crisis is develop a framework to articulate the labor of care that does not place nurturance in opposition to the other skills and labor required of paid care workers. Care work is a mix of human relationship, skilled intervention, and plain hard work. Building a vocabulary that adequately captures the whole of care is critical to creating strategies to address the care crisis. In the latter decades of the twentieth century, one of the trends that emerged was the reduction of time for the relational aspects of nurturant care work. In the context of neoliberal restructuring across the economy, workplaces are increasingly the sites of speedup and cost cutting. For businesses that want to get more bang for their buck out of care workers, the relational components of care are the easiest to squeeze. Relationship is unpredictable, not easily measured, and not easily controlled.

Describing and advocating for formal recognition of relational labor as part of paid care work is critical to addressing some of the problematic working conditions care workers now face. Timothy Diamond describes nursing homes in which the labor of CNAs is reduced to a series of physical tasks listed on a chart, relegating to invisibility the unpredictable and constant relational demands on a CNA. But as Diamond explains, those relational demands do not go away.[10] The result is a much heavier workload than CNAs' employers recognize. This scenario finds parallels in the experiences of teachers, nurses, mental health workers, home-care workers, and other care workers in the twenty-first century, and helps explain their difficult working conditions. The structural constraints on relationship also conflict with workers' perceptions of their role and often with their training, adding a layer of frustration and guilt to their daily work experience. Difficult working conditions contribute to high rates of burnout and turnover, two factors that undermine the quality and availability of care. Making relationality visible in the work of care is an important part of advocating for change in the care sector.

At the same time, basing claims for the value of care on relationality, to the exclusion of or in opposition to the other skills and labor involved in paid care, is problematic. Suzanne Gordon, a noted journalist who has chronicled the work of nurses, was once introduced at a conference in the following way: "Suzanne Gordon appreciates us not for our technical wizardry but for what we give of ourselves to our patients." Gordon says she demurred: "I appreciate you for your technical wizardry *and* for what you give of yourself to your patients. And I have to admit, although I would prefer the total package, if I were admitted to an ER and a nurse told me I had a choice between what she gave of herself to me and her technical wizardry I would say please, technical wizardry any day."[11] Gordon shares this anecdote to illustrate how the relational aspects of care work are often framed in contrast to skills, training, and labor—which are actually also very important parts of a care worker's job. Relationship, skills, and labor are not mutually exclusive, and our language needs to reflect that.

This oppositional framing is the legacy of the early process of feminization of many nurturant care occupations. At various points in history, nursing, teaching, and social work advocates sought to differentiate their occupations from male-dominated jobs. Nursing advocates characterized the job of nurses as maintaining the moral character of the hospital and engaging in daily interactions with patients, in contrast to the medical expertise of doctors. When teaching was feminized, the claim was made that teachers needed the capacity to connect with students. And in the face of the rising dominance of psychology, social workers tried to carve out a niche based on their warm and nurturing approach to mental health care and case management. In laying claim to these occupations for women, advocates emphasized their relational demands in contrast to the (presumably male) demands of other similar work. That relational skills were assumed to come naturally to women care workers contributed to rendering them invisible and to their categorization as something other than work.

In the context of economic cost cutting across the board, tying the requirements for care work to the character of women rather than to learned skills was a way to justify lower wages. As the century progressed, claims made for the value of care work tended to reinforce the dichotomy of relationship and skill. While some nurses argued for professionalization on the basis of the skills and labor required by their jobs, others resisted professionalization out of fear that it would undermine the essentially relational nature of their work. Similarly, some child-care workers oppose being labeled educators because they want to retain the caring nature of their jobs. Finding a path for advocacy that escapes this dichotomous thinking and recognizes relationality without reifying it is critical.

A few scholars have begun to articulate the labor of care outside these oppositional discourses. Cameron Macdonald and David Merrill have explored both theoretically and practically how care workers can integrate the language of virtue with the language of skill. They point to the Center for the Childcare Workforce (CCW) as an example of an organization that has worked to escape this false dichotomy. The CCW's Model Work Standards "acknowledge the complexity of childcare jobs which demand education and training, physical and emotional strength, constant vigilance, creativity, intense human interaction every day all day long, a high level of self-esteem and self-confidence in order to instill the same in children, and a commitment to fostering human development in children and the many adults involved in childcare."[12] This statement is an example of an advocacy position that does not adopt an oppositional frame. Valerie Adams and Julie Nelson have developed a model for articulating the labor of nurses in a way that uses "non-dualistic, practice enhancing rhetoric."[13] A well-developed framework that describes care work by integrating relational content with learned skills and physical, intellectual, and emotional labor allows advocates to argue for its value without falling into the traps on either side of the dichotomy between relationality and labor.

When relationality is invisible, workers are not recognized and care is compromised. But when nurturance is the linchpin, care work is associated with the essentialized feminine, reinforcing the feminization of paid care and diminishing its other equally important aspects. We should be able to value relationship without reducing care to the warm and fuzzy. We need a vocabulary that recognizes the relational components of care work and is not constrained by the gendered discourses of morality and motherhood. Only when we have developed this framework will we be able to advocate effectively for structural changes that reward all aspects of care work. A framework that integrates relationality with other aspects of skill and labor also acknowledges the time and energy required by the jobs of care workers, rather than using the rhetoric of relationship to extract extra labor from them. That is, as long as the evidence of relational connection lies in doing things on one's own time or nickel, the relational aspects of care work remain outside job descriptions and therefore uncompensated. Seeing relationship as part of the job rather than as in opposition to the work is the first step toward creating workplace structures that make paid care workers less vulnerable to exploitation and better able to provide quality care.

IT'S (ALSO) THE ECONOMY, STUPID

Bill Clinton's now iconic tagline from the 1992 election season reminds us that amidst all the complicated and competing issues that emerge in politics and policy, keeping the economy front and center is key. Care scholars and activists should heed a similar message. Understanding the unique characteristics of care work is critical, but equally important is examining and challenging the larger socioeconomic structures within which paid care is located. Gender, racial-ethnic, and class hierarchies in paid care reflect a society in which the economic gap between haves and have-nots has widened. Understanding and addressing care inequalities require facing these structural issues head on. Advocacy for care workers must be joined with a larger appeal for a basic minimum standard that should be a right of all workers.

The lowest-paid workers in the paid care sector include home-care aides, personal care attendants, hospital nursing aides, school cafeteria workers, cleaning workers in hospitals and schools, and child-care workers. These workers also often experience difficult working conditions and find few opportunities for advancement, job characteristics they share with low-wage workers across the economy. The last decades of the twentieth century saw a dramatic increase in the overall level of economic inequality in the United States and the expansion of the low-wage workforce.[14]

To resolve the problems of low-wage care work, we must challenge the structure of the labor market as a whole. The process that has led to the separation of tasks considered menial and unskilled from the more professionalized occupations of care is happening across the labor market. Focusing solely on the ways in which society does not value care to explain the low-wage care sector obscures the connections between the professionalization of some paid care occupations and the degradation of others. In an economic structure in which training and credentialing are the keys to recognition, occupational groups that want to advance must show that their labor is skilled. But to define one group of workers as skilled, both advocates and employers simultaneously define another group as unskilled: nurses are not performing the menial (unskilled) tasks of care work but the more advanced health-care tasks that require training; educators are not (unskilled) babysitters or child-care providers but skilled teachers who have been trained to impart knowledge to children. This is the process by which occupations become divided along the lines of skill and wages, and by which organizations can relegate an increasing amount of work to low-wage employees.

As long as we live in a society that accepts a high degree of economic inequality based on training and credentials as markers of skill, the best care advocates and scholars can hope for is to move a particular occupation from one side of the divide to the other. Addressing more broadly the problems of low-wage care work requires challenging the nature and scale of the divide itself. Without denying the market principles of rewarding workers for investment in their human capital, we should establish a reasonable minimum standard of living to which all workers are entitled. Living wages, access to benefits, and opportunities for advancement should be basic rights of workers rather than privileges afforded only to those who succeed in professionalizing their occupations.

Unionization efforts such as the Justice for Janitors campaign provide an important model for advocacy using a framework based on worker rights and social justice. Unions can be instrumental not only in securing adequate compensation and benefits, but also in increasing job security and protecting worker health and safety. These critical issues for low-wage care workers, which may be addressed for certain groups by pursuing professionalization, will be guaranteed for all only by a model that argues for a minimum standard across the board. Among the rights that all workers should be entitled to is the right to care, which includes the opportunity not only to care for one's own health and well-being, but also to participate in care for others. Despite the growth in paid care occupations, families still provide an enormous amount of unpaid care for young children, the elderly, and individuals who are ill or disabled. Acknowledging these near-universal experiences of workers would mean fighting for a range of benefits, including access to health care, paid sick days for workers to care for themselves or for ill family members, paid family leave for families with the need for longer-term absences, and worker-centered scheduling flexibility.[15]

Support for unpaid care is not only key to maintaining a basic standard of living for all workers, but also a critical ingredient in solving the care crisis in the United States. In some cases, unpaid family care and paid care can substitute for one another—but more often, paid care and unpaid care comprise complementary parts of a complex web of care. A family who is caring for an elderly relative at home may depend on visiting nurses or physical therapists for medical advice and treatment, social workers for mental health support and assistance navigating the tangle of social programs, and workers at a local senior center for stimulation and companionship. A teacher can more effectively educate a child whose parents are able to provide adequate nutrition, help with homework, and emotional support.[16] During the twentieth century, as expert care became the norm, the roles of paid workers and unpaid care providers in some cases became more differentiated. A well-functioning system of paid care depends on adequately supported unpaid care—and vice versa. And adequately supporting unpaid care requires providing all workers with basic rights and benefits. In addition, like all workers, low-wage care workers cannot perform their jobs as well when hampered by health problems or unsupported unpaid care demands. Ensuring these workers basic rights and benefits also increases the quality of their work, providing better care in the end.

Although the notion of providing workers with a broadly defined basic set of rights and benefits challenges the way most organizations currently conceptualize labor, in practice it does not have to mean a loss for business. Economists argue that organizations face a series of choices in their quest to achieve efficiency (which for businesses translates into profits). The prevailing model in the last decades of the twentieth century was a "low-road" strategy that emphasized cutting labor costs as much as possible, despite the resulting high turnover and poor-quality work. The alternative "high-road" strategy accepts some increased labor costs in return for higher levels of worker effort and stability.[17] In the short run, adopting a high-road approach requires some investment by government agencies, nonprofit organizations, and for-profit corporations. But in the long run, organizations benefit from having a stable workforce that produces a high-quality product or service. For the care sector, this approach means not only better working conditions for paid care workers but also higher quality care.

Challenging the fundamental structures of work and economic competition in the United States is necessary not only to address the problems of the low-wage care workforce, but also to unravel the gendered and racialized hierarchies in the care sector. The rise of neoliberalism led to a cost-cutting model and a resultant deskilling and speedup of work that has been closely linked to exacerbating gender and racial-ethnic hierarchies in the care sector. Gender and race-ethnicity as well as citizenship have become associated with the divides in our economy. Raising the value of relationality without simultaneously challenging larger labor-market structures could add relationality to the skilled side of the divide—which would move some workers over but leave many behind, especially those whose labor is not included by a nurturant care perspective. In addition, in the context of an economic model that strives to minimize labor costs above all else, any movement to formally recognize the relational components of care work will be difficult.

The government has an important role to play in setting standards for worker protection, compensation, and benefits. Within the care sector, some groups of workers lack even minimal standards of protection. Large numbers of home-care aides, personal care attendants, child-care workers, housecleaners, and domestic workers have no formal legal protections as workers either because their occupations are not covered by labor legislation or because of the informal status of their employment arrangements.[18] Bringing these workers under the umbrella of legal protection is critical. Government must also strengthen legislation to protect the right of workers to unionize.[19] And in the absence of a large-scale voluntary shift in organizational culture, government intervention through regulation, incentives, and support will be important in motivating employers to move to a high-road approach. Without this kind of shift in the overall structure of the labor market, we cannot hope to fully address the problems of the low-wage care workforce.

PUBLIC INVESTMENT, SOCIAL RESPONSIBILITY

Nurturant care theory focuses on the labor process of care work and its relational content. Although at its most broad, this frame includes a wide range of occupations that are relational in nature, I agree with Kari Waerness that the most pressing focus for feminists and policy makers should be care for dependents, which I have argued lies at the intersection of reproductive labor and nurturant care.[20] Nurturant care theory emphasizes the ethical responsibility of a society to care for dependents—and by extension for their caregivers. But a focus on reproductive labor emphasizes the ways in which providing that care supports the functioning of our families, our communities, and our economy. Combining these two perspectives illuminates the idea that a sense of social responsibility for care should come both out of a sense of moral obligation to others and out of the self-interest of every member of a society.

Randy Albelda, Nancy Folbre, and I have used the metaphor of human infrastructure to describe the essential role of care work in a society: "Care work is not just a cornerstone of our economy—it is a rock-bottom foundation. Care work provides the basis for our human infrastructure, and we need it to navigate through life as surely as we need our roads and bridges."[21] While the nature of what care is "needed" at any given moment in history may vary, every society has a set of care tasks that must be performed in order for everyone to go on working, volunteering, and being part of communities.

This characteristic of care—its position as foundational to the economy and the larger society—is an important argument for why care should be of concern to all. But it also points to a critical way in which paid care work is unique in the labor market. When someone gets good care, the benefits of that care reach far beyond that individual. For example, a child who receives high-quality child care and education may grow up to be a more productive worker, a better spouse, and a stronger community leader. The parents of that child are able to contribute to the labor force because the child is being cared for. The benefits of care are diffuse, which makes it problematic for a market system based on individual exchange.

Because the provision of care creates what economists call "positive externalities"—the benefits to all those other people besides the individual directly involved in the exchange—left to the market, care will be underproduced and costly. If we as a society want to ensure we have enough good care, we have to invest public dollars in care. We understand this need when we invest in roads and bridges, and our human infrastructure requires the same kind of support. In addition, it is uniquely difficult to define and monitor quality in care work. Consumers in need of care who lack clear information cannot make the kinds of choices that drive markets to meet demand, and the quality of care can be undermined. These characteristics of care work mean that we need public investment and government oversight of care in order to be sure not only that paid care workers have decent jobs, but also that there is enough care for everyone. Focusing on the labor process of care without considering its position in the economic structure does not clearly identify the ways in which care must be a social responsibility.

F. Scott Fitzgerald famously wrote that "the test of a first-rate intelligence is the ability to hold two opposed ideas in mind at the same time and still retain the ability to function."[22] The history of paid care work is full of contradictions and complexities. We must resist the urge to simplify this history into neatly tied-up narratives. Addressing the contemporary care crisis and the multiple layers of inequalities both reflected by and perpetuated in the structure of the paid care labor force will require sustained dialogue across all sorts of boundaries—academic disciplines, occupational groups, paid and unpaid care work, race-ethnicity, gender, and class. Let's get to it.

Appendix: Data and Methods

Data

The Integrated Public Use Microdata Series (IPUMS) project at the University of Minnesota was designed to facilitate historical analysis of decennial U.S. Census data.[1] For each year in the series, IPUMS provides access to a computerized sample drawn from the entire population of census respondents. The IPUMS datasets are very large, high-precision, national random samples of the U.S. population. U.S. Census data include many detailed labor-force variables as well as information about gender, race-ethnicity, and immigration status at an individual level.

Table A.1 provides labor-force sample sizes for the IPUMS datasets used in this project, which span the period 1900 to 2007. For the decades between

Table A.1.
Sample Sizes for IPUMS Datasets

Year	*Labor Force N*
1900	274,700
1910	362,300
1920	401,500
1930	468,900
1940	541,300
1950	687,400
1960	699,700
1970	827,500
1980	1,057,500
1990	1,236,200
2000	1,366,700
2007	1,487,200

Sources: The samples for 1900–2000 are from the U.S. Census. The sample for 2007 is from the American Community Survey.

1900 and 2000, samples are drawn from the decennial U.S. census; the 2007 sample is drawn from the American Community Survey (ACS), an annual survey designed by the U.S. Census Bureau to provide ongoing data comparable to that collected by the decennial census. The datasets used in this project have a sample density of 1-in-100, meaning that the sample includes a randomly selected 1 percent of cases from the total U.S. Census (or ACS) population. The resulting sample sizes range from 366,000 to over 2.8 million cases. Unless otherwise stated in the text, I have limited my analysis to the paid labor force. The size of the labor-force samples ranges from about 275,000 to over 1.4 million cases.

For any project involving data that range over a period of one hundred years, comparability is a major concern. Since the goal of the IPUMS project is to facilitate historical analysis, comparability issues have been addressed in a number of ways. First, IPUMS provides extensive documentation of potential comparability problems with particular variables. In addition, for many variables, IPUMS has assigned uniform codes across decades. For example, the coding scheme for the variable recording an individual's occupation has changed significantly over the history of the U.S. Census. Every IPUMS sample contains a new variable recoding an individual's occupation according to the 1950 categorization scheme, and samples since 1950 include an additional occupation variable that is matched to the 1990 coding. In all cases, the original variable is preserved, allowing for accurate historical comparison without the loss of detailed information provided by contemporary codes. While this process does not eliminate all comparability issues, IPUMS has created a system that allows unprecedented levels of consistency in historical analysis with such a wealth of data.

Variables Used in the Analysis

Person weight (PERWT) is a weighting variable included in every IPUMS dataset. I used this variable to generate national population estimates from the samples.

Labor force status (LABFORCE) is a dichotomous variable that indicates whether the individual was part of the labor force—working or seeking work. The universe for this variable is limited to persons sixteen and older between 1900 and 1930 and 1980 and 2007, and fourteen and older between 1940 and 1970.

Occupation (OCC1950, OCC1990, and OCC) is measured in three different variables. Each sample contains a variable that categorizes occupation into the contemporary occupational coding system (which has changed each census year). Each IPUMS dataset also contains a standardized occupation variable that categorizes the occupation of each individual according to the 1950 coding scheme. After 1950, the samples include an additional standardized variable based on the 1990 coding scheme. These standardized variables permit more consistent historical comparison, and I have used them extensively in the analysis. I also draw on the contemporary occupation variable to provide more information about the particularities of the labor force in any given year.

Industry (IND1950, IND1990, and IND) is measured in three variables that parallel the occupational variables. I have used these codes in a similar way. Every individual in the labor force is assigned both an occupational code (that identifies the kind of work that person is engaged in) and an industrial code (that captures the location or type of workplace where the work is happening).

Sex is a dichotomous variable contained in every IPUMS dataset.

Race-ethnicity is a measure for which I created a new variable combining three variables available in the IPUMS samples: race (RACE), Hispanic origin (HISPANIC), and birthplace (BPL). The U.S. Census identifies people according to detailed racial categorizations that vary from year to year. The IPUMS samples contain a standardized variable that categorizes individuals into between five and nine racial categories. Since 1980, the census has included a separate question asking individuals to identify if they are of Hispanic origin. IPUMS has also imputed values to a Hispanic origin variable previous to 1980 based on a combination of eight criteria including birthplace, parental birthplace, and Spanish surname.[2] Every sample also contains a variable (BPL) that records the birthplace of each individual (by country or by U.S. state). I combined information from these three variables to create a race-ethnicity and immigration measure with the following mutually exclusive categories: White (non-Hispanic) U.S. born; Black (non-Hispanic) U.S. born; Hispanic U.S. born; Other (non-Hispanic) U.S. born; and foreign born. Most of the analysis relies on this new variable, although I use BPL to provide additional details about the origin of the foreign-born population.

Marital status (MARST) provides information not only about legal marital status but also about whether the spouse is present or absent.

Children ever born (CHBORN) records the number of children born to a respondent.

Age (AGE) reports the person's age in years as of the last birthday.

Relationship to household head (RELATE) describes an individual's relationship to the person listed as head of household by the U.S. Census. I used this variable to identify live-in domestic servants.

Wage levels were reported using a variable that measures earned income (INCEARN), which is a total of income earned from wages or from a person's own business or farm in the past year. For domestic servants, wage levels were calculated only for full-time year-round workers. Full-time year-round workers were defined as those who reported working at least thirty-five hours of the preceding week (using the variable HRSWORK1) and at least fifty weeks of the preceding year (using the variable WKSWORK1).

Explanation of Figures

Figures 2.1 through 2.4 use OCC1950 to identify those coded as housekeepers, private household; laundresses, private household; and private household workers (n.e.c.). "N.e.c." refers to workers "not elsewhere classified," a more general category of private household workers much larger than the category that includes workers identified specifically as housekeepers or laundresses

Figure 2.5 uses IND1990 to identify those coded as working in the industrial category private households, and then identifies within that group workers whose occupations are coded housekeepers, maids, butlers, stewards, and lodging quarters cleaners; private household cleaners and servants; and child-care workers. In 2000 and 2007, there are no workers identified in the private household cleaners and servants category (due to the change in coding that does not allow these workers to be separately identified as an occupational category in that year). In those years, these workers were subsumed into the larger category of housekeepers, etc.

Figures 3.1 and 3.2 use OCC1950 to identify nurturant care workers, a category that includes the following occupational titles: chiropractors; clergymen; dentists; nurses, professional; nurses, student; optometrists; osteopaths; physicians and surgeons; recreation and group workers; religious workers; social and welfare workers, except group; psychologists; teachers; therapists and healers; attendants, physicians' and dentists' office; attendants, hospital and other institution; attendants, professional and personal service; midwives; and practical nurses.

Figures 3.3 through 3.6 use OCC1950 to identify workers in specific health-care occupations. All occupational titles are listed on the figure legend as they appear in the U.S. Census category names.

Figures 3.7 and 3.8 use OCC1950 to identify workers reported as teachers. Although later iterations of the U.S. Census allow differentiation among kinds of teachers, in the OCC1950 codes all teachers are grouped in a single category.

Figures 3.9 through 3.12 use OCC1950 to identify workers in specific social service occupations. All occupational titles are listed on the figure legend as they appear in the U.S. Census category names. Although the term "clergymen" is outdated and has since been changed in the census categories, I use it in order to maintain the consistency of representing census categories as they were recorded at the time. In Figure 3.9, in 1940 an additional small category of workers (recreation and group workers) was folded into the category of social workers rather than separately identified. As a result of this aberration, the growth in the number of social workers between 1930 and 1940 is an overestimation, and the rate of growth between 1940 and 1950 is an underestimation. Although a category of psychologists is identifiable in 1900 through 1950, the numbers are so small as to be unreliable. Psychiatrists cannot be identified separately from the larger category of physicians.

Figures 4.1 and 4.2 use OCC1990 to identify nurturant care workers. "Health care workers" includes physicians; dentists; optometrists; podiatrists; other health and therapy; registered nurses; licensed practical nurses; health aides, except nursing; nursing aides, orderlies, and attendants; respiratory therapists; occupational therapists; physical therapists; speech therapists; therapists (n.e.c.); physicians' assistants; dental hygienists; and dental assistants.

"Teachers" includes kindergarten and earlier school teachers; primary school teachers; secondary school teachers; special education teachers; teachers (n.e.c.); and teachers' aides.

"Mental health and social services" includes social workers; psychologists; vocational and educational counselors; recreation workers; welfare service aides; and clergy and religious workers.

"Child-care workers" includes the single category by the same name. Child-care workers cannot be separately identified in 1950. The category identified by OCC1990 as child-care workers includes some of the workers identified by OCC1950 as private household workers (n.e.c.), so these numbers show some overlap with the calculations in figures 2.1 through 2.4. Figure 2.5 also uses the OCC1990 category of child-care workers and so also shows some overlap. The overlap is as large as 300,000 workers in 1960 and as small as 125,000 workers in 2000.

Figures 4.3 through 4.6 use OCC1990 to identify workers in specific health-care occupations. All occupational titles are listed on the figure legend as they appear in the U.S. Census category names.

Figure 4.7 uses OCC1990 to identify specific categories of teachers and child-care workers. "Primary and secondary school teachers" includes primary school teachers, secondary school teachers, special education teachers, and teachers (n.e.c.). Inconsistencies in enumerator instructions and the large number of teachers (n.e.c.) make it difficult to create reliable estimates of the overall numbers of teachers in each of these categories. Kindergarten and preschool teachers and child-care workers cannot be separately identified before 1960 and 1970 respectively.

Figures 4.8 and 4.9 use OCC1990 to identify workers in education and child-care occupations. All occupational titles are listed on the figure legend as they appear in the U.S. Census category names. Note that these calculations exclude the large number of workers in the teachers (n.e.c.) category. While the exclusion is likely to have less impact on the proportional representation of various demographic groups than on overall counts, there may be some inaccuracy in these estimates due to the omission.

Figures 4.10 through 4.13 use OCC1990 to identify workers in specific mental health and social service occupations. All occupational titles are listed on the figure legend as they appear in the U.S. Census category names.

Figures 5.1 and 5.2 use OCC1950 to identify cleaning, food, and laundry workers outside of private households. "Janitors and cleaners" includes charwomen and cleaners; housekeepers and stewards, except private household; and janitors and sextons.

"Food preparation and service" includes cooks, except private household; counter and fountain workers; waiters and waitresses; and service workers, except private household (n.e.c.). This last category includes very few workers in the earlier years of the century. In the years following 1950, as food service and food preparation workers are enumerated in more detailed categories, a comparison of the OCC1950 category of service workers, except private household, reveals that the majority of these workers are involved in some form of food preparation or service.

"Laundry and dry cleaning" includes laundry and dry cleaning operatives.

Figure 5.3 uses IND in the 2007 American Community Survey sample to identify workers within the industry code hospitals. The variable OCC is then used to identify particular occupational groups within this industry. All occupational titles represent U.S. Census categories except "cleaning workers" and "food preparation and service." "Cleaning workers" includes first-line supervisors of janitors and cleaners; janitors and building cleaners; and maids and housekeeping cleaners.

"Food preparation and service" includes chefs and head cooks; first-line managers of food preparation and serving workers; cooks; food preparation workers; combined food preparation and serving workers, including fast food; counter attendant, cafeteria, food concession, and coffee shop; waiters and waitresses; food servers, nonrestaurant; miscellaneous food preparation and serving related workers; dishwashers; and host and hostesses, restaurant, lounge, and coffee shop.

Notes

Introduction

1. For more discussion of this, see Mignon Duffy, "Reproducing Labor Inequalities: Challenges for Feminists Conceptualizing Care at the Intersections of Gender, Race, and Class," *Gender and Society* 19 (February 2005): 66–82; and Evelyn Nakano Glenn, "From Servitude to Service Work: Historical Continuities in the Racial Division of Paid Reproductive Labor," *Signs: Journal of Women in Culture and Society* 18 (Autumn 1992): 1–43.
2. For examples of this perspective, see Janet Chafetz, "The Gender Division of Labor and the Reproduction of Female Disadvantage," *Journal of Family Issues* 9, no. 1 (1988): 108–131; and Heidi Hartmann, "Capitalism, Patriarchy, and Job Segregation by Sex," *Signs: Journal of Women in Culture and Society* 1, no. 3, pt. 2 (1976): 137–169.
3. Arlie Hochschild, *The Second Shift* (New York: Viking, 1989).
4. Nakano Glenn, "From Servitude to Service Work," 3.
5. Arlie Hochschild, *The Commercialization of Intimate Life: Notes from Home and Work* (Berkeley: University of California Press, 2003), 214.
6. Deborah Stone, "Caring by the Book," in *Care Work: Gender, Labor, and the Welfare State*, ed. Madonna Harrington Meyer (New York: Routledge, 2000), 89.
7. Caitlin Flanagan, "How Serfdom Saved the Women's Movement: Dispatches from the Nanny Wars," *Atlantic Monthly*, March 2004, 109–130; Mona Harrington, *Care and Equality: Inventing a New Family Politics* (New York: Knopf, 1999), 21.
8. For additional discussion of the importance of historical sociology in understanding inequalities, see Teresa Amott and Julie Matthaei, *Race, Gender, and Work: A Multi-cultural Economic History of Women in the United States* (Boston: South End Press, 1996), 5; and Alice Kessler-Harris, *A Woman's Wage: Historical Meanings and Social Consequences* (Lexington: University Press of Kentucky, 1990), 488.
9. Steven Ruggles, Matthew Sobek, Trent Alexander, Catherine A. Fitch, Ronald Goeken, Patricia Kelly Hall, Miriam King, and Chad Ronnander, *Integrated Public Use Microdata Series: Version 4.0* [Machine-readable database]. Minneapolis: Minnesota Population Center [producer and distributor], 2009. For more details, see www.ipums.org.
10. Nakano Glenn, "From Servitude to Service Work," 115. See also Barbara Laslett and Johanna Brenner, "Gender and Social Reproduction: Historical Perspectives," *American Sociological Review* 15 (1989): 381–404.
11. Kessler-Harris, *A Woman's Wage*, 488.
12. Nakano Glenn, "From Servitude to Service Work," 41.

Chapter 1   Conceptualizing Care

1. Concurring opinion in *Jacobellis v. Ohio* (1964).
2. Francesca Cancian and Stacey Oliker, *Caring and Gender* (Thousand Oaks, Calif.: Pine Forge Press, 2000), 2.
3. The label "nurturant care" is not used by all scholars in this field. While this group of scholars may use the language of "care" more generally, I use the "nurturant care" label to distinguish this particular understanding of relational care from other definitions of care work. I borrow the term "nurturance" from Paula England, *Comparable Worth: Theories and Evidence* (New York: Aldine de Gruyter, 1992).
4. For a more detailed discussion of the theoretical and practical limitations of using a nurturance definition of care, see Mignon Duffy, "Reproducing Labor Inequalities: Challenges for Feminists Conceptualizing Care at the Intersections of Gender, Race, and Class," *Gender and Society* 19 (February 2005): 66–82.
5. For detailed documentation on this bifurcation of activities, see Jeanne Boydston, *Home and Work: Housework, Wages, and the Ideology of Labor in the Early Republic* (New York: Oxford University Press, 1990).
6. Friedrich Engels, *The Origins of the Family, Private Property, and the State* (New York: International Publishers, 1972 [1884]).
7. See Mariarosa Dalla Costa, *The Power of Women and the Subversion of the Community* (Bristol, U.K.: Falling Wall Press, 1972); Karen V. Hansen and Ilene J. Philipson, *Women, Class, and the Feminist Imagination: A Socialist-Feminist Reader* (Philadelphia: Temple University Press, 1990); Heidi Hartmann, "Capitalism, Patriarchy, and Job Segregation by Sex," *Signs: Journal of Women in Culture and Society* 1, no. 3, pt. 2 (1976): 137–169; Wally Secombe, "The Housewife and Her Labour under Capitalism," *New Left Review* 83 (1974): 3–24; Barbara Laslett and Johanna Brenner, "Gender and Social Reproduction: Historical Perspectives," *American Sociological Review* 15 (1989): 381–404.
8. See Cancian and Oliker, *Caring and Gender*, for a nice discussion of the naturalization of women's caring labor.
9. Arlene Kaplan Daniels, "Invisible Work," *Social Problems* 35, no. 5 (1987): 408.
10. Evelyn Nakano Glenn, "From Servitude to Service Work: Historical Continuities in the Racial Division of Paid Reproductive Labor," *Signs: Journal of Women in Culture and Society* 18 (Autumn 1992): 115. See also Laslett and Brenner, "Gender and Social Reproduction."
11. See Carol Gilligan, *In a Different Voice: Psychological Theory and Women's Development* (Cambridge, Mass.: Harvard University Press, 1982), for the origins of this strain of analysis in psychology. Sara Ruddick, *Maternal Thinking: Toward a Politics of Peace* (Boston: Beacon Press, 2002 [1995]), further developed an idea of "maternal thinking" unique to those engaged in the practice of mothering. Nel Noddings, Suzanne Gordon, and Patricia Benner, eds., *Caregiving: Readings in Knowledge, Practice, Ethics, and Politics* (Philadelphia: University of Pennsylvania Press, 1996), also discuss the practice of care and its impact on those who do it.
12. See Joan Tronto, *Moral Boundaries: A Political Argument for an Ethic of Caring* (New York: Routledge, 1993); Diemut Grace Bubeck, "Justice and the Labor of Care," in *The Subject of Care: Feminist Perspectives on Dependency*, ed. Eva Feder Kittay and Ellen K. Feder (Lanham, Md.: Rowman and Littlefield, 2002), 160–185; Deimut Elisabet Bubeck, *Care, Gender, and Justice* (Oxford: Clarendon Press, 1995); Eva Feder Kittay, *Love's Labor: Essays on Women, Equality, and Dependency* (New York: Routledge, 1999); Nel Noddings, *Starting at Home: Caring and Social Policy* (Berkeley: University of California Press, 2002); and Noddings et al., *Caregiving*.

13. See Nancy Folbre, *The Invisible Heart: Economics and Family Values* (New York: New Press, 2001); and Nancy Folbre and Julie A. Nelson, "For Love or Money— Or Both?" *Journal of Economic Perspectives* 14, no. 4 (2000): 123–140.

14. See essays in Nancy J. Hirschmann and Ulrike Liebert, eds., *Women and Welfare: Theory and Practice in the United States and Europe* (New Brunswick, N.J.: Rutgers University Press, 2001); Linda Gordon, ed., *Women, the State, and Welfare* (Madison: University of Wisconsin Press, 1990); and Theda Skocpol, *Social Policy in the United States: Future Policy in Historical Perspective* (Princeton: Princeton University Press, 1995). Also see June Axinn and Herman Levin, *Social Welfare: A History of the American Response to Need* (New York: Longman, 1992), for a history of the distrust of dependency in U.S. social welfare.

15. Joan Tronto, "Who Cares? Public and Private Caring and the Rethinking of Citizenship," in *Women and Welfare: Theory and Practice in the United States and Europe,* ed. Nancy J. Hirschmann and Ulrike Liebert (New Brunswick, N.J.: Rutgers University Press, 2001), 71.

16. See Martha Albertson Fineman, "Dependencies," in *Women and Welfare: Theory and Practice in the United States and Europe,* ed. Nancy J. Hirschmann and Ulrike Liebert (New Brunswick, N.J.: Rutgers University Press, 2001), 23–37; and Tronto, *Moral Boundaries.* Other authors have shown that the very concepts of need and dependency have changed over time and are historically contingent ideas rather than universal categories. See Nancy Fraser and Linda Gordon, "A Genealogy of Dependency: Tracing a Keyword of the US Welfare State," *Signs: Journal of Women in Culture and Society* 19 (Winter 1994): 309–336; and Viviana A. Rotman Zelizer, *Pricing the Priceless Child: The Changing Social Value of Children* (New York: Basic Books, 1985).

17. Joan Tronto and Berenice Fisher, "Toward a Feminist Theory of Caring," in *Circles of Care: Work and Identity in Women's Lives,* ed. Emily K. Abel and Margaret K. Nelson (Albany: State University of New York Press, 1990), 35–62.

18. Ibid., 40.

19. Kari Waerness, "The Rationality of Caring," in *Caregiving: Readings in Knowledge, Practice, Ethics, and Politics,* ed. Suzanne Gordon, Patricia Benner, and Nel Noddings (Philadelphia: University of Pennsylvania Press, 1996), 235. Tronto also acknowledges the importance of these differences in Tronto, "Who Cares?"

20. See Fineman, "Dependencies," 28.

21. For more on this argument see Fineman, "Dependencies"; Eva Feder Kittay, "From Welfare to a Public Ethic of Care," in *Women and Welfare: Theory and Practice in the United States and Europe,* ed. Nancy J. Hirschmann and Ulrike Liebert (New Brunswick, N.J.: Rutgers University Press, 2001), 38–64; Bubeck, "Justice and the Labor of Care"; and Tronto, "Who Cares?"

22. Cancian and Oliker, *Caring and Gender,* 2.

23. See Timothy Diamond, *Making Gray Gold: Narratives of Nursing Home Care* (Chicago: University of Chicago Press, 1995); and Deborah Stone, "Caring by the Book," in *Care Work: Gender, Labor, and the Welfare State,* ed. Madonna Harrington Meyer (New York: Routledge, 2000), 89–111.

24. Arlie Hochschild, *The Managed Heart: Commercialization of Human Feeling* (Berkeley: University of California Press, 2003 [1983]), 7.

25. See Amy Wharton, "The Sociology of Emotional Labor," *Annual Review of Sociology* 35 (2009), 147–165, for a discussion of the links between care work scholarship and the concept of emotional labor.

26. Dorothy Roberts, "Spiritual and Menial Housework," *Yale Journal of Law and Feminism* 9, no. 51 (1997): 52.

27. Nakano Glenn, "From Servitude to Service Work," 32.

28. For a discussion of racialized notions of care and motherhood in the formation of the U.S. welfare state, see Linda Gordon, ed., *Women, the State, and Welfare* (Madison: University of Wisconsin Press, 1990), especially Barbara J. Nelson, "The Origins of the Two-Channel Welfare State: Workmen's Compensation and Mothers' Aid." Also see Sherry Wexler, "Work/Family Policy Stratification: The Examples of Family Support and Family Leave," *Qualitative Sociology* 20, no. 2 (1997): 311–322.

29. Paula England, Michelle Budig, and Nancy Folbre, "Wages of Virtue: The Relative Pay of Care Work," *Social Problems* 49, no. 4 (2002): 455–473. Although I used the criteria England and her colleagues developed, I made my own decisions about which occupations met the criteria. Because I drew on data from multiple years, I used a number of different sets of occupational codes. For each year, I chose occupations from the occupational list that I judged met the criteria. Where I had questions, I consulted the *Dictionary of Occupational Titles* for descriptions of job responsibilities of particular groups of workers. I thank Paula England for being willing to answer my questions as I went through the decision-making process.

30. Laslett and Brenner, "Gender and Social Reproduction," and Nakano Glenn, "From Servitude to Service Work." I relied heavily on Nakano Glenn's categorization in her article when making coding decisions. I thank Evelyn Nakano Glenn for responding to my queries as I went through that decision-making process.

31. Practically, the groups of workers not included in my analysis that England and her colleagues do include are postsecondary teachers and librarians. Although we may be approaching a time when a college education is considered socially necessary, we are not there yet, so I have limited my discussion to activities that involve care of children and youth rather than education more broadly defined.

Chapter 2   Domestic Workers: Many Hands, Heavy Work

1. Barbara Ryan, *Love, Wages, Slavery: The Literature of Servitude in the United States* (Urbana: University of Illinois Press, 2006), 17.

2. Marilyn Richardson, *Maria W. Stewart: America's First Black Woman Political Writer* (Bloomington: Indiana University Press, 1987), 47.

3. These statistics appear in Daniel E. Sutherland, *Americans and Their Servants: Domestic Service in the United States from 1800 to 1920* (Baton Rouge: Louisiana State University Press, 1981).

4. It is important to note that slaves and indentured servants had been part of reproductive labor for the entire history of the United States, so nonfamily members' involvement in care work has a much longer history than I discuss here, and many of the patterns of inequality I trace have roots as far back as slavery.

5. Sutherland, *Americans and Their Servants*, 11.

6. Several authors have described in detail the daily labor of domestic servants. In particular, see David M. Katzman, *Seven Days a Week: Women and Domestic Service in Industrializing America* (Urbana: University of Illinois Press, 1981). For descriptions of this work in the nineteenth and early twentieth centuries, see Faye E. Dudden, *Serving Women: Household Service in Nineteenth-Century America* (Middletown, Conn.: Wesleyan University Press, 1983); and Sutherland, *Americans and Their Servants*. For a description of a slightly later period in rural areas, see Karen V. Hansen, *Taking Back the Day: The Historical Recovery of Women's Household Work Experience* (M.A. thesis, University of California at Santa Barbara, 1979).

7. See Dudden, *Serving Women*, for a description of the less rigid boundaries that characterized hiring help in the early nineteenth century. See Hansen, *Taking*

Back the Day, for a description of servants working alongside the women and children of the house in early twentieth-century rural areas.

8. Dudden, *Serving Women*.

9. For a description of the evolution of the domestic service model, see ibid.

10. See Jacqueline Jones, *Labor of Love, Labor of Sorrow: Black Women, Work, and the Family, from Slavery to the Present* (New York: Vintage Books, 1985), for an excellent analysis of the labor of Black women from slavery through the twentieth century.

11. For a discussion of the changes in family ideology, see Dudden, *Serving Women*; and Jeanne Boydston, *Home and Work: Housework, Wages, and the Ideology of Labor in the Early Republic* (New York: Oxford University Press, 1990).

12. For a discussion of these practices in the context of a shift from hired girls to domestic servants, see Dudden, *Serving Women*. Sutherland, in *Americans and Their Servants*, also talks about the symbolic gestures meant to reinforce class boundaries. In particular he identifies uniforms, architecture (e.g., the use of the back door), separate eating spaces, and the use of separate china as means to minimize contact between family and servants.

13. See Hansen, *Taking Back the Day*; Dudden, *Serving Women*; and Sutherland, *Americans and Their Servants*. For more discussion on why the hired-girl model persisted longer in rural areas, see Genevieve Leslie, "Domestic Service in Canada, 1880–1920," in *Women at Work, Ontario, 1850–1930*, ed. Janice Acton, Penny Goldsmith, and Bonnie Shepard (Toronto: Canadian Women's Educational Press, 1974), 71–126. Leslie points to the greater need for help, the more difficult work, the lower wages, and the increased likelihood that the hired girl would be a friend or neighbor.

14. This number is almost certainly an underestimation. Many who took temporary domestic work as hired girls probably did not report the occupation of domestic service. Furthermore, this number includes only the labor force, and therefore excludes anyone under sixteen. In rural areas where the hired-girl model persisted, many hired girls were quite young women. For more on this point, see Katzman, *Seven Days a Week*.

15. The statistical breakdowns in this section rely on an analysis using the variables BPL and MARST, measuring birthplace and marital status, respectively.

16. Several scholars have noted the transitional nature of domestic service during this time. In particular see Dudden, *Serving Women*, and Sutherland, *Americans and Their Servants*.

17. Sutherland, *Americans and Their Servants*.

18. I calculated these statistics using the variable RELATE, which captures the relationship of each individual in the household to the household head.

19. The decline in absolute numbers of domestic servants in 1920 is the first in a hundred years of U.S. Census data collection, and is followed by another period of increasing numbers. This decline has been partially attributed to fluctuations in data collection, in particular to differences in enumerator instructions dealing with housewives in 1920. Katzman, however, has argued that the decline may also reflect a real temporary downturn. See Katzman, *Seven Days a Week*, 48, for more information.

20. Katzman, in *Seven Days a Week*, discusses these shifts in the supply of domestic servants.

21. For more information on changing immigration laws in this time period, see Elliott Robert Barkan, *And Still They Come: Immigrants and American Society, 1920 to the 1990s* (Wheeling, W.Va.: H. Davidson, 1996).

22. See Sutherland, *Americans and Their Servants*; Leslie, "Domestic Service in Canada, 1880–1920"; Ruth Schwartz Cowan, *More Work for Mother: The Ironies of Household Technology from the Open Hearth to the Microwave* (New York: Basic Books, 1993); and Phyllis M. Palmer, *Domesticity and Dirt: Housewives and Domestic Servants in the United States, 1920–1945* (Philadelphia: Temple University Press, 1990).

23. Cowan, *More Work for Mother*.

24. See Sutherland, *Americans and Their Servants*; and Leslie, "Domestic Service in Canada, 1880–1920."

25. See Stephanie Coontz, *The Way We Never Were: American Families and the Nostalgia Trap* (New York: Basic Books, 1992); and Cowan, *More Work for Mother*.

26. For a history of the social construction of childhood, see Viviana A. Rotman Zelizer, *Pricing the Priceless Child: The Changing Social Value of Children* (New York: Basic Books, 1985), and Philippe Ariès, *Centuries of Childhood: A Social History of Family Life* (New York: Knopf, 1962).

27. Cowan, in *More Work for Mother*, has argued that while technological and ideological changes for women in this era decreased the household labor force, the net effect was actually an increase in the amount of unpaid reproductive labor expected from women. Hansen, in *Taking Back the Day*, makes the argument that in the early twentieth century, the size of the household labor force was significantly reduced, increasing the burden on individual women. She cites a study by Vanek that shows that the average full-time housewife in 1924 spent fifty-two hours a week doing household work, compared to fifty-five hours in 1965.

28. For fascinating oral histories of Black women domestic workers who participated in the "great migration" of Blacks from the rural South to the urban North in the early twentieth century, see Elizabeth Clark-Lewis, *Living In, Living Out: African American Domestics and the Great Migration* (New York: Kodansha, 1996).

29. See Judith Rollins, *Between Women: Domestics and Their Employers* (Philadelphia: Temple University Press, 1985). Pierrette Hondagneu-Sotelo, in *Doméstica: Immigrant Workers Cleaning and Caring in the Shadows of Affluence* (Berkeley: University of California Press, 2001), uses the term "occupational ghetto" to describe the severe constraints on mobility for Black female domestics during the 1950s. On regional variations, see Evelyn Nakano Glenn, "From Servitude to Service Work: Historical Continuities in the Racial Division of Paid Reproductive Labor," *Signs: Journal of Women in Culture and Society* 18 (Autumn 1992): 1–43; and Evelyn Nakano Glenn, *Issei, Nisei, Warbride: Three Generations of Japanese-American Women in Domestic Service* (Philadelphia: Temple University Press, 1986).

30. See Palmer, *Domesticity and Dirt*; Ryan, *Love, Wages, Slavery*; and Sutherland, *Americans and Their Servants*.

31. Sutherland, *Americans and Their Servants*.

32. Palmer, *Domesticity and Dirt*.

33. For descriptions of the conditions of domestic workers at midcentury, see Rollins, *Between Women*; Mary Romero, *Maid in the U.S.A.* (New York: Routledge, 1992); and Dorothy Roberts, "Spiritual and Menial Housework," *Yale Journal of Law and Feminism* 9 (1997): 51–80.

34. See Hondagneu-Sotelo, *Doméstica*.

35. While it is certain that these numbers do not fully capture the extent of domestic service, they are good estimates of the trend direction and overall magnitude. The U.S. Census Bureau has improved its data collection over time, implementing efforts to include immigrants as well as informal economic arrangements, so any undercount of these groups should not be greater in later than in earlier years. See

Karen Woodrow-Lafield, "Undocumented Residents in the United States in 1990: Issues of Uncertainty in Quantification," *International Migration Review* 32, no. 1 (1998): 145–173.

36. Teresa Amott and Julie Matthaei, *Race, Gender, and Work: A Multicultural Economic History of Women in the United States* (Boston: South End Press, 1996), gives detailed accounts of the movement of various racial-ethnic groups of women in and out of different occupations.

37. This term appears in Lewis A. Coser, "Servants: The Obsolescence of an Occupational Role," *Social Forces* 52 (1973): 31–40.

38. See Hondagneu-Sotelo, *Doméstica*, on cooking; on the transformation of health care from domestic labor to hospital care, see Paul Starr, *The Social Transformation of American Medicine* (New York: Basic Books, 1982), and Susan Reverby, *Ordered to Care: The Dilemma of American Nursing, 1850–1945* (Cambridge: Cambridge University Press, 1987). Chapters 3 and 4 in this volume describe the development of these care industries.

39. For more information on this migration, see Barkan, *And Still They Come.*

40. It is not possible to use U.S. Census data to obtain a directly comparable number for 1900, as at that timethe universe for the variable indicating whether or not a woman had a child was limited to married women—and in 1900 very few domestic servants, especially those who were immigrants, were married.

41. This term appears in Arlie Russell Hochschild, "Importing Motherhood: The Global Nanny Chain," *American Prospect* 11, no. 4 (2000): 32–36. For more on the global migration of care workers, see Rhacel S. Parreñas, *Servants of Globalization: Women, Migration, and Domestic Work* (Stanford: Stanford University Press, 2001); and Hondagneu-Sotelo, *Doméstica.* In some cases the chain gets extended even further: the U.S. domestic sends money home, which allows her own family to hire care for her children, which requires the caretaker to provide alternate care for her own children.

42. Hondagneu-Sotelo, in *Doméstica*, finds that most live-in nanny/housekeepers have been in the United States for fewer than five years. Although new immigrants with no housing may initially find a live-in position attractive, the conditions of live-in work prompt most of them to move into live-out work or daywork as soon as they can.

43. Hondagneu-Sotelo, *Doméstica.*

44. Hondagneu-Sotelo, *Doméstica*, contains a section entitled "The Growth of Domestic Work." Ruth Milkman's "The Macrosociology of Paid Domestic Labor," *Work and Occupations* 25, no. 4 (1998): 483–510, starts with the assumption that the occupation is on the rise. For other examples, see Caitlin Flanagan, "How Serfdom Saved the Women's Movement: Dispatches from the Nanny Wars," *Atlantic Monthly*, March 2004, 109–130; and Hochschild, "Importing Motherhood."

45. Milkman, "The Macrosociology of Paid Domestic Labor."

46. The industry category "private households" includes any worker employed in the service of a single household, such as lawyers, gardeners, et cetera. Maids and housekeepers, along with child-care workers, make up the largest number of these workers (between 70 and 80 percent), but there is also a significant number of nursing aides in this group. Some have argued that personal care assistants and home health-care aides are in some ways disguised domestic servants, and I believe there are important continuities. But I have confined this discussion to the nannies and housekeepers that are most often the center of the debate around the rise in domestic service; I discuss nursing aides in the context of the overall trajectory of health-care jobs in the next chapter.

47. Sutherland, *Americans and Their Servants*, 61. The scenario Sutherland describes is very similar to that in the twentieth century, when "generally women who took domestic jobs in this period had no other choices; they were socially peripheral and politically powerless and took housework jobs as a last resort when other employment failed" (Palmer, *Domesticity and Dirt*, 67).

48. This particular vulnerability in domestic service has been widely documented. Coser, in "Servants," identifies the diffuse nature of the work and its individualistic structure as part of what makes the domestic servant role incompatible with egalitarian ideologies. For descriptions of these constraints in the nineteenth and early twentieth centuries, see Lucy Maynard Salmon, *Domestic Service* (New York: Macmillan, 1897); Sutherland, *Americans and Their Servants*; Palmer, *Domesticity and Dirt*; Katzman, *Seven Days a Week*; and Dudden, *Serving Women*. For descriptions of contemporary situations, see Hondagneu-Sotelo, *Doméstica*; Mary Romero, *Maid in the U.S.A.*; Hochschild, "Importing Motherhood"; and Rollins, *Between Women*. These authors all describe similar challenges associated with the amount of work, the difficulty of enforcing boundaries, and the unique isolation of the job.

49. Katzman, *Seven Days a Week*, 111.

50. Hochschild, "Importing Motherhood," 33.

51. Salmon, *Domestic Service*, 145. Also on this point see historian Clark-Lewis, *Living In, Living Out*, who refers to the "soul-destroying hollowness of live-in domestic work" and reports that most Black women in her study had tried to escape live-in positions as soon as they were able.

52. These sample calculations appear in Hondagneu-Sotelo, *Doméstica*. Also see Rollins, *Between Women*; and Romero, *Maid in the U.S.A.*, on expanding hours for domestic workers.

53. Rollins, *Between Women*.

54. On this point see Rollins, *Between Women*. Describing heterosexual couples, Rollins explains that even when the wife is employed outside the home, generally the employer-employee relationship is between her and the domestic.

55. Numerous scholars have described this isolation as a major source of distress for domestics over the course of the century. See Salmon, *Domestic Service*; Katzman, *Seven Days a Week*; Rollins, *Between Women*; Romero, *Maid in the U.S.A*; and Hondagneu-Sotelo, *Doméstica*. Significantly, there is counterevidence that especially among nannies there may be more vehicles for connection than once thought. On this point see Amada Armenta, "Creating Community: Latina Nannies in a West Los Angeles Park," *Qualitative Sociology* 32, no. 3 (September 2009): 279–292.

56. For a description of some organizing efforts by domestic workers, see Rosalyn Terborg-Penn, "Survival Strategies among African American Women Workers: A Continuing Process," in *Women, Work, and Protest: A Century of U.S. Women's Labor History*, ed. Ruth Milkman (Boston: Routledge and Kegan Paul, 1985), 139–155; Peggie R. Smith, "Organizing the Unorganizable: Private Paid Household Workers and Approaches to Employee Representation," *North Carolina Law Review* 79 (2000): 46–109; and Romero, *Maid in the U.S.A.* Also see Domestic Workers United, who have had some success at the local level in pushing for a domestic workers' bill of rights in New York (www.domesticworkersunited .org).

57. See Hondagneu-Sotelo, *Doméstica*, for a discussion of this in the contemporary context.

58. For detailed descriptions of the relationship between domestics and employing women in the latter half of the twentieth century, see Cameron Macdonald,

"Manufacturing Motherhood: The Shadow Work of Nannies and Au Pairs," *Qualitative Sociology* 21, no. 1 (1998): 25–53; Rollins, *Between Women*; Hondagneu-Sotelo, *Doméstica*. Katzman, in *Seven Days a Week*, describes the uniqueness of the intensely personal relationship between employer and employee.

59. See Salmon, *Domestic Service*, 131, for a list of the "advantages" of domestic work given by her survey respondents in 1890, which included health factors, better pay, and a place to live. However, by far the most respondents noted their primary reason for entering domestic service was that "it was most available."

60. Rollins, *Between Women*.

61. Romero, *Maid in the U.S.A.*, 12. Hondagneu-Sotelo, in *Doméstica*, finds similar discussions in her sample of some of the advantages of domestic service relative to other occupations open to Hispanic women.

62. Salmon, *Domestic Service*, 131.

63. Katzman observes the irony of a caste system that confined Black women and immigrant women to these jobs, which often paid more than other unskilled or semi-skilled positions, and concludes: "This factor more than any other underscores the degree to which domestic service must be examined primarily within the social, not the economic structure." Katzman, *Seven Days a Week*, 273. Similarly, Sutherland, in *Americans and Their Servants*, finds that wages were not a frequent complaint of nineteenth- and early twentieth-century servants; their complaint was rather that no amount of wages could make up for the loss of dignity and lack of control over one's life experienced by domestic workers.

64. W.E.B. Du Bois, "The Philadelphia Negro," in *The Social Theory of W.E.B. Du Bois*, ed. Phil Zuckerman (Thousand Oaks, Calif.: Pine Forge Press 2004 [1889]), 113–115.

65. Salmon, *Domestic Service*, 140.

66. Hondagneu-Sotelo, *Doméstica*; Rollins, *Between Women*; and Romero, *Maid in the U.S.A.*, all document a range of experiences vis-à-vis wages among the domestic workers in their studies.

67. Rollins, *Between Women*, 72–73.

68. Hondagneu-Sotelo describes the variation in the earnings of nannies and housekeepers in Los Angeles in the mid 1990s. For live-in nannies/housekeepers, weekly earnings ranged from $100 a week to $450 a week; for live-out positions, the average wage was $5.90 an hour. Hondagneu-Sotelo, *Doméstica*, 35–38.

69. Full-time, year-round workers are those who have worked at least fifty weeks of the previous year and at least thirty-five hours of the previous week. Conversions to 2010 dollars were calculated using the Consumer Price Index as reported by the U.S. Bureau of Labor Statistics.

70. Romero, *Maid in the U.S.A.*, 13.

71. According to Rollins in *Between Women*, while her respondents differed in their assessment of the fairness of their wages, they were universal in their grievances about the lack of benefits and security of private household work.

72. Hondagneu-Sotelo, *Doméstica*; Rollins, *Between Women*; and Romero, *Maid in the U.S.A.*

73. Hondagneu-Sotelo, *Doméstica*, 217.

74. Arlene Kaplan Daniels, in "Invisible Work," *Social Problems* 34, no. 5 (1987), notes that recognition of an activity as work gives it a "moral force and dignity— something of importance in a society" (408).

75. See Roberts, "Spiritual and Menial Housework"; also Jill Quadagno, *The Color of Welfare: How Racism Undermined the War on Poverty* (New York: Oxford University Press, 1996).

76. Rollins, *Between Women*, 78.
77. Daniels, in "Invisible Work," discusses this dynamic.
78. Roberts, "Spiritual and Menial Housework." This division of labor is also described by Nakano Glenn, "From Servitude to Service Work"; and Palmer, *Domesticity and Dirt*.
79. Cowan, in *More Work for Mother*, says this is expectation increased the burden on women, despite technological advances.
80. Sutherland, *Americans and Their Servants*, 11.
81. Palmer, in *Domesticity and Dirt*, outlines the process from 1920 to 1945, exploring how the division of housework involved the assignment of meanings of whiteness and nonwhiteness, as well as of class. She argues that women learned appropriate social identities through assignment of tasks and the cultural significance of those tasks. Also on this point see Nakano Glenn, "From Servitude to Service Work"; and Roberts, "Spiritual and Menial Housework."
82. Palmer, *Domesticity and Dirt*.
83. Palmer, in *Domesticity and Dirt*, argues that this identification of menial housework with undesirable and unfeminine qualities was so intense that in later decades when domestic servants became less available and more housewives were forced to do the menial as well as the spiritual work, it felt untenable and left many feeling conflicted. It is her assertion that these conflicts were a large source of the unrest identified by Betty Friedan in *The Feminine Mystique* (New York: Laurel, 1963).
84. Simone de Beauvoir, *The Second Sex* (New York: Vintage Press, 1959).
85. Palmer, *Domesticity and Dirt*.
86. Nakano Glenn, in "From Servitude to Service Work," has described the regional variation in which groups dominated domestic service.
87. Hondagneu-Sotelo, *Doméstica*.
88. Hondagneu-Sotelo, *Doméstica*; Rollins, *Between Women*; Hochschild, "Importing Motherhood."
89. Flanagan, "How Serfdom Saved the Women's Movement," 5.

Chapter 3 *Transforming Nurturance, Creating Expert Care*

1. The occupations included as nurturant care in this 850,000 are based on a coding system that standardizes all occupational data to the 1950 categories and are as follows: chiropractors; clergymen; dentists; nurses, professional; nurses, student; optometrists; osteopaths; physicians and surgeons; recreation and group workers; religious workers; social and welfare workers, except group; psychologists; teachers; therapists and healers; attendants, physicians' and dentists' office; attendants, hospital and other institution; attendants, professional and personal service; midwives; and practical nurses.
2. For a discussion of the transformation of health care from home to hospital, see Susan M. Reverby, *Ordered to Care: The Dilemma of American Nursing, 1850–1945* (Cambridge: Cambridge University Press, 1987); Paul Starr, *The Social Transformation of American Medicine* (New York: Basic Books, 1982); and Karen Buhler-Wilkerson, *No Place Like Home: A History of Nursing and Home Care in the United States* (Baltimore: Johns Hopkins University Press, 2001). Unless otherwise cited, the discussion in the text that follows draws on Reverby for descriptions of changes in nursing care and on Starr for the role of physicians.
3. The discussion of the professionalization of medicine in the text that follows draws heavily on Starr's detailed discussion in *The Social Transformation of American Medicine*.

4. Ehrenreich and English have argued that the professionalization of medicine amounted to a take-over of healing expertise by men (doctors) from women (midwives and traditional healers). See Barbara Ehrenreich and Deidre English, *For Her Own Good: 150 Years of Experts' Advice to Women* (Garden City, N.Y.: Anchor Books, 1979).

5. For a description of the characteristics of a profession as developed in the health-care field, see Starr, *The Social Transformation of American Medicine*; and Barbara Melosh, *The Physician's Hand: Work Culture and Conflict in American Nursing* (Philadelphia: Temple University Press, 1982). For a more general treatment of the characteristics of a profession, see Andrew Abbott, *The System of Professions* (Chicago: University of Chicago Press, 1988).

6. Starr, *The Social Transformation of American Medicine*.

7. See Reverby, *Ordered to Care*; and Melosh, *The Physician's Hand*.

8. See Reverby, *Ordered to Care*; Starr, *The Social Transformation of American Medicine*; and Buhler-Wilkerson, *No Place Like Home*.

9. Reverby, in *Ordered to Care*, reports the use of the term "short course nurse." Buhler-Wilkerson, in *No Place Like Home*, talks about the various iterations of care for the ill in the home.

10. Starr, *The Social Transformation of American Medicine*.

11. Ibid.

12. Kathleen Gow, in *How Nurses' Emotions Affect Patient Care: Self-Studies by Nurses* (New York: Springer, 1982), makes the argument that emphasis on feminine traits was part of an explicit professionalization strategy to differentiate nurses from doctors.

13. For a description of the day-to-day working conditions of nurses during this period, see Reverby, *Ordered to Care*; and Melosh, *The Physician's Hand*.

14. Reverby, *Ordered to Care*.

15. See Darlene Clark Hine, *Black Women in White: Racial Conflict and Cooperation in the Nursing Profession, 1890–1950* (Bloomington: Indiana University Press, 1989), for a detailed account of the experiences of Black nurses during this time.

16. Dorothy Roberts discusses this continuity of roles in "Spiritual and Menial Housework," *Yale Journal of Law and Feminism* 9 (1997): 51–80; as does Evelyn Nakano Glenn in "From Servitude to Service Work: Historical Continuities in the Racial Division of Paid Reproductive Labor," *Signs: Journal of Women in Culture and Society* 18 (Autumn 1992): 1–43.

17. Melosh, *The Physician's Hand*, 195, 196.

18. See ibid., and Suzanne Gordon, *Nursing against the Odds: How Health Care Cost Cutting, Media Stereotypes, and Medical Hubris Undermine Nurses and Patient Care* (Ithaca, N.Y.: Cornell University Press, 2005).

19. Reverby, *Ordered to Care*, 195.

20. See Viviana A. Rotman Zelizer, *Pricing the Priceless Child: The Changing Social Value of Children* (New York: Basic Books, 1985), 3.

21. See Martin Carnoy and Henry M. Levin, *Schooling and Work in the Democratic State* (Stanford: Stanford University Press, 1985).

22. Jo Anne Preston, "Domestic Ideology, School Reformers, and Female Teachers: Schoolteaching Becomes Women's Work in Nineteenth Century New England," *New England Quarterly* 66, no. 4 (1993): 532. Among others who describe the transformation of teaching to women's work are Carnoy and Levin, *Schooling and Work*; 531–551; and Kate Rousmaniere, *City Teachers: Teaching and School Reform in Historical Perspective* (New York: Teachers College Press, 1997).

23. See Zelizer, *Pricing the Priceless Child*.

24. See Carnoy and Levin, *Schooling and Work*.

25. Priscilla Ferguson Clement, "The City and the Child, 1860–1885," in *American Childhood: A Research Guide and Historical Handbook*, ed. Joseph M. Hawes and N. Ray Hiner (Westport, Conn.: Greenwood Press, 1985), 186–235.
26. The link between Mann and the feminization of teaching is discussed by Carnoy and Levin in *Schooling and Work*, Preston in "Domestic Ideology," and Rousmaniere in *City Teachers*.
27. See Carnoy and Levin, *Schooling and Work*.
28. Rousmaniere, *City Teachers*, 35.
29. John L. Rury, "Who Became Teachers? The Social Characteristics of Teachers in American History," in *American Teachers: Histories of a Profession at Work*, ed. Donald Warren (New York: Macmillan, 1989), 9–49.
30. Preston, "Domestic Ideology," 532.
31. Zelizer, *Pricing the Priceless Child*, 6. This section draws heavily on Zelizer's analysis.
32. Clement, "The City and the Child."
33. Rury, "Who Became Teachers?" 25.
34. Carnoy and Levin, *Schooling and Work*. Rury, in "Who Became Teachers?" argues that the increased length of the school term made teaching less attractive to men, who often combined teaching with other professional work. He describes this as part of the economic push for feminization of the occupation.
35. See Carnoy and Levin, *Schooling and Work*; Rousmaniere, *City Teachers*. Carnoy and Levin point out that the movement toward "scientific management" in schools also led to tracking and specialized curricula, which were inextricably linked to racial segregation.
36. Rury, "Who Became Teachers?" 27.
37. For descriptions of early teacher organizing, see Rousmaniere, *City Teachers*. James W. Fraser, in "Agents of Democracy: Urban Elementary-School Teachers and the Conditions of Teaching," in *American Teachers: Histories of a Profession at Work*, ed. Donald Warren (New York: Macmillan, 1989), 118–156, has argued that the centralization of schools, while decreasing teachers' autonomy, actually increased their ability to organize by moving them from patronage-based situations into workplace settings.
38. Rousmaniere, *City Teachers*; and Fraser, "Agents of Democracy."
39. Rousmaniere, *City Teachers*, 28.
40. See Carnoy and Levin, *Schooling and Work*; and Rousmaniere, *City Teachers*.
41. For a discussion of the working conditions for teachers in the early twentieth century, see Preston, "Domestic Ideology"; and Rousmaniere, *City Teachers*.
42. Rousmaniere, in *City Teachers*, talks about the segregation of schools, Black women's role as teachers, and the role of some immigrant women as teachers. Jacqueline Jones, in *Labor of Love, Labor of Sorrow: Black Women, Work, and the Family, from Slavery to the Present* (New York: Vintage Books, 1985), discusses the particular hardships and activism of Black teachers.
43. See Barbara Finkelstein, "Casting Networks of Good Influence: The Reconstruction of Childhood in the United States, 1790–1870," in *American Childhood: A Research Guide and Historical Handbook*, ed. Joseph M. Hawes and N. Ray Hiner (Westport, Conn.: Greenwood Press, 1985), 58–111.
44. Ibid.
45. This point is discussed by Clement in "The City and the Child." Intellectual exposure was thought to be damaging to young children, so kindergarten had to be framed in a particular way.
46. Barbara Beatty, "Child Gardening: The Teaching of Young Children in American Schools," in *American Teachers: Histories of a Profession at Work*, ed. Donald Warren (New York: Macmillan, 1989), 65.

47. See Regina Kunzel, *Fallen Women, Problem Girls: Unmarried Mothers and the Professionalization of Social Work, 1890–1945* (New Haven: Yale University Press, 1993).
48. See Irene Philipson, *On the Shoulders of Women: The Feminization of Psychotherapy* (New York: Guilford Press, 1993).
49. The charity organization movement is described by June Axinn and Herman Levin in *Social Welfare: A History of the American Response to Need* (New York: Longman, 1992), and by Kunzel in *Fallen Women, Problem Girls*. Kunzel uses the term "benevolence."
50. See Kunzel, *Fallen Women, Problem Girls*, for a description of the coordinating work of the COS.
51. An extensive body of scholarship describes the development of social welfare policy in the United States and these competing frames. See, for example, Axinn and Levin, *Social Welfare*; and Walter I. Trattner, *From Poor Law to Welfare State: A History of Social Welfare in America* (New York: Free Press, 1974).
52. Axinn and Levin, *Social Welfare*, 103.
53. The process of the professionalization of social work is described by Kunzel, *Fallen Women, Problem Girls*.
54. In 1940 an additional small category of workers (recreation and group workers) was folded into the category of social workers. As a result of this aberration, the growth in the number of social workers between 1930 and 1940 is an overestimation, while the rate of growth between 1940 and 1950 is an underestimation (see figure 3.9).
55. Kunzel, *Fallen Women, Problem Girls*.
56. Teresa Amott and Julie Matthaei, *Race, Gender, and Work: A Multicultural Economic History of Women in the United States* (Boston: South End Press, 1996), 163. On Black women's clubs, see also Angela Davis, *Women, Race, and Class* (New York: Random House, 1983). On early Black female social reformers, see Iris Carlton-LeNay, "African American Social Work Pioneers' Response to Need," *Social Work* 44, no. 4 (1999): 311–321.
57. Clement, "The City and the Child."
58. The approaches to child welfare are described by Hamilton Cravens in "Child-Saving in the Age of Professionalism, 1915–1930," in *American Childhood: A Research Guide and Historical Handbook*, ed. Joseph M. Hawes and N. Ray Hiner (Westport, Conn.: Greenwood Press, 1985), 377–415.
59. Cravens, in "Child-Saving in the Age of Professionalism," describes the development of child-guidance clinics. Philipson, in *On the Shoulders of Women*, also identifies child-guidance clinics as one of the earliest forms of modern psychotherapy.
60. Dorothea Dix's work and her role in mental health reform are described in many introductory social welfare textbooks, including Howard Jacob Karger and David Stoesz, *American Social Welfare Policy: A Pluralist Approach* (Boston: Allyn and Bacon, 2009).
61. Philipson, in *On the Shoulders of Women*, points out that mental health care before World War II consisted of institutional treatment for the seriously psychotic and psychoanalysis for the wealthy neurotic.
62. See Cravens, "Child-Saving in the Age of Professionalism"; and Philipson, *On the Shoulders of Women*.
63. Cited in Kunzel, *Fallen Women, Problem Girls*, 167.
64. See Ruth Schwartz Cowan, *More Work for Mother: The Ironies of Household Technology from the Open Hearth to the Microwave* (New York: Basic Books, 1999).

Chapter 4   Managing Nurturant Care in the New Economy

1. Luis L. M. Aguiar and Andrew Herod, eds., *The Dirty Work of Neoliberalism: Cleaners in the Global Economy* (Malden, Mass.: Blackwell, 2006), 3.

2. Ilene J. Philipson, *On the Shoulders of Women: The Feminization of Psychotherapy* (New York: Guilford Press, 1993), 67. See Harry Braverman, *Labor and Monopoly Capital: The Degradation of Work in the Twentieth Century* (New York: Monthly Review Press, 1974).

3. For a summary of this argument, see Ronnie J. Steinberg, "Social Construction of Skill: Gender, Power, and Comparable Worth," *Work and Occupations* 17, no. 4 (1990): 449–482.

4. See Paula England, *Comparable Worth: Theories and Evidence* (New York: Aldine de Gruyter, 1992); and Joan Acker, *Doing Comparable Worth: Gender, Class, and Pay Equity* (Philadelphia: Temple University Press, 1990).

5. Jo Anne Preston, "Domestic Ideology, School Reformers, and Female Teachers: Schoolteaching Becomes Women's Work in Nineteenth Century New England," *New England Quarterly* 66, no. 4 (1993): 531–551; Margery W. Davies, *Woman's Place Is at the Typewriter: Office Work and Office Workers, 1870–1930* (Philadelphia: Temple University Press, 1984); and Samuel Cohn, *The Process of Occupational Sex-Typing: The Feminization of Clerical Labor* (Philadelphia: Temple University Press, 1985).

6. Conversations with Dan Egan were crucial in helping me crystallize this piece of the argument.

7. See U.S. Department of Health and Human Services, *Medicare: Long-Term Care*. Retrieved January 18, 2010, from http://www.medicare.gov/LongTermCare/Static/Home.asp.

8. The variable measured in figure 4.1 is standardized to the 1990 occupational codes and therefore provides more detail for occupations that became more important in the second half of the century. This variable is not available for datasets before 1950. Small inconsistencies in population estimates are due to the differences in the ways the variables capture occupations. In general, the 1990 measure is more accurate in this later period. The categories included in these measures: "Healthcare workers" includes physicians; dentists; optometrists; podiatrists; other health and therapy; registered nurses; licensed practical nurses; health aides, except nursing; nursing aides, orderlies, and attendants; respiratory therapists; occupational therapists; physical therapists; speech therapists; therapists n.e.c. [not elsewhere categorized]; physicians' assistants; dental hygienists; and dental assistants. "Teachers" includes kindergarten and earlier school teachers; primary school teachers; secondary school teachers; special education teachers; teachers n.e.c.; and teachers' aides; "Mental health and social services" includes social workers; psychologists; vocational and educational counselors; recreation workers; welfare service aides; and clergy and religious workers. "Child-care workers" includes the single category of the same name.

9. Philipson, *On the Shoulders of Women*, 6.

10. Elizabeth Arias, "United States Life Tables, 2004," *National Vital Statistics Report* 56, no. 9 (2007).

11. Suzanne Gordon, *Nursing against the Odds: How Health Care Cost Cutting, Media Stereotypes, and Medical Hubris Undermine Nurses and Patient Care* (Ithaca, N.Y.: Cornell University Press, 2005).

12. Richard Nixon first used the term "health maintenance organization" and introduced federal endorsement, certification, and assistance to such organizations in the 1970s. See *Healthcare Crisis: Who's at Risk?* Healthcare Timeline, PBS,

produced by Issues TV (2000). Retrieved January 18, 2010, from http://www.pbs
.org/healthcarecrisis/history.htm.

13. Barbara Melosh, *The Physician's Hand: Work Culture and Conflict in American
Nursing* (Philadelphia: Temple University Press, 1982), 198; and Ester C. Apesoa-
Varano and Charles S. Varano, "Nurses and Labor Activism in the United States:
The Role of Class, Gender, and Ideology," *Social Justice* 31, no. 3 (2004): 77–104.

14. Melosh, in *The Physician's Hand*, argues that the pressure of unions played a critical role in the emergence of the primary nursing care model.

15. Melosh, in *The Physician's Hand*, describes this model. See also Suzanne Gordon,
Life Support: Three Nurses on the Front Lines (Ithaca, N.Y.: Cornell University
Press, 2007); Dana Beth Weinberg, *Code Green: Money-Driven Hospitals and the
Dismantling of Nursing* (Ithaca, N.Y.: Cornell University Press, 2003); and Gordon,
Nursing against the Odds.

16. Gordon, in *Nursing against the Odds*, and Weinberg, in *Code Green*, talk about this
trend toward cost cutting, although they both focus on its impact on nursing. On
the rise of evidence-based medicine, see Stefan Timmermans and Marc Berg, *The
Gold Standard: The Challenge of Evidence-Based Medicine and Standardization in
Health Care* (Philadelphia: Temple University Press, 2003).

17. See Michael J. Carter and Susan Boslego Carter, "Women's Recent Progress in the
Professions, or Women Get a Ticket to Ride after the Gravy Train Has Left the
Station," *Feminist Studies* 7, no. 3 (1981): 477–504.

18. Barbara F. Reskin and Patricia A. Roos, *Job Queues, Gender Queues: Explaining
Women's Inroads into Male Occupations* (Philadelphia: Temple University Press,
1990).

19. Jerry Jacobs and Ann Boulis, *The Changing Face of Medicine: Women Doctors and
the Evolution of Health Care in America* (Ithaca, N.Y.: Cornell University Press,
2008).

20. Gordon, *Nursing against the Odds*; and Weinberg, *Code Green*.

21. Barry T. Hirsch and David A. Macpherson, "Union Membership and Coverage
Database from the Current Population Survey: Note," *Industrial and Labor Relations
Review* 56, no. 2 (January 2003): 349–354. Updated data retrieved from
www.unionstats.com, July 2009.

22. Philip Dine, *State of the Unions: How Labor Can Strengthen the Middle Class,
Improve our Economy, and Regain Political Influence* (New York: McGraw-Hill,
2008), 101.

23. Gordon, *Nursing against the Odds*.

24. Weinberg, *Code Green*, 49.

25. This list of some of the tasks that used to be performed by nurses comes from
Gordon, *Nursing against the Odds*.

26. Gordon, in *Nursing against the Odds*, and Weinberg, in *Code Green*, both describe
how restructuring and cost cutting at Beth Israel and elsewhere have impacted
nursing practice.

27. Timothy Diamond titles a chapter "If It Is Not Charted It Didn't Happen" in
Making Gray Gold: Narratives of Nursing Home Care (Chicago: University of
Chicago Press, 1992); Deborah Stone, in "Caring by the Book," in *Care Work:
Gender, Labor, and the Welfare State*, ed. Madonna Harrington Meyer (New York:
Routledge, 2000), 89–111, describes a similar dynamic for home-care aides.

28. Several scholars have documented the importance to the workers they interviewed
of relationships as well as of the emotional and relational aspects of the job. See
Stone, "Caring by the Book"; Diamond, *Making Gray Gold*; and Gordon, *Nursing
against the Odds*.

29. Linda C. Andrist, "The History of the Relationship between Feminism and Nursing," in *A History of Nursing Ideas*, ed. Linda C. Andrist, Patrice K. Nicholas, and Karen A. Wolf (Sudbury, Mass.: Jones and Bartlett, 2006), 19.

30. Diamond, *Making Gray Gold*, 18.

31. Lisa Dodson and Rebekah M. Zincavage, "'It's Like a Family': Caring Labor, Exploitation, and Race in Nursing Homes," *Gender and Society* 21, no. 6 (2007): 912; Stone, in "Caring by the Book," has described a very similar process for home-care aides, who end up doing things for their clients on their own time that are not part of their official duties.

32. Robert Moroney, in *Caring and Competent Caregivers* (Athens: University of Georgia Press, 1998), has pointed out that despite the popular perception that these institutions emerged in response to a decline in family responsibility and care, research data suggest that family members in earlier eras did not have to make institutionalization decisions, as fewer people survived to old age and most who were born with a severe disability died very young.

33. Karen Buhler-Wilkerson makes this point in *No Place Like Home: A History of Nursing and Home Care in the United States* (Baltimore: Johns Hopkins University Press, 2001), an excellent history of home care.

34. Eileen Boris and Jennifer Klein describe the development of these two different models in "Organizing Home Care: Low-Waged Workers in the Welfare State," *Politics and Society* 34, no. 1 (2006): 81–108. Buhler-Wilkerson, in *No Place Like Home*, also discusses the different models of home care.

35. Nona Y. Glazer, "Between a Rock and a Hard Place: Women's Professional Organizations in Nursing and Class, Racial, and Ethnic Inequalities," *Gender and Society* 5, no. 3 (1991): 351–372.

36. See Susan M. Reverby, *Ordered to Care: The Dilemma of American Nursing, 1850–1945* (Cambridge: Cambridge University Press, 1987); Boris and Klein, "Organizing Home Care"; and Glazer, "Between a Rock and a Hard Place."

37. See Nancy Guberman, Éric Gagnon, Denyse Côté, Claude Gilbert, Nicole Thivièrge, and Marielle Tremblay, "How the Trivialization of the Demands of High-Tech Care in the Home Is Turning Family Members into Para-Medical Personnel," *Journal of Family Issues* 26, no. 2 (2005): 247–272. One of the authors' main arguments is that shifting some of this high-tech labor (injections, IVs, et cetera) to family members trivializes the knowledge and skills involved, and so is part of the degrading of professional workers. Cameron Macdonald is investigating this phenomenon in the United States in an as yet unpublished project. Gordon, in *Nursing against the Odds*, also mentions this trend toward trivialization as part of the deskilling of nursing.

38. Stone, "Caring by the Book."

39. These observations are from a chart recording the work of a home-care worker from the agency Home Instead, a large national home-care provider, and from the Web site of the Medicaid program.

40. Boris and Klein, "Organizing Home Care."

41. *Long Island Care at Home, Ltd., v. Coke*, 127 S. Ct. 2339 (2007).

42. See Peggie Smith, "Protecting Home Care Workers under the Fair Labor Standards Act." Direct Care Alliance Policy Brief No. 2 (2009). Retrieved January 18, 2010, from http://blog.directcarealliance.org/wp-content/uploads/2009/06/6709-dca_policybrief_2final.pdf.

43. Charles E. Strickland and Andrew M. Ambrose, "The Baby Boom, Prosperity, and the Changing Worlds of Children, 1945–1963," in *American Childhood: A Research Guide and Historical Handbook*, ed. Joseph M. Hawes and N. Ray Hiner (Westport, Conn.: Greenwood Press, 1985), 533.

44. See Strickland and Ambrose, "The Baby Boom"; and John L. Rury, "Who Became Teachers? The Social Characteristics of Teachers in American History," in *American Teachers: Histories of a Profession at Work*, ed. Donald Warren (New York: Macmillan, 1989), 9–48.

45. Strickland and Ambrose, "The Baby Boom."

46. Rury, "Who Became Teachers?"

47. In figure 4.7 "primary and secondary school teachers includes those categorized as primary school teachers, secondary school teachers, teachers (n.e.c. [not elsewhere categorized]), and special education teachers. Inconsistencies in enumerator instructions and the large number of teachers in the n.e.c. category make it difficult to create reliable estimates of the overall number of teachers in each category.

48. Even at the height of the idealization of motherhood, women were still thought to need plenty of advice from experts like Dr. Benjamin Spock and other (mostly male) psychologists. On this point see Strickland and Ambrose, "The Baby Boom."

49. Strickland and Ambrose, "The Baby Boom," 538.

50. Bronfenbrenner is cited in ibid., 540. See Urie Bronfenbrenner, "Reality and Research in the Ecology of Human Development," *American Philosophical Society Proceedings* 119, no. 6 (December 1975): 439–469.

51. Kate Rousmaniere, *City Teachers: Teaching and School Reform in Historical Perspective* (New York: Teachers College Press, 1997).

52. William R. Johnson, "Teachers and Teacher Training in the Twentieth Century," in *American Teachers: Histories of a Profession at Work*, ed. Donald Warren (New York: Macmillan, 1989), 240.

53. Susan Carter, "Incentives and Rewards to Teaching," in *American Teachers: Histories of a Profession at Work*, ed. Donald Warren (New York: Macmillan, 1989), 57.

54. Rury, "Who Became Teachers?"

55. The statistics for 1900 and 1940 were calculated using the standardized 1950 occupation code for teachers, while the 1960 statistic was calculated using standardized 1990 occupation codes for primary school teachers, secondary school teachers, special education teachers, and teachers n.e.c. [not elsewhere categorized]. This coding is consistent with the way the numbers in the rest of the book are calculated.

56. Wayne J. Urban, "Teacher Activism," in *American Teachers: Histories of a Profession at Work*, ed. Donald Warren (New York: Macmillan, 1989), 190–209.

57. Rury, "Who Became Teachers?"

58. Urban, "Teacher Activism."

59. Rury, "Who Became Teachers?"

60. Urban, "Teacher Activism."

61. Ibid.

62. Rousmaniere, *City Teachers*, 28.

63. The subtitle of this section borrows from Nel Noddings, "Caring and Competence," in *The Education of Teachers*, ed. Gary A. Griffin (Chicago: National Society for the Study of Education, 1999), 205–220.

64. Doug Selwyn, "Highly Quantified Teachers: NCLB and Teacher Education," *Journal of Teacher Education* 58 (2007): 131.

65. Carolyn Bunting, "Teaching to Survive NCLB," *Education Digest* 72, no. 5 (2007): 12–15; Monty Neill, "Preparing Teachers to Beat the Agonies of No Child Left Behind," *Education Digest* 71, no. 8 (2006): 8–12; and June Million, "Nurturing Teachers in the Famine of NCLB," *Education Digest* 70, no. 9 (2005): 16–18.

66. This calculation includes primary school teachers, secondary school teachers, special education teachers, and teachers (n.e.c. [not elsewhere categorized]).

67. Hirsch and Macpherson, "Union Membership and Coverage Database." Updated data available at http://www.unionstats.com. According to Julia E. Koppich, in "A Tale of Two Approaches—The AFT, the NEA, and NCLB," *Peabody Journal of Education* 80, no. 2 (2005): 137–155, in 2005, 90 percent of public school teachers paid dues to either the NEA or the AFT.

68. Koppich, "A Tale of Two Approaches."

69. Koppich, in ibid., describes in detail the responses of the two major teacher unions to NCLB.

70. Barbara Beatty, "Child Gardening: The Teaching of Young Children in American Schools," in *American Teachers: Histories of a Profession at Work*, ed. Donald Warren (New York: Macmillan, 1989), 65–92.

71. Lynet Uttal, *Making Care Work: Employed Mothers in the New Childcare Market* (New Brunswick, N.J.: Rutgers University Press, 2002).

72. Edward Zigler, "By What Goals Should Head Start Be Assessed?" *Children's Services: Social Policy, Research, and Practice* 1, no. 1 (1998): 5–17.

73. Uttal, *Making Care Work.*

74. These are workers in the private household industry whose occupation is identified as child-care worker.

75. Mary C. Tuominen, *We Are Not Babysitters: Family Child Care Providers Redefine Work and Care* (New Brunswick, N.J.: Rutgers University Press, 2003), 61. See also Cameron Macdonald and David A. Merrill, "'It Shouldn't Have to Be a Trade': Recognition and Redistribution in Care Work Advocacy," *Hypatia* 17, no. 2 (2002): 78, for a discussion of a similar dynamic among child-care center workers.

76. Tuominen, *We Are Not Babysitters.*

77. Uttal, *Making Care Work*, 51.

78. For other examples of studies that show parents and child-care workers speaking explicitly about having and wanting relationships between providers and children, see Margaret K. Nelson, *Negotiated Care: The Experience of Family Day Care Providers* (Philadelphia: Temple University Press, 1990); Rosanna Hertz, "A Typology of Approaches to Child Care: The Centerpiece of Organizing Family Life for Dual-Earner Couples," *Journal of Family Issues* 18, no. 4 (1997): 355–385; and Julia Wrigley, *Other People's Children: An Intimate Account of the Dilemmas Facing Middle-Class Parents and the Women They Hire* (New York: Basic Books, 1995).

79. Uttal, *Making Care Work.* Tuominen, in *We Are Not Babysitters*, also found that cultural stereotypes often identified women of color as more emotional and loving—and less skilled—than White women.

80. Lynet Uttal and Mary Tuominen, "Tenuous Relationships: Exploitation, Emotion, and Racial Ethnic Significance in Paid Child Care Work," *Gender and Society* 13, no. 6 (1999): 755–777.

81. It is not clear whether these notions are motivational in the choice of child-care provider or are "interpretive acts" that serve to justify choices after the fact. Cameron Macdonald, in "Manufacturing Motherhood: The Shadow Work of Nannies and Au Pairs," *Qualitative Sociology* 21 (1998): 25–53, discusses how nannies and mothers who employ them engage in these kinds of interpretive acts to preserve the ideology of intensive motherhood.

82. Wrigley, *Other People's Children*, 20. While Wrigley does not use the labels "spiritual" and "menial," her discussion parallels this distinction made by Dorothy Roberts in "Spiritual and Menial Housework," *Yale Journal of Law and Feminism* 9, no. 51 (1997). Macdonald, in "Manufacturing Motherhood," also distinguishes between spiritual and menial child care and reports a similar dynamic.

83. See Nelson, *Negotiated Care*, for discussion of this division of labor.

84. Macdonald, "Manufacturing Motherhood"; Nelson, *Negotiated Care*. For further discussion about how transferring the labor of motherhood is perceived as problematic, see Rosanna Hertz and Faith Ferguson, "Childcare Choice and Constraints in the United States: Social Class, Race, and the Influence of Family Views," *Journal of Comparative Family Studies* 27, no. 2 (1996): 249–280; Mary Tuominen, "Gender, Class, and Motherhood: The Legacy of Federal Child Care Policy," *AFFILIA* 7, no. 4 (1992): 8–25; and Lynet Uttal, "Racial Safety and Cultural Maintenance: The Child Care Concerns of Employed Mothers of Color," *Ethnic Studies Review* 19, no. 1 (1996): 43–59.

85. Annette Lareau, *Unequal Childhoods: Class, Race, and Family Life* (Berkeley: University of California Press, 2007).

86. See Sherry Wexler, "Work/Family Policy Stratification: The Examples of Family Support and Family Leave," *Qualitative Sociology* 20, no. 2 (1997): 311–322.

87. Uttal, "Racial Safety and Cultural Maintenance," 51.

88. Macdonald and Merrill, "It Shouldn't Have to Be a Trade," 78.

89. Tuominen, *We Are Not Babysitters*.

90. I focus the discussion on these two occupational groups because they are the largest separately identifiable groups in the data (psychiatrists cannot be separately identified) and because their intersecting histories tell a very interesting story about race-ethnicity and gender.

91. Note that because the data do not allow the separation of clinical psychologists from this more general category, this number includes some psychologists not engaged in clinical practice.

92. Regina Kunzel, *Fallen Women, Problem Girls: Unmarried Mothers and the Professionalization of Social Work, 1890–1945* (New Haven: Yale University Press, 1993).

93. See Philipson, *On the Shoulders of Women*. The discussion that follows draws heavily on Philipson's argument about the feminization of psychology.

94. On the process of medicalization in mental health and the move toward increased drug treatment, see, for example, Allan Horwitz and Jerome Wakefield, *The Loss of Sadness: How Psychiatry Transformed Normal Sorrow into Depressive Disorder* (London: Oxford University Press, 2007); David Herzberg, *Happy Pills in America: From Milltown to Prozac* (Baltimore: Johns Hopkins University Press, 2009); and Christopher Lane, *Shyness: How Normal Behavior Became a Sickness* (New Haven: Yale University Press, 2007).

95. Philipson, *On the Shoulders of Women*.

96. Iris Carlton-LeNay, "African American Social Work Pioneers' Response to Need" *Social Work* 44, no. 4 (1999): 315.

97. Preston, "Domestic Ideology."

98. Philipson, *On the Shoulders of Women*.

99. Reskin and Roos, *Job Queues, Gender Queues*.

100. In some local areas the teaching workforce and nursing workforce are more racially-ethnically diverse—but on a national level the inroads made into these occupations by Blacks and Hispanics have been relatively small.

Chapter 5   *Doing the Dirty Work*

1. For conciseness, I use "food workers" to refer to "food preparation and service workers."

2. Pierrette Hondagneu-Sotelo, in *Doméstica: Immigrant Workers Cleaning and Caring in the Shadows of Affluence* (Berkeley: University of California Press, 2001), reports that the roles of nannies and housekeepers often overlap, as mentioned in chapter 2.

3. Evelyn Nakano Glenn, "From Servitude to Service Work: Historical Continuities in the Racial Division of Paid Reproductive Labor," *Signs: Journal of Women in Culture and Society* 18 (Autumn 1992): 1–43.

4. These data use standardized 1950 occupation codes to calculate totals. "Janitors and cleaners" includes charwomen and cleaners; housekeepers and stewards, except private household; and janitors and sextons. "Food preparation and service" includes cooks, except private household; counter and fountain workers; waiters and waitresses; and service workers, except private household (this category contains primarily miscellaneous kitchen workers). "Laundry and dry cleaning" is a single category of the same name.

5. Industry breakdowns calculated using industry codes standardized to 1950 categories.

6. The proportion in 1900 is much higher than that in 1910, again showing a pattern of fluctuation.

7. These category names and the calculations that follow use the 2007 American Community Survey occupational categories, which duplicate the categories in the 2000 U.S. Census.

8. U.S. Department of Commerce, Bureau of Census (2000), "Classified Index of Occupations." Retrieved January 18, 2010, from http://www.census.gov/hhes/www/ioindex/view.html.

9. Barbara Ehrenreich, *Nickel and Dimed: On (Not) Getting By in America* (New York: Metropolitan Books, 2001), 90.

10. On this point, see Niklas Krause, Teresa Scherzer, and Reiner Rugulies, "Physical Workload, Work Intensification, and Prevalence of Pain in Low-Wage Workers: Results from a Participatory Research Project with Hotel Room Cleaners in Las Vegas," *American Journal of Industrial Medicine* 48, no. 5 (2005): 326–337. Peter Milburn and Rod Barrett, in "Lumbosacral Loads in Bedmaking," *Applied Ergonomics* 30, no. 3 (1999): 263–373, document the heavy and risky work involved in repetitive bed making, especially in light of the hospitality industry's shift toward heavier and larger beds.

11. Timothy Diamond, in *Making Gray Gold: Narratives of Nursing Home Care* (Chicago: University of Chicago Press, 1992), also describes the work of nursing assistants who do some of the cleaning in nursing homes as physically backbreaking.

12. Ehrenreich, *Nickel and Dimed*, 70. The data available in the American Community Survey cannot be broken down to separately identify workers employed by housecleaning services.

13. Mary Romero, *Maid in the U.S.A.* (New York: Routledge, 1992). See also Hondagneu-Sotelo, *Doméstica*; and Judith Rollins, *Between Women: Domestics and Their Employers* (Philadelphia: Temple University Press, 1985).

14. Hondagneu-Sotelo, *Doméstica*, 47. The ways in which independent housecleaners sometimes organize cooperative structures to help find jobs has also been explored in Leslie Salzinger, "A Maid by Any Other Name: The Transformation of Dirty Work by Central American Immigrants," in *Ethnography Unbound: Power and Resistance in the Modern Metropolis*, ed. Michael Buroway (Berkeley: University of California Press, 1991), 139–160.

15. Ehrenreich, in *Nickel and Dimed*, has argued that the procedures used by the maid service she worked for in Maine did not achieve true cleanliness, but rather a surface-level shine that could be produced quickly. Jennifer Bickham-Mendez, in "Of Mops and Maids: Contradictions and Continuities in Bureaucratized Domestic Work," *Social Problems* 45, no. 1 (1998): 114–135, has also documented the routinization of housecleaning work in corporate franchise operations.

16. Bickham-Mendez, "Of Mops and Maids." For more discussion of the characteristics of service work, see Cameron Macdonald and Carmen Sirianni, eds., *Working in the Service Society* (Philadelphia: Temple University Press, 1996); and Marek Korczynski and Cameron Macdonald, eds., *Service Work: Critical Perspectives* (New York: Routledge, 2009).

17. Bickham-Mendez documents this in "Of Mops and Maids."

18. Ehrenreich, in *Nickel and Dimed,* and Bickham-Mendez, in "Of Mops and Maids," both point this out, and my informal search of some of the major Web sites confirms it. Every Web site I visited either shows a picture of a maid on her hands and knees scrubbing a floor, advertises that specific service, or both.

19. See Cynthia Cranford, "Networks of Exploitation: Immigrant Labor and the Restructuring of the Los Angeles Janitorial Industry," *Social Problems* 52, no. 3 (2005): 379–397; and Roger Waldinger, Chris Erickson, Ruth Milkman, Daniel B. J. Mitchell, Abel Valenzuela, Kent Wong, and Maurice Zeitlin, "Helots No More: A Case Study of the Justice for Janitors Campaign in Los Angeles," in *Organizing to Win: New Research on Union Strategies,* ed. Kate Bronfenbrenner, Sheldon Friedman, Richard W. Hurd, Rudolph A. Oswald, and Ronald L. Seeber (Ithaca, N.Y.: Cornell University Press, 1998), 102–119.

20. Cranford, "Networks of Exploitation," 390.

21. Both Cranford in "Networks of Exploitation," and Waldinger et al. in "Helots No More" argue that Latinos did not push African Americans out of these jobs, but rather were used by companies as cheaper and more controllable replacements as African Americans left an occupation with deteriorating working conditions.

22. Cynthia Cranford, "It's Time to Leave Machismo Behind! Challenging Gender Inequality in an Immigrant Union," *Gender and Society* 21, no. 3 (2007): 409–438.

23. Cranford, "Networks of Exploitation," and Waldinger et al., "Helots No More."

24. Preston Rudy, "'Justice for Janitors' Not 'Compensation for Custodians': The Political Context and Organizing in San Jose and Sacramento," in *Rebuilding Labor: Organizing and Organizers in the New Union Movement,* ed. Milkman and Voss (Ithaca, N.Y.: Cornell University Press, 2004), 133–149.

25. Based on standardized 1950 occupation codes for nurses, professional, and nurses, student professional, combined within the standardized 1950 industry code for hospitals.

26. Nona Y. Glazer, "Between a Rock and a Hard Place: Women's Professional Organizations in Nursing and Class, Racial, and Ethnic Inequalities," *Gender and Society* 5, no. 3 (1991): 351–372.

27. The percentages in figure 5.3 do not exactly parallel the percentages presented in earlier chapters for two reasons. First, these calculations include only workers in hospitals; previously presented data include workers in these occupations across a range of settings. Second, these data use contemporary occupation and industry codes for 2007 in order to preserve as much detail as possible.

28. Pat Armstrong, Hugh Armstrong, and Krista Scott-Dixon, *Critical to Care: The Invisible Women in Health Services* (Toronto: University of Toronto Press, 2008), 96; while this is a study of the Canadian health-care system, there are important parallels to dynamics within the U.S. system. The title of this subsection is drawn from the title of this book.

29. Ibid, 98, 97.

30. Nakano Glenn, in "From Servitude to Service Work," has made a similar argument. She shows that the construction of certain jobs as primarily manual ignores the relational content of the labor of workers on the lower rungs of the hospital hierarchy.

Chapter 6   Making Care Count

1. Robert Moroney makes this point in *Caring and Competent Caregivers* (Athens: University of Georgia Press, 1998).
2. Ibid.
3. In 2008, columnist Lenore Skenazy allowed her nine-year-old son, Izzy, to ride the subway home from Bloomingdale's after he had asked for many months to do this. She wrote a column about it and received national attention—most of it negative, some of it suggesting she should be brought up on child-abuse charges.
4. Mona Harrington, *Care and Equality: Inventing a New Family Politics* (New York: Knopf, 1999), 21.
5. Evelyn Nakano Glenn, "From Servitude to Service Work: Historical Continuities in the Racial Division of Paid Reproductive Labor," *Signs: Journal of Women in Culture and Society* 18 (Autumn 1992): 1–43; and Dorothy Roberts, "Spiritual and Menial Housework," *Yale Journal of Law and Feminism* 9, no. 51 (1997): 51–80.
6. Roberts, "Spiritual and Menial Housework"; and Daniel E. Sutherland, *Americans and Their Servants: Domestic Service in the United States from 1800 to 1920* (Baton Rouge: Louisiana State University Press, 1981).
7. This construction ignores the many women who employed domestic servants and worked side by side with them to complete the formidable tasks of household labor. The construction had strong ideological power, despite its applying only to upper-class households where a cadre of servants could be hired.
8. Susan Reverby, *Ordered to Care: The Dilemma of American Nursing, 1850–1945* (Cambridge: Cambridge University Press, 1987), 195.
9. Proportions calculated using 1990 U.S. Census data for private household workers and 2007 American Community Survey data for nursing aides, orderlies, and attendants; child-care workers; and cleaning, food, and laundry workers. See the appendix for discussion of occupational categories included as cleaning, food, and laundry workers.
10. Timothy Diamond, *Making Gray Gold: Narratives of Nursing Home Care* (Chicago: University of Chicago Press, 1995).
11. Suzanne Gordon, *Nursing against the Odds: How Health Care Cost Cutting, Media Stereotypes, and Medical Hubris Undermine Nurses and Patient Care* (Ithaca, N.Y.: Cornell University Press, 2005), 221. Emphasis added.
12. Cameron Macdonald and David Merrill, "'It Shouldn't Have to Be a Trade': Recognition and Redistribution in Care Work Advocacy," *Hypatia* 17, no. 2 (2002): 77.
13. Valerie Adams and Julie Nelson, "The Economics of Nursing: Articulating Care," *Feminist Economics* 15, no. 4 (2009): 3.
14. For more details see Sheldon Danziger and Peter Gottschalk, *America Unequal* (New York: Russell Sage Foundation, 1995).
15. For a discussion of the potential confluences between a labor movement and calls for a care movement, see Mignon Duffy, "'We are the Union': Care Work, Unions, and Social Movements," *Humanity and Society* 34, no. 2 (2010): 125–140.
16. This discussion of paid and unpaid care as interdependent draws on conversations with Nancy Folbre and Randy Albelda.
17. Nancy Folbre describes these models in "Demanding Quality: Worker/Consumer Coalitions and 'High-Road' Strategies in the Care Sector," *Politics and Society* 34, no. 1 (March 2006): 11–31. For more general discussion of high-road strategies, see Stephen Herzenberg, John Alic, and Howard Wial, *New Rules for a New Economy: Employment and Opportunity in Postindustrial America* (Ithaca, N.Y.: Cornell University Press, 1998); and Eileen Appelbaum, *Manufacturing Advantage: Why*

High Performance Work Systems Pay Off (Ithaca, N.Y.: Cornell University Press, 2000).

18. Peggie Smith, "Protecting Home Care Workers under the Fair Labor Standards Act," *Direct Care Alliance Policy Brief No. 2* (June 2009, www.directcarealliance.org), provides an excellent discussion of home-care workers' exclusion from a number of basic legal protective frameworks.

19. Harley Shaiken, "Unions, the Economy, and Employee Free Choice," Economic Policy Institute Briefing Paper No. 181 (February 2007, www.epi.org), describes the ways in which workers' right to organize has been curtailed in recent decades and makes a strong argument for strengthening legal protection of that right.

20. Kari Waerness, "The Rationality of Caring," in *Caregiving: Readings in Knowledge, Practice, Ethics, and Politics*, ed. Suzanne Gordon, Patricia Benner, and Nel Noddings (Philadelphia: University of Pennsylvania Press, 1996), 231–256.

21. Randy Albelda, Mignon Duffy, and Nancy Folbre, *Counting on Care Work: Human Infrastructure in Massachusetts* (September 2009, www.countingcare.org). This section draws on our argument in this report.

22. F. Scott Fitzgerald, *The Crack-Up* (New York: New Directions, 1945[1931]), 69.

Appendix: Data and Methods

1. Descriptive information about the IPUMS samples and variables can be found at www.ipums.org.

2. For a full description of the criteria and method used for this imputation, see Brian Gratton and Myron Gutmann, "Hispanics in the United States, 1850–1990: Estimates of Population Size and National Origin," *Historical Methods* 33 (2000): 137–153.

Index

Adams, Valerie, 140
Albelda, Randy, 144
American Association of Social Workers (AASW), 65
American Community Survey (ACS), 6, 148
American Federation of Labor (AFL), 82
American Medical Association (AMA), 48
American Nurses Association (ANA), 55, 82
Armstrong, Pat, 126–127

Beauvoir, Simone de, 39
"benevolence," 63–64
Beth Israel Hospital, 87–88
Bickham-Mendez, Jennifer, 120–121
Black workers: in child-care occupations, 100; in cleaning jobs, 122; domestic service and, 23–24, 27–29, 35, 38–39; gendered division of labor and, 11; in health care occupations, 85–87; in hospital jobs, 125–126; menial labor performed by, 136; in mental health occupations, 108–110; in nonnurturant care occupations, 114–115; in nurturant care occupations, 44, 79–80; as practical nurses, 54–55; in social work occupations, 67–69, 108–110; in teaching occupations, 62, 94–95, 97–98
Boulis, Ann, 83

Braverman, Harry, 76
Bronfenbrenner, Urie, 93
Budig, Michelle, 18
bureaucratic control, 7, 76, 83–84, 108; in education, 60, 71, 97; of nursing, 86

cafeteria workers, 114, 136, 141
Cancian, Francesca, 9, 15–16
care work. *See* child care; health care; nonnurturant care; nurturant care; *individual occupations*
Carlton-LeNay, Iris, 110
Carter, Michael, 83
Carter, Susan, 83
Center for the Childcare Workforce (CCW), 139
certified nursing assistants (CNAs), 88–89, 112
Charity Organization Society (COS), 64–65
charity work, 42, 63–67, 69, 108, 137
child care, 27, 56–63, 98–105, 132–133; demographics of, 2007, 97–98, 100; for poor children, 103; professionalization of, 104; racial-ethnic representation in, 101–102; relationality in, 102–103; twentieth-century changes in, 7
child-care workers, 1–2; associated with reproductive labor, 121; challenges faced by, 141; changing expectations for, 45; as educators, 104, 139–140; growth in numbers of, 78, 93;

child-care workers (continued) interpersonal skills of, 16; lacking legal protection, 143; nonnurturant work done by, 113; as nurturant care workers, 6, 9; racial-ethnic women as, 137; relational care and, 127; unionization of, 104–105, 123. *See also* day care workers

child-centered environments, 93–94

childhood, 56–59, 132–133; as sacred, 56–59, 63, 69, 93, 132. *See also* infancy

child labor, 26, 59

child welfare, 69

citizenship, 7, 34, 136, 137, 143

civil rights movement, 28–29, 94

class inequality, 2–3, 5, 129; domestic work and, 33; among women, 40–41

cleaning services, 119–121, 122, 172n15

cleaning workers, 115–128; challenges faced by, 141; demographics of, 122, 125–126; gendered division of labor and, 117–119; in hospitals, 125, 126–127; importance of, 124; list of occupations, 172n4; as nonnurturant care workers, 19; racial-ethnic women as, 135, 137; relational skills of, 127; rise in number of, 115; social organization of, 119–121. *See also* housecleaners; housekeepers; janitors; maids

clergy, 66–68, 106–107, 109

clerical workers, 76, 126

Clinton, Bill, 140

cold-modern model of care, 4

commercialization, 4

commodification, 4, 130

Common School movement, 58, 134

companionship services, 91–92

"concerted cultivation," 102–103

Congress of Industrial Organizations (CIO), 82

cost containment, 81, 83

cost cutting, 7, 76–77, 84, 86, 112, 138–139, 143; cleaning and, 122; in health care, 87–88, 125; in mental health care, 108

Cowan, Ruth Schwartz, 72

Cranford, Cynthia, 122

data collection, 147–152

day care workers, 1, 15, 99–102, 105

dehumanization, 39

deinstitutionalization, 90

dependency, 13–15, 17

dependents, 18, 144

deskilling, 76–77, 86, 91, 143; feminization linked to, 108, 111–112

Diamond, Timothy, 88–89, 138

Dine, Philip, 86

Dix, Dorothea, 69–71

doctors. *See* physicians

Dodson, Lisa, 89

domestic service, 6–7, 20–41; associated with menial tasks, 17; child care and, 63; demography of, 1900, 23–24; demography of, 1950, 27–28; demography of, 1990, 29–30; employer-employee relationship and, 34–35; invisibility of workers, 36–37; lack of legal protection for, 37, 143; modern equivalents, 135–136; in the nineteenth century, 20–24; as nonnurturant care, 113–115; as nurturant care, 10; racialization of, 27–28, 38–39; relational nature of, 34–35; reproductive labor and, 10–11; spiritual/menial division of labor in, 162n83; stigma associated with, 35–36; temporary workers and, 157n14; twenty-first-century growth of, 31–33; twentieth-century decline of, 24–31, 157n19; undesirability of, 33–34; vulnerability of workers in, 119–120; wages for, 35–36

Du Bois, W.E.B., 35

economic inequality, 31, 137, 140–141

economic restructuring, 75–76. *See also* cost cutting

education: nonnurturant care in, 124; twentieth-century changes in, 7. *See also* schools; teaching elderly, care of, 1, 3, 81, 90, 113–114, 142; institutionalization and, 132. *See also* nursing homes

emotional labor, 16, 102–103, 140

Engels, Friedrich, 11

England, Paula, 18

expert care, 43, 75, 136, 142

expert knowledge, 45, 131; in education, 60, 71; in medicine, 48; in mental health, 133; nurturant care and, 71–72; of physicians, 51, 56

exploitation, 3, 123, 136, 140; domestic service and, 22, 29, 33, 119; relationality and, 89, 105, 121; among women, 5, 40

factory work, 25–26, 35, 72

Fair Labor Standards Act (FSLA), 91

family care, 131, 142

family day care providers, 101

"family wage," 59

femininity, 13, 38, 111–112, 133–134; associated with homemaking, 37, 162n83; gendered division of labor and, 136; nursing and, 52–54, 56; nurturant care and, 42, 45–46, 78, 119, 140; relationality and, 72–73, 127; reproductive labor and, 11; social work and, 63–64; teaching and, 61

feminism, 40, 133–134

feminization: linked to deskilling, 108, 111–112; loss of autonomy and, 83–84, 97; of menial hospital tasks, 86; of mental health care, 106–108; of nurturant care, 7, 78–79, 110–111, 119, 133–135, 139; of teaching, 57–58, 97, 164n34

Fineman, Martha Albertson, 14

Fisher, Berenice, 14

Fitzgerald, F. Scott, 144

Folbre, Nancy, 18, 144

food service workers, 7, 114–117; demographics of, 2007, 125–126; in hospitals, 127; importance of, 124; list of occupations, 172n4; as nonnurturant care workers, 6, 9, 18, 19; racial-ethnic women as, 135, 137;

relational skills of, 127; rise in number of, 115–116

gendered division of labor, 1–2, 10–12, 26, 59, 133, 136; deskilling and, 76–77; domestic service and, 37–38; in nonnurturant care occupations, 117–119; in social work, 66–67. *See also* separate spheres ideology

gendered segregation, 73

gender inequality, 2–3, 5, 8, 129; cost cutting and, 143; domestic service and, 21, 33; hospital hierarchies and, 51; in hospitals, 51, 124–126; in nonnurturant care, 117; persistence of, 21; spiritual *vs.* menial labor distinction and, 39

Glazer, Nona, 124

Glenn, Evelyn Nakano, *see* Nakano Glenn, Evelyn

Gordon, Suzanne, 87, 138–139

Great Depression, 75

Guberman, Nancy, 91

Harrington, Mona, 5, 135

Head Start, 103

health care, 46–56, 80–92; cost-containment and, 81; demographics of, nineteenth century, 51; demographics of, 1950–2007, 85–87; demographics of, 1970–2007, 108–110; demographics of, 2007, 125–126; home care and, 89–92; hospitals and, 42; impact of neoliberalism on, 76, 87–88; nonnurturant care in, 124–128, 126–127; technological change in, 131; twentieth-century changes in, 7; as workers' right, 142

health care workers: growth in numbers of, 50, 78, 80; lacking legal protection, 91–92; list of occupations, 166n8; loss of autonomy of, 83–84; as nurturant care workers, 42; professionalization of, 47–48; relational skills of, 87–89; women as, 84. *See also* nursing; physicians; *individual occupations*

health maintenance organizations (HMOs), 81, 83, 134

helicopter parenting, 103

"high-road" strategies, 142–143

"hired girls," 21–23, 37–38, 157n12

Hispanic workers: in child-care occupations, 100; in domestic service occupations, 30, 35, 39–40; in hospital jobs, 125–126; in nonnurturant care occupations, 114–115; in nurturant care occupations, 79–80; in teaching occupations, 98

Hochschild, Arlie, 4, 16

home care, 32, 77, 90–91

home-care workers, 1–2, 90, 131–133, 138; association with reproductive labor, 12; challenges faced by, 141; changing expectations for, 45; demographics of, 2007, 125–126; as domestic servants, 159n46; interpersonal skills of, 16; lacking legal protection, 101, 143; unionization of, 123

Hondagneu-Sotelo, Pierrette, 39, 120

hospital attendants, 54–55, 86–87, 112, 124; women as, 84

hospitals, 42, 49–50; cleaning workers in, 118, 126–127; cost cutting and, 87–88; hierarchical organization of, 51; nonnurturant care in, 114–115, 124–128. *See also* health care

housecleaners, 119–121; association with reproductive labor, 12; lacking legal protection, 143; as nonnurturant care workers, 9; routinization and, 172n15. *See also* cleaning workers; housekeepers

housecleaning services, 32

housekeepers, 1–2, 41, 118–119, 159n46; immigrants as, 159n42; as nonnurturant care workers, 6, 18; racial-ethnic women as, 137; relational skills of, 127; twenty-first-century increase in numbers of, 32–33; wages of, 161n68. *See also* cleaning workers; housecleaners

human infrastructure, 144

immigrants: in child-care occupations, 100, 101–102; in cleaning occupations, 122; in domestic service, 22–24, 29, 31, 159n42; in early twentieth century, 26; exploitation of, 5, 39–40; in health care occupations, 85–87; in hospital jobs, 125–126; industrialization and, 58; in low-wage jobs, 135; menial labor performed by, 136; in nurturant care occupations, 43–44, 79–80; as physicians, 84; as practical nurses, 54–55; in social work occupations, 67–68; as teachers, 97–98

individualism, 12–13, 75–76

industrialization, 26, 58–59

inequality. *See* class inequality; economic inequality; gender inequality; racial-ethnic inequality

infancy, 62–63, 102

Integrated Public Use Microdata Series (IPUMS), 5–6, 8, 147–148

interdependence, 12, 14, 129

Jacobs, Jerry, 83

janitors, 114, 117–119, 136; as nonnurturant care workers, 16, 18; unionization of, 121–123, 141. *See also* cleaning workers

job queues, 83

Justice for Janitors, 122–123, 141

Kessler-Harris, Alice, 8

kindergarten, 63, 99–100, 102

kitchen workers, 12. *See also* food service workers

Kunzel, Regina, 70

Lareau, Annette, 102

laundry workers, 7, 114; demographics of, 2007, 125–126; in hospitals, 127; importance of, 124; as nonnurturant care workers, 6, 9, 19; racial-ethnic women as, 135, 137; rise in number of, 115–116

licensed practical nurses, 50, 73, 80, 85–87; demographics of, 2007,

84, 125–126. *See also* practical
nurses
living wage, 141
long-term care, 132
"low-road" strategies, 142
low-wage jobs, 2, 5, 87, 135–136,
141–143; cleaning work as, 120;
deskilling and, 77, 91, 126–127, 137;
domestic service as, 35–36; economic
dependency and, 15; feminization of,
46, 48, 111, 134; immigrants in, 58;
teaching as, 96

Macdonald, Cameron, 102, 139
maids, 114, 118–119, 121, 159n46.
See also cleaning workers; domestic
service
managed care, 81, 107
Mann, Horace, 58
marketization, 3–4, 130–133
Marx, Karl, 11
maternal care, 98–100, 101
Medicaid, 76–77, 81, 90–91
medical education, 48–50, 51
Medicare, 76–77, 81
menial jobs, 16–17, 73–74, 88, 124,
126; in child care, 102; feminization
of, 86, 112; in health care, 54–55,
87–88, 112, 136, 141; home care and,
90, 92. *See also* nonnurturant care;
spiritual *vs.* menial labor hierarchy
mental health care, 69–71, 105–110;
feminization of, 106–108, 111; growth
in numbers of workers, 78, 105;
loss of autonomy in, 107–108;
twentieth-century trends in, 133.
See also psychiatry; psychology;
psychotherapy; social work
mental hospitals, 69, 132–133
mental hygiene movement, 69–71
mental illness, 64, 69–71, 106; treatment
for, 105, 133
Merrill, David, 139
minimum standards, 140–142
morality, 49, 140
Moroney, Robert, 132
mothering, 63, 98, 102, 140

Nakano Glenn, Evelyn, 3, 17, 19, 114, 135
nannies, 1–2, 41, 102; immigrants as,
159n42; racial-ethnic women as,
137; relational obligations of, 35;
twenty-first-century increase in
numbers of, 32–33; wages of, 161n68
National Labor Relations Act, 37
Nelson, Julie, 140
Nelson, Margaret, 102
neoliberalism, 76–77, 83, 125, 138; cost
cutting and, 143
New Deal, 75
No Child Left Behind (NCLB) Act,
96–97
Noddings, Nel, 96–97
nonnurturant care, 6–7, 19, 113–123;
demographics of, 114–115; domestic
service and, 20; racial-ethnic workers
in, 18; twentieth-century rise in
numbers of workers, 115–116;
unionization and, 121–123. *See also*
cleaning workers; food service
workers; laundry workers
nursing, 1–2, 50–56, 86–87, 138–140;
changing expectations for, 45;
demographics of, 171n99;
demographics of, 1900–1950,
51–52; demographics of, 2007, 86–87,
125–126; deskilling of, 91; division
into spiritual and menial tasks, 136;
effect of cost cutting on, 84, 86–88;
femininity and, 52, 54; home care and,
90–91; interpersonal skills and, 16;
limited to White workers, 44;
nonnurturant care associated with,
124–125; as nurturant care, 6, 9, 42;
origins of, 46–47; predominance of
women in, 78, 111–112, 139;
professionalization and, 55–56, 82,
125, 136–137, 139; relational care
and, 72–73, 82, 127, 136; as skilled
labor, 141; training programs for, 52,
55; unionization of, 86. *See also*
licensed practical nurses; practical
nurses; primary nursing; professional
nurses; registered nurses; student nurses;
trained nurses

nursing aides, 54, 74, 91, 124–126; challenges faced by, 141; growth in numbers of, 80; menial tasks performed by, 136; as nurturant care workers, 42; racial-ethnic women as, 135; relational skills of, 127; women as, 84

nursing homes, 89–90, 114, 118, 131–132, 138

nursing schools, 50

nurturance, 9–10, 12, 15–16, 74, 138, 140; in child care, 59, 99, 102–103; cost cutting and, 112; devaluation of, 88; in health care, 7, 81, 87–89; home-care workers and, 91; mental health care and, 106–108; nursing and, 56, 82; overlap with technical knowledge, 77; teaching and, 61, 92; therapeutic work and, 108; unionization and, 123; women and, 126

nurturant care: association with women, 43–44; care of dependents and, 144; definition of, 6, 15–16, 18–19, 154n3; demographics of, 1900–1950, 43–44; demographics of, 1950–2007, 79–80; expert knowledge and, 45, 71–72; feminization of, 7, 78–79, 110–111, 119, 133–135, 139; gender segregation of, 46; growth of, 78; list of occupations, 162n1; predominance of women in, 116; relationality and, 18, 72–73, 127, 138; reproductive labor and, 12; theory of, 9–10, 12–16, 129, 143–144; twentieth-century changes in, 7, 71–74; twentieth-century growth of, 42–43; in twenty-first century, 75, 77–80, 110–112; unionization and, 123. *See also* health care; nursing; physicians; social work; teaching; *individual occupations*

Oliker, Stacey, 9, 15–16

orderlies, 54, 86–87; menial tasks performed by, 136; as nonnurturant care workers, 6; women as, 84, 135

outsourcing, 3–5, 40

Palmer, Phyllis, 38

parenting, 57, 102–103, 132

personal care attendants; challenges faced by, 141; as domestic servants, 159n46; home care and, 90; lacking legal protection, 143; as nurturant care workers, 9; relational skills of, 127; unionization of, 123

Philipson, Ilene, 76, 106–108, 111

physicians, 1, 49; expert judgment of, 72; foreign-born, 51, 84; growth in numbers of, 80; loss of autonomy by, 83; in nineteenth century, 47, 51; as nurturant care workers, 6, 9, 42; professionalism of, 48, 50, 55–56, 71; by race-ethnicity, 53, 85; women as, 52, 84, 86, 111

positive externalities, 144

postmodern model of care, 4

practical nurses, 50–55, 80, 86–87; demographics of, 73, 85, 125–126; women as, 84. *See also* licensed practical nurses

prepared food industry, 114

preschool, 93, 95, 98, 99–100

Preston, Jo Anne, 58

primary nursing, 82, 87–88

principals, 60

private household workers. *See* domestic service

professionalization, 136–137, 142; of child care, 104; contrasted with degradation, 141; of feminized jobs, 112; of health care, 47–48, 163n4; of nurses, 55–56, 82, 125, 139; of nurturant care occupations, 71; relational skills and, 72–73; of social work, 65–66, 72; of teaching, 61; unionization and, 123

professional nurses, 50–52, 55

psychiatry, 70, 108, 134; authority of, 71; demographics of, 2007, 125–126

psychoanalysis, 64

psychology, 70, 105–110, 134; authority of, 71; feminization of, 111; as nurturant care, 42

psychotherapy, 70, 105–106; cost cutting and, 112; feminization of, 111; as nurturant care, 9
public schools, 57, 76, 92, 98

queuing theory, 83

race, measurement of, 8
racial-ethnic inequality, 2–3, 5, 8, 129, 135–136; cost cutting and, 143; dependence and, 17; domestic service and, 21, 33, 38–39, 40–41; hospital hierarchies and, 51; in hospitals, 51, 124–126; in nonnurturant care, 117; in nursing, 54–55; in nurturant care, 7, 16–18, 42–44, 73–74; persistence of, 21; spiritual *vs.* menial labor distinction and, 39, 113, 126; among teachers, 94; among women, 40–41
racial-ethnic workers. *See* Black workers; Hispanic workers; immigrants
racial segregation, 28, 73, 87, 94, 164n35. *See also* racial-ethnic inequality
Reagan, Ronald, 75–76, 81, 96
registered nurses, 50, 86–87; cost cutting and, 112; demographics of, 2007, 125–126; growth in numbers of, 80; home care and, 90–91; White predominance in, 17; women as, 84
relational care, 72, 154n3
relationality, 9–10, 13, 91, 105, 127–128, 129, 135, 137–140, 143; associated with women, 66, 72–73, 113, 124, 126; in child care, 102–103; in health care, 82, 87–89; in mental health care, 108, 111; in teaching, 92, 97. *See also* relational skills
relational skills, 72–74; of child-care workers, 103; of mental health workers, 70; of nurses, 82, 88–89; of social workers, 105–106; of teachers, 96–97, of women, 139. *See also* relationality
religious workers, 65–68, 106–107

reproductive labor, 10–12, 13, 16, 18–19, 129; care of dependents and, 144; domestic service and, 20–21; nonnurturant care and, 19, 113; racial-ethnic divisions in, 16–18, 135; slavery and, 156n4; spiritual *vs.* menial labor distinction in, 38; technological change and, 158n27
residential care facilities, 131–132
Reskin, Barbara, 83
Reverby, Susan, 56, 137
Roberts, Dorothy, 16, 19, 38, 135
Rollins, Judith, 37
Romero, Mary, 36, 120
Roos, Patricia, 83
routinization, 7, 76, 86

"sacred child" concept, 56–59, 63, 69, 93, 132
Salmon, Lucy Maynard, 34, 35–36
school boards, 71
schools, 57–62, 92–95, 134, 136; educational reform in, 96–97; medical, 51, 55; nonnurturant care in, 114–116, 119, 124; twentieth-century growth in, 42; for young children, 62–63, 99–100. *See also* education; teaching
Sedgwick, Catharine Maria, 20
segmentation, 124–125
separate spheres ideology, 10–11, 26–27, 37–38, 133
"serfdom saved the women's movement" argument, 4–5, 40–41, 45, 135
Service Employees International Union (SEIU), 122–123
sex segregation, 42, 46, 73, 112, 116; in health care, 55, 73; in teaching, 61. *See also* gendered division of labor; gender inequality
"short course" nurses. *See* practical nurses
Skenazy, Lenore, 174n3
slavery, 22–23, 24, 156n4
social activism, 46, 60–61, 64, 67, 95, 133
social change, 7, 129, 137
Social Security, 37

social services, 64–66; effect of neoliberalism on, 76, 105; expert knowledge and, 71; list of occupations in, 166n8; training for, 133; twentieth-century changes in, 7; women in, 67, 107, 109. *See also* mental health care; social work
social valuation, 36
social welfare laws, 37
social work, 63–71, 105–110; Black women in, 110; demographics of, 1900–1950, 67–68; demographics of, 1950–2010, 108–110; external controls on, 108; female domination of, 78, 139; gender and, 66–67; mental health care and, 69–71; relational care and, 72–73, 134; White predominance in, 17, 44
social workers, 1; changing expectations for, 45; increasing numbers of, 66; measuring numbers of, 165n54; as nurturant care workers, 6, 9, 42; professionalization of, 65–66, 72, 136–137; specialized knowledge of, 71
spiritual parenting, 102
spiritual *vs.* menial labor hierarchy, 16–18, 19, 38–39, 112, 114, 136; in child care, 102; in domestic service, 162n83; racial-ethnic inequality and, 126
Spock, Benjamin, 93
standardized testing, 94, 96–97
Starr, Paul, 48
Stewart, Maria W., 20
Stewart, Potter, 9
Stone, Deborah, 4
"strategic personalism," 120–121
student nurses, 50

talk therapy, 106
"teacher-proof" curricula, 94
teacher-training schools, 61, 71, 96–97
teaching, 1, 57–58, 92–98, 111; association with reproductive labor, 12; changing expectations for, 45; cost cutting and, 112; demographics of, 171n99; demographics of, 1900–1950,

61–62; demographics of, 1970, 94–96; demographics of, 2007, 97–98; division into spiritual and menial tasks, 136; feminization of, 57–58, 97, 164n34; growth in numbers of teachers, 59–60, 78, 92–93; loss of professional autonomy in, 92; as nurturant care workers, 6, 42; predominance of women in, 78, 111–112, 139; professionalization of, 61, 136–137; relational skills and, 72–73, 96–97, 127; standardization and, 94, 96–97; unionization and, 60, 95–96, 98; White predominance in, 17, 44; women as, 134–135. *See also* education
teaching assistants, 137
technical knowledge, 77, 82
technological innovations, 45; in domestic work, 25–27; in health care, 47, 71, 81, 131; in house cleaning, 119; in medicine, 49; reproductive labor and, 158n27
Thatcher, Margaret, 76
therapists, 70, 106, 108. *See also* psychotherapy
trained nurses, 49–50, 54–55, 124
Tronto, Joan, 13–14
Tuominen, Mary, 100–101

unionization, 141–142; of child care, 104–105; of feminized jobs, 112; impact of neoliberalism on, 76; of nonnurturant care workers, 121–123; of nursing, 82, 86; of teachers, 60, 95–96, 98; as workers' right, 143
United States Census, 5–6
unpaid care, 17, 24, 31, 44–45, 142
Uttal, Lynet, 99, 101

Waerness, Kari, 14, 18, 143–144
wages, for domestic service, 35–36. *See also* low-wage jobs
welfare policy, 17, 37, 75
welfare reform, 13, 49, 70, 75–76, 104
Wells, Ida B., 67

women, 1–2; association of nurturant care with, 43–44, 78–79, 86; care of infants and, 62–63; as charity workers, 63–64; in child-care occupations, 99–100; entrance into medical schools, 51; entrance into the labor force, 4, 40, 45; in health care occupations, 52, 84, 134; inequality among, 16–17, 40–41; loss of professional autonomy and, 83–84, 134; in mental health care occupations, 106–108; in nonnurturant care occupations, 114, 116–118; predominance of in nurturant care, 116, 133–135; relationality and, 126; reproductive labor and, 10–12; in social work occupations, 66–67; as teachers, 57–58, 94; twentieth-century occupational choices of, 25–26. *See also* femininity; feminization; gendered division of labor; maternal care; mothering; separate spheres ideology

women's activism, 46, 61, 64, 133

women's movement, 29, 40, 46, 83. *See also* "serfdom saved the women's movement" argument

workers' rights, 140–143

Wrigley, Julia, 102

Zelizer, Viviana, 56–57

Zincavage, Rebekah, 89